Praise for
Showdown! Lionhearted Lawmen of Old California

"*Showdown!* is a remarkable look at some of the most noted, but now forgotten, lawmen of the California frontier. Once again Bill Secrest has aimed straight and hit the bullseye."

—John Boessenecker, author of *Gold Dust and Gunsmoke: Tales of Gold Rush Outlaws, Gunfighters, Lawmen, and Vigilantes*

"In his *Showdown!: Lionhearted Lawmen of Old California*, William B. Secrest has rescued a number of nineteenth-century California lawmen from an undeserved obscurity while providing the stories of their times as a backdrop for their truly amazing feats."

—Kevin J. Mullen, author of *Chinatown Squad*

"Well, Bill Secrest has done it again. Long recognized as a leading authority on frontier California violence, this author has dug out the long forgotten stories of a half dozen fabulous California characters: John J. Bogard, who 'would follow a criminal to Hell' and died in a shootout with bandits; ex-convict turned lawman Lafayette 'Punch' Choisser who died mysteriously; William J. Howard, the 'Last of the California Rangers'; Hiram L. Rapelje, a 'gunfighting lawman with a dark side'; Los Angeles Chief of Police Emil Harris, who was called 'one of the greatest detectives in the West'; and Sheriff Davis F. Douglass, of whom it was said he 'would die in his tracks before he would let his man get away,' and did go down with an outlaw bullet in his back. No recognizable household names here; only well told accounts of the exploits of remarkable men in remarkable times."

—Robert K. DeArment, author of *Deadly Dozen: Forgotten Gunfighters of the Old West*

SHOWDOWN!

Lionhearted Lawmen of Old California

By
William B. Secrest

CRAVEN
STREET
B O O K S

Fresno, California

Published by Craven Street Books
an imprint of Linden Publishing
2006 South Mary, Fresno, California 93721
559-233-6633 / 800-345-4447
CravenStreetBooks.com

Craven Street Books and Colophon are trademarks of
Linden Publishing, Inc.

ISBN 978-1-884995-65-1

135798642

Printed in the United States of America
on acid-free paper.

Cover art by Maynard Dixon
Overland Monthly, 1893

Library of Congress Cataloging-in-Publication Data

Secrest, William B., 1930-
   Showdown! : lionhearted lawmen of old California / William B. Secrest.
      p. cm.
   Includes bibliographical references and index.
   ISBN 978-1-884995-65-1 (pbk. : alk. paper)
   1. Peace officers--California--Biography. 2. Frontier and pioneer life--California. 3. Peace officers--California--History--19th century. 4. Law enforcement--California--History--19th century. 5. California--History--1850-1950. I. Title. II. Title: Lionhearted lawmen of old California.

F865.S43 2010
979.4'04--dc22

                                                                          2010024414

Contents

Introduction

For many years I have been researching the lives of the notorious characters who peopled frontier California. This includes the likes of the Dalton boys, Bill Miner, and yes, even Jesse and Frank James, who were out here in 1869 for a brief sojourn between robberies. My interests, however, run more toward the lesser-known characters. Still, in retrospect, I have done enough in this line to suddenly realize that it is time to emphasize the other side of the story.

California's pioneer lawmen have indeed been acknowledged by some of our best writers. Richard Dillon's *Wells Fargo Detective* is a splendid biography of James B. Hume, while John Boessenecker's *Lawman*, a biography of Harry Morse, is a model of how a Western biography should be researched and written. Boessenecker's *Badge and Buckshot* also contains biographies of various California lawmen, as does this author's *Lawmen & Desperadoes* and his *Dark and Tangled Threads of Crime*, a biography of San Francisco's famed lawman, Isaiah Lees. But there were many more early peace officers who have gone unchronicled and deserve recognition.

Showdown! is a reminder that California was not only where the Wild West began, but its history encompasses as much drama and excitement as is found in all those other overblown areas of the West. Early Los Angeles, for example, made Dodge City, Deadwood and Tombstone an amusement park by comparison. In his book, *Gold Dust and Gunsmoke*, California author John Boessenecker, calculated that in just over a year the homicide rate in 1851 Los Angeles, when adjusted for population, was 414 homicides per 100,000 population. This is a horrendous figure, but fully verified by statistics of the time.

Although in the past I have concentrated on various facets of California's rich past—desperadoes, grizzly bears, disasters, and biographies of colorful characters—*Showdown!* focuses on early, little-known California lawmen. Most are unknown to a modern generation, but the drama and showdowns in their lives place them on a level with any of the perhaps overly celebrated Earps and Mastersons of Kansas and Arizona fame.

Many years ago a few California historians discovered that California is particularly rich in colorful Western history and we have been proving it ever since! More than that, most Western writers gauge the Wild West period as being generated after the Civil War when so many veterans headed west for a new start. A transcontinental railroad was being constructed into vast, new territories, creating pioneer towns, ranches, and many opportunities for a war-weary country.

This is all true enough, except that California's Wild West was born and nurtured fully a decade *before* the Civil War, during the great 1849 Gold Rush…in roaring mining camps that came into being many years before Dodge City, Deadwood, and Tombstone.

In *Showdown!*, Sheriff John Bogard did not have time to weigh the dangers and consequences of facing two train robbers. He just instinctively knew what he must do.

Emil Harris is recalled as one of the greatest detectives of his time, yet today his story has faded into the mists of history. He was the personification of the immigrant success story, a Prussian Jew who tried various trades before finding his place as a lawman and far-famed detective in early Los Angeles.

Others took a very different course. As a very young man, "Punch" Choisser was a gambler and desperado who was banished from the state, yet he returned to redeem himself through a notable incident in California's history.

Although William J. Howard was not a career peace officer, his life was many-faceted and punctuated with gunsmoke. Besides careers as a lawyer, district attorney and deputy sheriff, he was unique in that he belonged to the California Rangers. This was that storied troop of manhunters who tracked down the murderous bandit Joaquin Murrieta. And yes, the Rangers brought back the dreaded outlaw's head as proof of their successful quest. Some, like Hi Rapelje, lived a long, respected, and exciting life, only to drift off course when direction was most needed. Although some lawmen did not have the benefit of long lives, when the time came, they went down fighting.

Towns and cities like Los Angeles, Stockton, and San Francisco served as supply centers to a mining country filled with tough, frontier villages with names like Sonora, Hangtown, and Mariposa. All were peopled by tough lawmen whose stories remind us of the triumph, tragedy, and drama of bringing the law to this unique corner of the Wild West.

Despite the burgeoning over-development and population explosion of today, vestiges of California's frontier environment can still be seen in the San Gabriel Mountains and surrounding deserts of the South. To the north are the comparatively sparsely settled plains and rolling hills of Tehama County and the vistas of the Shasta Mountains and the towering Sierra. The streets and tunnels of Fresno's old Chinatown may still be explored, while many of the colorful, foothill Gold Rush villages remain… if you can overlook the modern shopping centers and homes that now encompass them.

—William B. Secrest, Fresno, California

Acknowledgments

Several of these stories have appeared previously in an abb1reviated format. After the publication of my article on John Bogard in *Wild West* magazine, I was fortunate in being contacted in May 2000 by Richard Henry, a direct descendant of the sheriff. Rick and his family had seen my article and a correspondence and exchange of information was initiated. Later, a delightful visit with Rick, his mother, and other family members resulted in my handling the martyred sheriff's pistol. Along with the Tehama County Historical Society, Dick Chamberlain and Art Phelps were most cordial in helping to track down the pistol's present location.

My original story of Punch Choisser's ride was first published by *True West* magazine in August 1965. Since then much new information has been made available. My thanks to Bill Choisser, the custodian of the Choisser genealogy. In the course of research, Daisy Choisser Condrey and her son, John, were contacted through the pioneer Trabucco family of Mariposa. Daisy is not with us anymore, but she was able to read my original article and pronounced it the most accurate she had seen to date. John Condrey was most helpful in securing a copy for me of an unpublished early photo of "Punch." My brother, Jim Secrest, took the photograph of Punch's grave and was otherwise helpful, as always. My thanks also to Josh Reader, of Santa Cruz, for his aid on this chapter.

After writing a brief biography of Hi Rapelje for the *Fresno Historical Society Journal* some years ago, I set to work tracking down his full story. His trail took me back to Michigan, then to Canada, and finally to New York and his Huguenot roots. Elbert (Bill) Ayres, of Essexville, Michigan, has been working on his wife's Rapelje roots for some time and was very helpful, as was Mary Felton of the Saginaw, Michigan, Genealogical Society.

My thanks also to Gail Benjafield of the St. Catharines Public Library in Ontario, Canada and Pat Temple of the Elgin County Branch, Ontario

Genealogical Society, St. Thomas, Ontario. The resources of the Fresno County Library's California History and Genealogical Society Room aided my research immeasurably. Its collection of early California newspapers is a gold mine for those seeking the everyday life of our great valley and foothills.

The newspaper collections at the California State Library and the Bancroft Library at University of California, Berkeley, were richly mined for historical data. Many thanks to the helpful staffs. Jim Casey generously supplied a photo of an early Los Angeles badge from his wonderful collection. Thanks, Jim.

Captain William Howard's chapter should have been a cakewalk, since his biography was published many years ago. Unfortunately, it left much to be desired, but an assiduous scouring of newspaper archives and other resources turned up new information that was utilized for a colorful refocus on a fascinating character. Again, my brother Jim, who lives in Mariposa County, was very helpful in my research.

Emil Harris was the subject of a brief biography in my 1994 book, *Lawmen & Desperadoes* and I have been gathering material on him ever since. I can not imagine doing Emil Harris's story without the background provided by Harris Newmark's wonderful volume, *Sixty Years in Southern California.* Emil Harris's life underscores both his skills as a detective and his long career as a pioneer police officer and deputy sheriff.

For the David Douglass chapter, I want to thank both Orval Bronson of Nevada City, as well as the Searls Historical Library (Eric Roberts) for providing much data and information.

Last, but not least, my thanks to historian John Boessenecker for his always helpful advice and loan of materials. Bob McCubbin, a great name in things Western, also generously allowed my use of an unpublished image from his collection. Thanks, Bob and John...and anyone I may have overlooked.

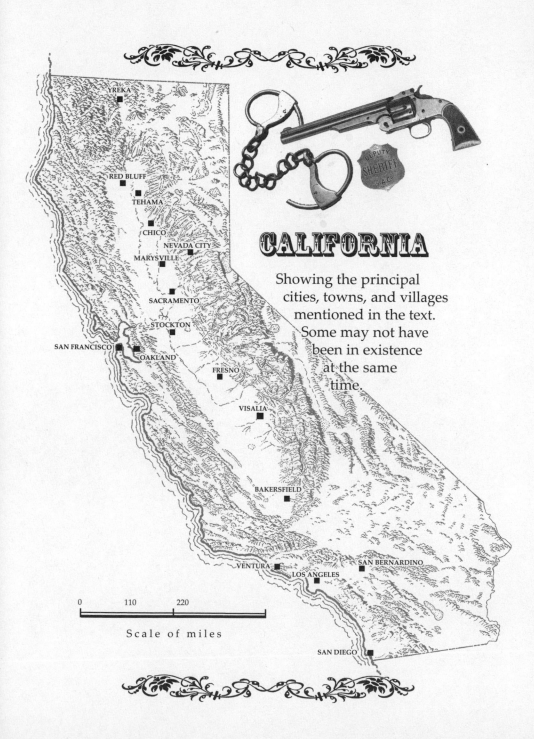

CALIFORNIA

Showing the principal
cities, towns, and villages
mentioned in the text.
Some may not have
been in existence
at the same
time.

YREKA

RED BLUFF
TEHAMA
CHICO
NEVADA CITY
MARYSVILLE
SACRAMENTO
STOCKTON
SAN FRANCISCO
OAKLAND
FRESNO
VISALIA
BAKERSFIELD
VENTURA
SAN BERNARDINO
LOS ANGELES
SAN DIEGO

0   110   220

Scale of miles

Chapter One

William J. Howard

He was the last of the California Rangers

Over the years, many writers have questioned the claim of William J. Howard that he was a member of the California Rangers. They were mistaken.

There is no doubt that William Howard and his brother were members of Captain Harry Love's organization. Contemporary newspaper accounts, a muster roll, and other documents prove this conclusively. One of Howard's favorite stories of the Joaquin Murrieta killing is his tale of the trunkless head of Joaquin being thrust in the face of one of Murrieta's men in an effort to identify the escaped members of the gang. The bandit was told to talk or his head would receive the same treatment. "Cut away!" he said, "I'll not tell." It is a good story and the implication is that Howard saw the incident himself. There is evidence, however, that he was in Stockton attending a horse race at this exact time. When he told this story to the *Merced Sun* in 1890, Howard thought he and his brother, who lived in Texas, were the only surviving Rangers. And, perhaps they were.

William J. Howard, as he appeared in his declining years. *California State Library.*

What does this incident mean? Was Howard a liar? My own theory is that he did not like the idea that although he was one of the famous Rangers, he missed out on the Murrieta killing—the whole purpose of the

Rangers. So, in his book, *The Last of the California Rangers*, dictated to Jill L. Cossley-Batt, and in various dictated newspaper articles, he placed himself with his comrades on Cantua Creek that hot July day in 1853. He had heard stories from his Ranger pals of what happened and saw nothing wrong in inserting these few stories into his own recollections. After all, he *was* a Ranger and had gone out on various bandit hunts, as reported in contemporary newspapers at the time. He and fellow Ranger Pat Connor had been sent on a separate mission looking for a killer and some horse thieves in the Stockton area and so had missed out on the great event of Gold Rush days—the death of California's most notorious outlaw. But, as long as he was near Stockton on the day of the race, Howard attended the event in which one of his thoroughbreds was entered. The date was July 25, 1853—the date of Murrieta's death!

No, Howard was not in the habit of lying, although in this particular instance he certainly played fast and loose with the truth. Still, in his biography and in various newspaper articles, Howard related incidents of his life that check out very well with the facts. He actually understated some of them, and omitted others. His story of the Rangers, his life as a rancher, and his public life as lawyer and lawman is well worth the telling and is verified in the records of the time.

Born on a Virginia plantation in 1826, William James Howard grew to manhood in a constantly changing environment. The family of Major Taliaferro Howard and his wife, Elisabeth, was well-off for the time. Slaves worked the fields and William would later recall that his mother's hair "was brushed by one maid and her shoes laced by another, while a third fanned her when she read or sewed." Still, there was much domestic work to be supervised: sewing, soap- and clothes-making, and cooking. The major always liked a challenge and the family would move every few years or so to a new plantation, which he would proceed to build up and improve.

When William was about six, the family moved to Mississippi, and after seven years there, traveled to Washington County in the new Republic of Texas. It was a swampy area, however, and they soon acquired a new farm on the Brazos River, near Austin. In 1843, the family moved once again, this time to the island of Galveston. President Sam Houston was a particular friend of the family and was elected U.S. Senator after the Republic was annexed to the United States in late 1844. "I knew Houston," Howard once remarked to an interviewer. "He came often to our home in those days. You see, father stumped the state with him. Ah, yes, there was a great deal of excitement then."

When the elder Howard died in 1846, William was studying law and had to take over the family business interests. A long-festering war with Mexico broke out that spring and troops were mustered around the country to bolster the army of General Zachary Taylor. Young William Howard formed a company at his own expense and was elected captain. When his mother reminded him of his responsibilities at home, he grudgingly assigned command of his company over to his cousin Robert Howard.

William Howard had missed the call to glory, but the war was of brief duration, ending in the Treaty of Guadalupe Hidalgo in early 1848. This same year, stories began filtering through the states about a gold discovery in the newly acquired territory of California. Great chunks of the Southwest, as well as California, now no longer belonged to Mexico. When the word spread and the gold discoveries were confirmed, the Mexicans in California and from the Mexican state of Sonora flocked to the foothills of the Sierra, and Mexican mining camps such as Sonora, Campo Seco, and Melones came into being. While there was a trickle of Americans arriving in late 1848, the following year they began arriving in hordes, along with others from around the world. It was the greatest gold rush in history, and the massive displacement of people created problems that are still with us today.

William Howard now saw another opportunity for adventure. His brother Tom promised to stay behind to look after their mother, and William left for San Antonio, where overland parties were being organized.

In the bustling town, Howard and his friend Edward Burns easily found thirty-two other adventurous souls and formed a company, electing William as their captain, a title he would retain throughout his life. The group was divided into five mess-groups to simplify feeding arrangements. One of the men was Philemon T. Herbert, also a lawyer, who sought opportunity, as well as gold, in the new land. They bought pack mules instead of wagons and supplied themselves for the journey. It was to be a long and dangerous trip through primitive territory.

In Arizona, at the Colorado River, the group built rafts to get their property across. During the crossing, several rafts and mules were lost, Howard losing his riding mule and all his equipment. On the California side, the party rested for a few days. Howard proceeded alone, keeping on the same compass reading as his friends would be taking. He very nearly died on the trip for lack of food and water, collapsing finally at the door of an adobe hut on the outskirts of Los Angeles.

Portsmouth Plaza, the public square in San Francisco, as it appeared when Howard and his companions arrived. Abandoned ships in the Bay can be seen in the distance. *Author's Collection.*

Nursed back to health by the owner of the hut, Howard walked into Los Angeles one day, where he encountered a party of men preparing to start for San Francisco. Having already secured information on traveling the coast to the Bay City, Howard agreed to guide them. They arrived in the sprawling village on July 4, 1849, finding a rapidly growing town filled with gold seekers from around the world. Prices were very high and Howard was anxious to leave for the gold country. Booking passage on a crowded schooner, he crossed the bay and traveled up the Carquinez Strait, enjoying the short trip up the San Joaquin River to the bustling village of Stockton.

With several companions, Howard walked up the Mokelumne River to the mining camp of Mokelumne Hill. He soon found mining a disappointing drudgery and lived with the Indians for a time, then began hunting for the market. After saving up enough money, Howard went to Sacramento and loaded a pack train with supplies to start a trading post in the gold country. At that time there were particularly good mining reports from the Mariposa region, and he headed south.

Stockton Times, September 14, 1850::

> *The accounts from the Mariposa are of a most glowing description. Some exceedingly rich specimens of gold quartz were exhibited yesterday…on Portsmouth Square, San Francisco. The pieces of quartz on exhibition were of brilliant richness, the gold permeating through every part… adjudged at one hundred dollars per pound.*

In Mariposa County, Howard bought 350 acres on Burns Creek and established his Buena Vista Ranch. Mariposa, at this time, was the largest county in the state, extending from the Merced River south to the Tehachapi Mountains. The mining camp of Agua Fria was the county seat. Howard put up a tent store on the Fort Miller road which led to the army post, Stockton, and the Mariposa mines. It was an ideal location. A steady procession of riders, miners on foot, and pack trains passed by. Soon, stagecoaches were stopping for their passengers' convenience. Later, Howard would recall that business was so good that after four months he sold the store and concentrated on his Buena Vista Ranch. By now, his brother Tom had arrived to share his brother's responsibilities. An indication of the Howard brothers' worth at this time is their appointment as Indian traders on the Tuolumne and Merced rivers, where they had previously bought land claims.

Always fond of fine horseflesh, Howard was beginning to establish a herd of good stock at his Buena Vista Ranch, when unexpected Indian trouble erupted. One night in early January 1851, Howard had some 72 of his horses stolen. It was a miserable, stormy night, but the following morning Howard and several companions were in pursuit. Along the way, they joined a citizen posse in charge of Mariposa sheriff James Burney who was tracking Indians responsible for an attack and massacre at Jim Savage's trading post on the Fresno River. Savage, himself, was along as tracker and guide for the group.

After tracking the Indians to a mountain near the Fresno River, there was a battle, with both sides taking casualties. Burney and his men retreated, but managed to destroy the Indians' village and food stores. The only fatality was Lieutenant Skeane S. Skeens, who died after the detachment reached a meadow at Ahwahnee, some miles below Yosemite. A small fort was built and several wounded were left there with a strong guard, while Burney and the others returned to Agua Fria for supplies. It was the beginning of the Mariposa Indian War.

Howard joined James Burney's party of volunteer Indian fighters. *Courtesy Pelk Richards.*

While Tom Howard ran the ranch, William joined the Mariposa Battalion that was now formed to bring all the local Indians into reservations on the San Joaquin Valley plains. Howard had always gotten along well with the Indians and employed many of them on his ranch. He did not like having to fight them, realizing that they were only striking back at invaders who were taking their women and land from them. But many whites had died now, too much stock had been stolen, and the raids had to be stopped.

Three recently arrived U.S. Indian commissioners were in the area, empowered to make treaties and place California's Indians upon reservations. Here, they would be cared for and kept away from contact with miners and other whites. The occupants of a few Indian *rancherias*, or villages, came in, but there was trouble when old Chief Tenaya, of the Grizzlies or Yosemite Indians, appeared in camp. It was his warriors, along with the Chauchila Indians, who had killed the three clerks at Savage's Fresno River store.

Tenaya did not want to bring his people to a reservation on the plains. "My people," he said, "do not want anything from the Great Father you tell me about. The Great Spirit is our father, and he has always supplied us with all we need. We do not want anything from the white men....Go then. Let us remain in the mountains where we were born, where the ashes of our fathers have been given to the winds. I have said enough."

Jim Savage, who had been given the title of major and

6

Men of the Mariposa Battalion were astounded at the beauty of the great Yosemite Valley. *Roy Radonovich Collection.*

voted commander of the battalion, now threatened to go out and kill all the Indians who would not come in. The chief relented and sent word that his people must come down from the mountains. When they failed to appear, Captain John Boling's company was sent high into the Sierra to take the Indians out of their great hidden valley. This was Howard's company, but he apparently was excused from duty and so missed out on the May 5, 1851, discovery of Yosemite Valley, one of the wonders of the world. There was some skirmishing in the valley, with Indian casualties, but most of the Yosemites were brought down to the plains.

The Howard brothers then returned to their ranch. They were putting out crops now and there was much work to be done, although there was always time for horse races and other entertainments, as reported in the press.

Sacramento Union, **November 3, 1851:**

> *Foot Race—An interesting foot race came off on Belt's Ranch near the Merced (River), a few days ago between Mr. William Howard and one of the fastest Indian runners in the country. The victory was gallantly won by Mr. Howard. Distance one mile.*

With the Indians quiet, if not totally pacified, William began building up his horse trade. He attended auctions in Stockton and Sacramento and purchased the best animals he could find. Likewise, he visited other ranchers and the horse races which were always well attended by locals and gamblers. Soon he was racing his own blooded stock.

There was a shadow falling over California at this time, however. Native Californios and Mexicans

A California Indian of the Sonora region. *Tuolumne County Historical Society.*

7

had been the original colonists in California and were the first to flock to the mines from the coastal pueblos of Los Angeles, Santa Barbara, and Monterey. They established many of the early mining camps, and when the first Americans and others arrived, the Mexican miners from Sonora often showed them the rudiments of mining to get them started.

But many of the early arrivals were American sailors and soldiers fresh from the Mexican War. California was their country now and they resented these Mexican intruders who were in control of some of the best mining properties. Soon there was friction and Mexicans were driven from their claims, often with violence. In those early days, there was no law, and bitter feelings turned many a Mexican into an outlaw. Most were inoffensive peons, but others were opportunists or just hard characters to begin with, men willing to take advantage of the unsettled times. When Canada's Sir George Simpson visited the West Coast in 1841–42, he wrote that Los Angeles was a "Den of thieves...and is the abode of the lowest drunkards and gamblers of the country."

By the winter of 1853, a Mexican named Joaquin Murrieta had emerged as the most predominant and desperate bandit leader. In late 1851, his gang had murdered and robbed a series of travelers along the Feather River, then barely escaped posses near Marysville after seriously wounding Yuba County sheriff Robert B. Buchanan. The following year, there were robberies and gun battles around Sonora, and a young farmer was murdered on the Stockton road.

San Francisco Herald, **April 7, 1852**

More murders, Mariposa, April 28, 1852

> *Mr. Editor—I have to send you the melancholy news of the death of one of our best citizens, Mr. [Allan] Ruddle, near the Merced River. He started for Stockton on Monday last to purchase goods, had with his person some five hundred dollars, and was attacked, it is believed, near Forbes' Ranch...by two Mexicans. The poor fellow was lassoed and shot....*

Several Mexicans had been seen in the area and were described to a local miner, Harry Love, who tracked them to Southern California. One of the suspects was killed while trying to escape. Murrieta and his men had apparently split off from these two bandidos and after stealing some horses, fled to San Gabriel, near Los Angeles.

When popular militiaman and saloon owner General Joshua Bean was killed one night near the San Gabriel Mission, there was a general roundup of undesirables, including some of Murrieta's gang. The confession of young Reyes Feliz, brother-in-law of Joaquin, is one of the very foundations of the Murrieta saga, as reported in the *Los Angeles Star* and later by the San Francisco *Alta*.

Daily Alta California, **December 15, 1852:**

> *My name is Reyes Feliz, am 15 or 16 years old, was born at the Real de Bayareca, State of Sonora; did not know General Bean; don't know who killed him. Here, in Los Angeles, I heard some gentlemen whose names I do not know say that Murie-ta's woman had said that Joaquin Murieta had killed him. …I belonged to the company of Joaquin Murieta and the late Pedro, who was killed by Americans in the "cuesta del conejo"[The one Love had trailed and killed]….We robbed, Joaquin Murieta, the late Pedro, and myself.*

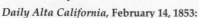

In the confession Feliz admitted to a local murder as well as to a previous killing in the mining town of Sonora. He also alluded to the Ruddle murder and was promptly hanged the next day. Two others were hung several days later. Murrieta had already left town with a herd of stolen horses, heading north through the Te-hachapi Mountains.

Harry Love, a Mexican War veteran and famed explorer and express rider in Texas. *From a woodcut in Ridge's* Life of Murieta.

Murrieta and his cohorts lost no time in getting to work again, as chronicled in dispatches from Calaveras County.

Daily Alta California, **February 14, 1853:**

> *At Big Bar on the Cosumnes on Tuesday, a party of five Mexicans killed six Chinamen and robbed them of $6000. The Mexicans were supposed to be headed by Joaquin. Citizens of the Cosumnes have offered $1000 for Joaquin, dead or alive.*

Other robberies and murders were reported in this same source, the Chinese being particular targets because they seldom carried guns to resist these assaults. Rumors were everywhere. Some fifty Chinese were chased from their camp and robbed, while the Stockton stage was report-ed stopped and two passengers killed. Joaquin was said to have "ridden through the town of San Andreas at a quick gallop and shot three Americans as he passed through the streets." A large party of Americans started in pursuit and overtook the outlaws at Cook's Gulch on Sutter Creek, but after a battle, the Mexicans escaped.

Joaquin is not known to have ever attacked a stagecoach, but the other incidents all took place. The *Calaveras Chronicle* published detailed reports by posse members of many of these events, as picked up by the Stockton, San Francisco, and Sacramento press.

Stockton San Joaquin Republican, **March 2, 1853:**

> *...We followed over a mountain, and on reaching the summit heard the report of several pistol shots in a Chinese camp at the foot of the hill. We rode down as quick as possible, and on arriving at the camp, we found three Chinamen dead and weltering in their blood, and five others mortally wounded; the Mexicans had been gone about 10 minutes, carrying with them $3000.*

> *23d—At daylight took the trail and followed them, passing through several China camps, and finding that each had been plundered....about five in the evening as we arrived on the summit of a hill, we saw them about three-quarters of a mile distant, robbing some Chinamen...There were five well-dressed Mexicans, well armed, and mounted on beautiful animals. We attempted pursuit, but our horses were worn out...*

Howard and the rest of California read about a big gun battle at the Phoenix Quartz Mill in Calaveras County, where several of the bandits had been wounded. A deputy sheriff from San Andreas received word of one of the injured outlaws and was quickly in the saddle, as reported in the *Republican* above.

> *He found him in a little camp on the other side of Angels, named Los Muertos. He arrested him and brought him to San Andreas where a trial by the people was had. He was found guilty and executed.... He made disclosures....*

> *He was of Joaquin's party, but not a conspicuous or leading member....He was compelled to be in readiness at all times, and to turn out immediately on receiving an order from any of his superiors....He was bound to shelter and protect any of the brethren who were in danger, to procure horses and assist them in their escape at all hazards...*

This was all startling news and it was now known that these marauders were not to be taken by ordinary means. Editorials and petitions from anxious miners were sent to legislators, and Governor John Bigler finally authorized a reward of $1,000 for the bandit "Joaquin Carrillo." This did nothing to calm the situation, but the pressure of the posses at least kept Joaquin and his men moving south into the next county.

In Mariposa County there was a shooting scrape at Hornitos over some stock stolen by Joaquin and his men. More petitions were gotten up, one of them calling for the previously mentioned Harry Love to be named head of a state police Rangers unit.

Love was well known in California as a veteran of the Mexican War and a daring express rider, guide, and explorer. He arrived in California in December 1850, and eventually drifted to Mariposa County, where many former soldiers were mining. On May 17, 1853, an act creating a company of twenty California Rangers under Captain Harry Love was signed by Governor John Bigler. It was time for some effective action at last, and Love sought the advice and help of William J. Howard.

As one of the signers of the "Ranger" petition, Howard was well advised of the events of the past few months. Howard would later recall Love contacting him to solicit aid for the coming campaign. "Howard," Love suggested, "you are more familiar with the fighting men of this part of the country. I wish you would pick the men you consider best suited for this undertaking."

Howard was anxious to help out with the project, but went even further. He put all his horses at Love's disposal; if Joaquin was to be captured, good animals would be of vital importance. Further, he invited the Rangers to make his ranch their headquarters for the three months term of their enlistment.

Portion of the Mariposa petition signed by Howard and others for the creation of the California Rangers. *California State Archives.*

Mexican War veteran Patrick Connor, a good friend of Howard. *California State Library.*

There are various lists of the Rangers—mainly because some dropped out and were replaced during the campaign. Since both Bigler and Howard were good Democrats, probably most of the Rangers were also of that persuasion, especially out-of-work politicians such as Walter Harvey and Philemon T. Herbert. A list of the original Rangers as reported in the press in June 1853, obviously reflects the original group, while Love's final muster roll of July 28, 1853, reflects those present when they disbanded. Most of Howard's list published in articles over the years is present on the final muster roll as shown here. Spelling has been corrected.

Joaquin Murrieta Papers, California State Archives:

Harry Love, Capt.	John W. Chiles	Robert H. Masters
P. Edward Connor	William A. Campbell	James M. Norton
William Byrnes	George Chase	John Nuttall
George W. Evans	William J. Howard	George A. Nuttall
Charles F. Bludworth	D. S. Hollister	John Sylvester
N. L. Ashmore	Thomas J. Howard	Edw. B. Van Born
Lafayette Black	William J. Henderson	John S. White

Except for Love, Howard, Connor, and several others, little is known of these men. Many were ex-soldiers and all were familiar with guns. The recovery of stolen bandit loot was certainly not the least of the motivations to join the group.

Charles Bludworth was another valuable addition to Love's Rangers. *Jerry and Joyce Wilson Collection.*

The Rangers were quickly in the saddle, fanning out over the countryside seeking horse thieves, but more importantly looking for information. A serious problem was the listing of five Mexicans named "Joaquin" in the legislation creating the Rangers; Joaquin Muriati, Joaquin Ocomorena, Joaquin Valenzuela, Joaquin Botellier, and Joaquin Carrillo.

Bill Byrnes was a noted gunman and a valuable addition to the Ranger ranks. *Author's Collection.*

Of these "Joaquins," only one was the real bandit chief—Murrieta, misspelled as "Muriati." His identification in Los Angeles at the time of the Bean murder was enough to get his name to head the list. Joaquin Carrillo was perhaps an alias or his stepbrother. Joaquin Valenzuela, another gang member, was also known as "Ocomorena" or "Nacamereno," and was a well-known desperado. The identity of "Botellier" is unclear.

Newspaper reports on the Ranger's activities appeared sporadically. Pat Connor scribbled this note to a Stockton newspaper.

San Joaquin Republican, **June 5, 1853:**

> *Tomorrow we start for the mountains—We have taken the horse that Mr. James Welch rode when he was shot, between San Jose and Santa Clara, about two months since, and we are now in pursuit of the Mexican who sold the animal in this place.*

There would be many such notices in the months to come—and the inevitable rumors.

San Joaquin Republican, **June 8, 1853:**

> *A member of Captain Love's company who are in search of Joaquin's gang, sends us the report of the death of Major Harvey and Mr. [Coho] Young. Their bodies were found yesterday on the trail between the San Joaquin and the Frezno [rivers].*

The report was not true. Harvey was elected delegate to the new county of Tulare and jumped at the chance to get out of the saddle and the summer heat. Coho Young had fallen from his horse and was, indeed, seriously injured. Assemblyman Phil Herbert soon found he also had business elsewhere and was replaced along with Harvey and Young.

There was a steady stream of letters to the press reporting on the progress of the Rangers and the movements of Joaquin and his men. When Love received a report that Joaquin had pillaged a ranch in Southern California, the Rangers headed south. They would also look into a reported band of horse thieves in the Coast Range. Bill Howard and Pat Connor were detailed to stay on the trail of James Welch's killer.

The past winter had seen much snow fall in the mountains, resulting in floods in the spring. An army topographical party coming out into the plains from the Bay Area reported "the [San Joaquin] Valley was one vast sheet of water, from 25 to 30 miles broad." Perhaps they found a ferry still in operation, but they may have had to swim their horses across the San Joaquin River. Either way, they were soon filing through Pacheco's Pass and on to San Juan [Bautista].

At San Juan, Love had a real piece of luck. Someone pointed out a suspicious character in town who was seized and questioned by several Rangers. Terrified when told he was in the presence of Harry Love and his Rangers, the suspect quickly admitted to being Jesus Feliz, Joaquin's brother-in-law. He was not a member of the gang, but carried messages and supplies to them as needed. Love bullied him into agreeing to show the Rangers where Joaquin's horse camp was on the San Joaquin plains. Feliz thought the gang would have been gone by now, but he insisted he must not be seen in any case. That evening, Love penned a letter to the governor, then sent it north by courier.

Joaquin Murrieta Papers, California State Archives:

> *San Juan, July 12, 1853*
>
> *To his Excellency Govr Bigler*
>
> *Sir—I leave this place this night for the mountains. I have arrested a Mexican, Jesus, a brother-in-law of Joaquin's. He says he will take & show us to Joaquin if we will release him. I will try him a while to see what it will end in. There appears to be quite a number of horse thieves hid in the mountains back of this place…. I hope I may make him useful to me in hunting them out. We get a few stray stock ever few days, but nothing of importance has occurred.*
>
> *Your obedient Servant*
>
> *Harry Love, Capt Cala Rangers*

Harry Love, some years after his appointment as captain of the California Rangers. *Author's Collection.*

Taking a surreptitious route out of the village that night, the group traveled to the edge of the foothills, where Feliz pointed out large herds of mustangs that were being branded for the drive south. He was startled, however, to see that the bandit gang was still there, along with many other mustang hunters. Love turned Feliz loose while he pondered what to do. Facing some sixty vaqueros, not all of whom were Murrieta men, Love and his men rode down among the dusty men and horses, picking out obviously stolen animals. They also took down the names of many of the vaqueros, realizing most would be fictitious. The Rangers then began herding the stolen stock north, up the edge of the valley towards Stockton. It was another blistering hot day.

Making sure they were out of sight of the mustangers, Love directed two Rangers to take the horses on to Stockton. With what Rangers he had left, Love then rode back into the mountains and circled back to where the mustang runners were camped. They were surprised to find their quarry gone. From this point on, it is mostly conjecture as to what happened, since the Ranger reports were brief and vague.

William Howard, who was not there, claimed that the Mexican vaqueros and their mustangs were all gone and that the Rangers now tracked their quarry as far south as the Tejon. Considering the time involved, this does not seem likely, however. Joaquin and six or seven of his men split off from the group and again headed north as the horse herd kept on to the Tejon Pass and Los Angeles. The Rangers, who had taken a different route, discovered what had happened and reversed their course, also.

The next morning, July 25, 1853, Love and his men spotted smoke from a campfire on Cantua Creek. Some half dozen Rangers now surprised the small group of vaqueros who were lounging around the campfire wrapped in their serapes. As Love and several others walked through the camp asking questions, a young man who was grooming his horse nearby shouted, "Talk to me! I am the leader here." All of the Rangers had weapons in their hands. Just then Bill Byrnes walked up.

"That's him, boys. We've found Joaquin at last!"

As Bill Henderson kept his shotgun pointed at several of the vaqueros, the leader swiftly looped a lariat around his horse's nose and leaped upon the animal's bare back. All was now confusion as Three-fingered Jack, Joaquin's lieutenant, drew his pistol and fired at Love, cutting off a chunk of hair. Others bandits went for their pistols, but were quickly cut

Cantua Creek was a stream meandering down out of the foothills of the Coast Range in what is now western Fresno County. *Photo by the author in the 1960s.*

down by the Rangers. Love and others promptly killed the three-fingered bandit as two other outlaws rushed to their horses and managed to escape in the gunsmoke.

Joaquin, meanwhile, had clung to his horse's neck, lying low on his back as he dug his heels into the animal's flanks. Galloping along the creek bank, he jumped his mount down into the dry creek bed and, having no saddle, he fell to the ground. A quick glance over his shoulder showed one of the Rangers, William T. Henderson, was close behind him. Henderson later described the events.

Fresno Expositor, **November 12, 1879:**

> *...Almost as quick as a flash Joaquin sprang to his feet and again mounted his horse. Henderson dropped his shotgun and pulled out his revolver, and not desiring to kill Joaquin, shot at his horse with a view of breaking one of his thighs, but the ball missed the bone. They were both riding at a break-neck pace down the bed of the creek. Coming to a low place in the bank of the creek, Joaquin turned his horse to ride out. As he did so, Henderson fired again at the horse, striking him in the same leg and very nearly the same place. The blood streamed from the wound, the ball having evidently cut an artery. Henderson was now convinced that his only chance to capture Joaquin was to shoot him, as the Mexicans in the rear were already shooting at him. He fired at the fleeing desperado and hit him in the small of the back, the ball passing through him, still he clung to his horse and urged the animal forward. At this time Ranger John White rode up and he also fired at Joaquin, who was leaning forward on his horse, and the ball struck him just above the one fired by Henderson, and ranged upward. This shot caused him to fall from his horse, but mortally wounded as he was, he still tried to escape, running...toward the hills. Henderson then fired...and shot him through the heart..... .*

A rope was slipped under the bandit chief's arms and he was dragged back to the camp where the other Rangers were searching for any stolen loot in the outlaws' camp. Bill Byrnes then cut off Joaquin's and Three-fingered Jack's heads and Jack's hand for identification. It was now, if Bill Howard's story was true, that Byrnes shook the severed head of Joaquin in the face of one of the prisoners and demanded he talk or he would get the same treatment. This was totally in character for Byrnes, who was a thoroughly seasoned frontiersman and gunman. The prisoner refused to talk, however. The heads and hand were then bundled up in a captured serape and Byrnes and John Sylvester headed across the San Joaquin Valley for Fort Miller with the two prisoners.

Meanwhile, Rangers Bill Howard and Pat Connor were in the foothills of San Joaquin County looking for a horse stolen by one of Joaquin's gang. They had traced the animal to a horse race near Stockton. The race was being promoted by a man named Dawson and his partner, who had made plans to fix the contest. The two Rangers also discovered that Dawson had been one of the robbers of an express company at Mormon Island. Connor then rode to Stockton and returned with Deputy Sheriff Canavan, who confronted Dawson. Refusing to be arrested, Dawson attempted to draw his pistol and escape, and the deputy was forced to shoot and mortally wound him. Dawson's partner was also taken into custody, while Connor and Howard took possession of the horse.

Love and his Rangers returned to Mariposa, having lost one of their prisoners who had drowned in a slough. The remaining captive, José Ochoa, identified the head as that of Joaquin. The head was then placed in a large jar and exhibited throughout Central California and the Gold Rush country. Many affidavits were collected further identifying the hideous trophy and the Rangers were paid their reward and disbanded.

The death of Joaquin Murrieta was denied by some at the time, and uninformed modern writers still dispute it, mainly as a ploy to make him a patriot and hero. The plain facts are that Murrieta was a vicious killer who richly deserved his fate. The gunfight and Joaquin's attempted flight at the time of his discovery are proof enough of his death, but the captured

The death of Murrieta as pictured by 1850s artist Charles Nahl in the *Police Gazette*. It was one of the more dramatic scenes in Gold Rush history. *Authior's Collection.*

17

bandit, Ochoa, also readily identified his late chieftain. When Love and several of his men exhibited the head throughout the Gold Rush country, a former mining partner of Joaquin living in the town of Columbia recognized the head immediately.

Stockton *San Joaquin Republican,* **October 25, 1853:**

> *Joaquin was probably better known here than in any other section of California, having long resided in this vicinity. A number of Mexicans and Americans recognized the head upon first sight. Among the number of those who recognized the head as that of Joaquin Muriatta [sic], was a Mexican who had known him in the state of Sonora, Mexico, from boyhood, and had been his partner in this vicinity. A number of Chinese, who had seen him in his forays against their countrymen in Calaveras, recognized the head instantly, and gave certificates to that effect....*

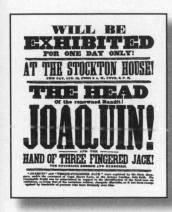

Many of the affidavits collected by Love and his Rangers can still be seen in the California State Archives.

The Howard brothers were eager to get back to work, although it seems Tom was minimally involved with the Rangers in lieu of having furnished horses and supplies to Love's men.

Bill Howard later maintained that Murrieta's wife, or a mistress, prior to the organization of the Rangers, had a mining claim she worked with several other Mexican women near the Buena Vista Ranch. "Rosita," Howard would later state, "whose beauty earned for her the name of 'Queen Victoria,' took up her abode at Tulita, a short distance from the Howard ranch." Here, with the assistance of two other Spanish women, she made a success at mining, and at the same time kept an intelligence station for her husband.

Jill Cossley-Batt, *The Last of the California Rangers,* **1828:**

> *...'Queen Victoria' loved to discuss shooting with Captain Howard, and one morning when he was riding along the dusty trail she came out of her tent, motioned to him, and said, "Captain Howard, I hear you are the best shot in the neighborhood, and I bet you a bottle of champagne that I can make the best two out of three at a distance of fifty yards."*

The head of Murrieta as sketched directly from the display.
Overland Monthly, November 1893.

Champagne being then sixteen dollars a bottle, William dismounted and agreed to take on the bet. It was decided that both should use [Colt] 'Navy six-shooters.' One of the women helpers placed a target fifty yards away, and when everything was in readiness the handsome Senora appeared anxious that William should have the first shot. He, however, had the presence of mind to suggest tossing for the first, thereby avoiding the danger of possible treachery.

When Howard won the coin toss, he gallantly insisted Victoria take the first shot anyway, which she did. She shot three times, missing the target each time. When she presented the champagne to Howard, he insisted she keep it as a gift since he did not drink.

It was a good story with indications that it was true. Murrieta was known to take his women along on his travels. These were tough, hard women who were expected to keep up with and aid their paramours. Some validation for the incident, however, is a brief notice in the local newspaper, which was established in late January 1854.

Mariposa Chronicle, **February 17, 1854:**

Court of Sessions — The People vs. Victoria, (Mexican Woman,) Allison for People, counsel refused by defendant – Indicted for intent to kill. Verdict, not guilty.

When the Rangers disbanded, most of the men returned to their normal pursuits although some sought to take advantage of their new-found fame. Several took up politics; Bill Byrnes obtained a position as a guard at San Quentin State Prison, while Pat Connor paid a call on Jack Hays, the noted Texas Ranger of Mexican War fame. Connor had met Hays during the late war and both men had joined the gold rush to California.

Hays had been elected the first sheriff of San Francisco County in 1851; then in late 1852, he attended the inauguration of the newly-elected President, Franklin Pierce. In Washington, Hays sought and obtained the appointment of U.S. surveyor general for California, and it was in this capacity that Pat Connor called on him. Hays was glad to give his friend a contract to survey land in the Tejon Pass area. Since he would be stationed in the area, Connor was also made a deputy customs agent, as was Bill

Howard, who accompanied Connor to the Tejon with a surveying party. The two former Rangers now toured the nearby Sebastian Indian Reserve and praised the operation, declaring the "Indians appear to be happy and contented." But, managed by dishonest agents, the new reservation system was doomed to fail by the end of the decade. Writing to his customs supervisor in Stockton, Connor reported on some of their activities.

Stockton *San Joaquin Republican*, March 11, 1854:

> Capt. Billy Howard had a big talk with the chiefs of Tuolumne, Merced, King's River and Four Creek Indians on his way up. Some of them have been to this place and expressed themselves highly gratified with the arrangement. They are now collecting their people in order to move....I shall start in a day or two, in company with my friend Howard, to examine the different passes leading into and diverging from the Tejon....

The Tejon area was noted for its grizzly bears, and when Howard went out with a posse after some horse thieves in late March, he had some firsthand experiences with bears rather than outlaws.

Mariposa Chronicle, May 5, 1854:

> Near the Tehachapi Pass the party encountered a grizzly, which they killed. Passing on, they encountered three more of these formidable animals. One of them made an attack on Captain Howard, and seized his stirrup. A well directed shot, however, broke one of its fore legs, and as the animal rolled on the ground, two other shots entered its body and all was over. Three bears were killed in all. One of the paws measured ten inches across.

Later that month Howard was surprised to read about his own death in a Stockton newspaper. It seems that several of his friends, on their way to the Tejon, had stopped to chat with Howard while he and Tewatchee, an Indian boy who helped around camp, were traveling in the opposite direction toward Stockton. Later, as the Tejon travelers were camped for the night, two men rode by with Howard's Indian boy riding between them. When they were hailed and asked to stop, they ignored the callers and rode on. A rider rode back to Howard's ranch to ask Tom if his brother had been there, but he had not.

Stockton *San Joaquin Republican*, March 20, 1854:

> ...We fear the report that he has been murdered, is too true. Our informant says that a party left Quartzburg and Mariposa immediately, in

search of him. Captain Howard had many warm friends and acquaintances in this city.

Captain Howard was pleased to read, a short time later, that he was still alive after all. When their surveying contract ran out, Connor returned home to Stockton and Howard again immersed himself in farming and stock herds at the Buena Vista Ranch. In late July, tragedy struck, however.

Sacramento Daily Union, July 29, 1854:

...A destructive fire occurred on the afternoon of the 25th inst., at Buena Vista Ranch, Mariposa County, owned by William J. Howard and Brother, by which they lost one hundred tons of Hay, their hay press and corral. It is supposed that the fire originated from the throwing of a lighted cigar into some loose hay near the stack. Loss $4,000.

Nothing more was heard concerning this incident, but destroying crops had always been a nasty means of revenge. It might have been a payback for the Howard brothers participating in the hunt for Joaquin, or merely the act of a disgruntled neighbor.

Fortunately, the Buena Vista had been quite profitable for the brothers. Their store and tavern at the ranch had also proved to be a cash cow, catering to the steady stream of prospectors stopping by as they headed into, or out of, the Mariposa mines.

Sometime in mid-April 1855, three men stopped by the Howard ranch. They were returning from the Kern River mines and asked who

Tejon Indians on their rancheria. *Williamson's Report on railroad routes in California, 1853.*

owned a nearby small, frame house. Captain Howard stated that he did. The leader of the party, named Chamberlain, said they were worn out from their trip and asked if they could stay in the empty house for a few days before they moved on. The men's clothes were quite ragged and dirty, and Howard, always the soul of Southern hospitality, readily agreed to let them stay, provided they did no damage.

A short time later, the Howard brothers decided to remodel the house and went over to the place only to find the occupants still there. Entering the house, they were surprised and angered to find the occupants had been tearing up the floorboards to make mining equipment. When Captain Howard told Chamberlain he and his party must leave immediately, there was hell to pay. Chamberlain and his cronies not only refused to leave, but insisted they were going to hold the claim as their own. The resulting incident was reported in newspapers throughout the area.

San Joaquin Republican, May 7, 1855:

>*...Captain Howard told Mr. Champlain [sic] ...that he would let him have a horse to go to Mariposa and satisfy himself that the land in dispute was recorded, surveyed and paid for; and that if he did not find the title to the property good, he would get free possession. But nothing would do; he had possession of the house and intended to keep it. Capt. Howard then remarked to him that both parties could not live in the same house; at which time, Champlain grabbed his pistol and attempted to rise and draw. The captain fired at Champlain and killed him instantly. He immediately gave himself up to the civil authorities.*

In later years, Howard remembered calling Chamberlain "a coward" to force the issue. "This was enough to start a fight," he recalled, and as "Champlain raised his pistol...William had drawn a derringer from his coat pocket and shot Champlain through the forehead. As he fell into the fireplace, William said to Tom, who now had entered the house, 'Pull that man out of the fire.' "

The sheriff and a coroner's jury were summoned and after hearing all the witnesses, Howard was easily acquitted. Chamberlain's partners, shaken by the incident, were now eager to get away from Howard and immediately left the area.

As early as 1855, Yosemite was already being visited by curious hunters and tourists. Although there were only rough trails and a few

Indian guides to take them into what was called the "Yo-Semity" Valley, individuals and groups were gradually discovering one of the most scenic vistas in the world. "Old Adams," the hunter and trapper later known as "Grizzly Adams," had gone into the valley with another hunter and had taken out all the game their pack animals could carry. The valley floor was covered with forests and wide meadows of lush grasses. A newspaper description of the time indicates the rapidly growing appreciation of what would eventually become something of a national shrine.

Mariposa Gazette, **October 11, 1855:**

> *Embowered in the mountains in its wildness and beauty, it seems desecration for civilization to intrude upon its loveliness. Even the poor Indian, with all his apathy and ignorance, shows his love for the spot the "Great Spirit" has made so lovely, and hallowed as the hunting ground of his forefathers.*

William Howard had visited the great valley several times and, like most others, was overwhelmed with its beauty. If it were ever possible, he wanted to live there one day, but for now it was not possible. The Buena Vista Ranch was his home now and was described in the local press.

Mariposa Democrat, **July 1857:**

> *A capacious adobe building furnished a pleasant retreat for the attendants on the rancho from the summer heat, while a well, at convenient distance from the house, affords water of a most pure and excellent quality to satisfy the thirst of the industrious laborer or the passing stranger, Near the road stands a very large corral built of rock taken from a neighboring sand-stone quarry, which affords most admirable slabs for building purposes. Higher up the valley is seen the barley field, embracing with its ditched fence some two hundred acres of land....*

With some fifty or sixty Indians at a nearby rancheria to draw on for his labor pool, Tom Howard probably ran the ranch at this time. Now William could spend as much time as he desired buying and racing his horses. When friends secured the nomination in 1856 for him to run for the state legislature from Mariposa and Merced counties, he decided he should visit his mother in Texas before becoming immersed in politics.

Travel was much easier now. Instead of the terrible desert journey across the Southwest, Howard now took passage at San Francisco on a ship down the coast to the Isthmus of Panama. A railroad made the crossing to Aspinwall and the Gulf of Mexico. A few more days' voyage up the coast to Galveston and he was home again. It was a joyous reunion, but all too short, and he was soon on his way back to California.

Home again, Howard plunged into his political campaign and quickly found that as a teetotaler he was at a decided disadvantage. Campaigning was done in saloons. Still, he did what he had to do, buying drinks for the crowds and giving speeches. The popular rancher found himself elected to the state assembly by a comfortable majority.

In Sacramento, Howard discovered his new job allowed him plenty of time to socialize, make new friends, and attend banquets and parties. At one of these events, the new legislator met sixteen-year-old Isabelle Holton, daughter of a prominent local judge. There was a mutual attraction, the young city girl being fascinated by Howard's tales of frontier ranch life in Mariposa County. When the new legislator received a card inviting him to Judge Holton's residence a few days later, the couple talked like old friends and began a friendly relationship.

When the legislature shut down that winter, Howard returned home to Mariposa. He reappeared in Sacramento in the spring and immediately began calling on "Belle" Holton. The judge saw what was happening and very much approved of the handsome young rancher. They were married in June 1857, and the following month made the trip to their home in the hills of Mariposa. Their first child, Ida, was born in 1859. Others soon followed.

Howard's horse breeding and stable of blooded stock led to his building a good racetrack, and during the racing season both he and others promoted contests at the ranch. When his horse "Trafalgar" won a

The town of Mariposa grew slowly, as shown in this 1860 view, but it was still the county seat and a supply center for the area. *Author's Collection.*

rousing race there in late October 1860, the editor of the *Gazette* ended his account with this notice.

Mariposa Gazette, **October 9, 1860:**

> *...Before closing it would not be amiss to state that Bill Howard has some number one horses. His three year-old stallion, "Black Prince" is the finest horse ever in this section of country; "you bet." But don't bet on anything against anything on Howard's ranch.*

Realizing that eventually his children must have access to a school, Howard moved to the Merced County seat of Snelling. The move was significant also because Howard's old Ranger companion, Charles Bludworth, had a horse track there. With their love of good horse-

Howard and his beautiful bride as photographed on their wedding day. *California State Libary.*

flesh, it was perhaps only natural that the Howard brothers were operating a Snelling livery stable in early 1864. When a flood inundated the town in 1867, the Howard family again moved. The 1870 census shows them living in Stanislaus County, near Knight's Ferry. Their family by now had grown to three boys and three girls. Later, he returned with his family to Mariposa County, taking up residence in the small community of Bridgeport, a worked-out mining camp. He had read the law in Texas, and now he resumed his legal studies and was soon ready to hang out his shingle.

In the spring of 1874, Howard met his friend James C. Lamon, who had rode down from Yosemite for a trip to the East. Lamon had first visited the great valley in 1859 and had been so impressed he determined to live there. He built a comfortable log cabin and became Yosemite's first homesteader. A bachelor, Lamon was taking a trip that summer and he invited Howard to utilize his cabin while he was gone. A great admirer of Yosemite, Howard jumped at the chance, planning to take his whole family on a vacation they would never forget.

25

There were several hotels in the valley now, one owned by J. M. Hutchings, who lived there with his family. Supplies, like tourists, were conveyed from Mariposa to Clark and Moore's small hotel at Wawona, then to the valley floor by horse or mule back. It was a hard and exhausting journey, but the thrill of the first sight of the valley of Yosemite made it all worthwhile. When Horace Greely made the 57-mile saddle trip to the valley in 1859, it nearly killed him, but he was awe-struck at the view.

"I know no single wonder of nature on earth," wrote Greely later, "which can claim a superiority over the Yosemite."

Preparations were made for the trip, supplies of food and clothes packed, and animals selected. With Captain Howard leading their train of twenty-one animals (including a milk cow and her calf), they struck out for the Hite's Cove trail to the great valley. There were seven children now; the younger ones rode double, and within three days the party arrived safely in the valley at Lamon's cabin and settled in for their vacation. It was a "beautiful, and never to be forgotten summer," as Mrs. Howard later described the family's scenic holiday.

The grandeur of Yosemite overwhelmed visitors from the very earliest days. Captain Howard's family was no exception. *Roy Radanovich Collection.*

The return trip was something else, as Belle Howard later recalled in a letter to editor Reynolds of the *Gazette*. She gives no reason for leaving so late in the season, but it was November 12 and the valley was already blanketed with snow. The party began their ascent up the walls of their summer retreat, the rocky trails only allowing for a single-file of animals. Howard had just warned his caravan that they had to get off this trail before nightfall, when he heard his son's voice calling from up ahead.

Mariposa Gazette, **December 5, 1874:**

> *"Papa, Papa! Come quick!" Soon in the dusk twilight our frenzied eyes were riveted upon a fallen animal, which our eldest son was leading when we last saw him. "Quick , papa, come quick!" came quivering back to us. How those words thrilled us! There was the child clinging to those treacherous rocks, with the mule's weight upon his slender arms, dragging him down to destruction, while waiting for "papa" to pass on a trail where there was no visible room for his foot to press… but pass he did, I following closely. Should we fall, seven helpless children would be left to the mercy of the cloudy night on those fearful, lonely heights… .*

Willie Howard had tied one of the pack mules to the horse he was leading when the mule slipped and tumbled over the edge. The mule had been killed, but they saved Willie's horse. Later the cow and her calf were lost, also. That night the family rested in a high meadow, then continued in the early morning.

"The second day," continued Mrs. Howard, "was filled with more startling events even than the first, for two horses and the boy went over together on the Hite's Cove precipice, but were happily rescued; not, however, till my poor tired mother heart had suffered ages of agony."

The Lamon cabin in Yosemite Valley. James C. Lamon became the first resident of the valley in 1859 when he filed his homestead. This is where the Howard family stayed. *Courtesy Yosemite Museum.*

Despite the travails of the return trip, the family had enjoyed their summer so much that the following year Howard began building his own cabin at Mirror Lake, at the eastern end of the valley. In 1875, a stage road was finally completed into the valley making access much easier to the increasing number of tourists. At the large celebration of the event, Captain Howard gave an address, while his eldest daughter read a poem composed by Mrs. Howard. A grand ball was held that evening.

As he grew older, Howard enjoyed his title of "Captain Howard," acquired during 1849 as the result of his election as captain of the party he had accompanied to California.

The first wagon road into Yosemite was a huge boost to tourism. *Author's Collection.*

When the Mariposa County district attorney resigned in early 1876, Howard was appointed to the position, although he accepted the job knowing it would adversely affect his other interests. In 1878 he was elected to a seat at the constitutional convention and saw to Mariposa's interests in the newly created constitution. But whatever his current occupation, Howard always saw to it that his family's summers were spent at their Mirror Lake cabin. The captain himself was elected justice of the peace for Yosemite, so his presence there was now official.

In late July 1882, Captain Howard had to return home from Yosemite to look after some business. He took his twelve-year-old daughter Delia along as company, and the two rode side by side, thoroughly enjoying the familiar mountain scenery. Passing through Mormon Bar, they were in Cathey's Valley on the last leg of their trip when they stopped just below the crest of a hill to check their saddle cinches. Howard later told young James Cunningham, a neighbor, just what happened.

J. C. Cunningham, *The Truth about Murietta*, 1938:

> I heard the sound of a horse's feet in the soft dust of the trail and looked up and there not over eight or ten feet away was a man riding to-

wards me who I knew was gunning for me. I immediately pulled my gun, noticing that he was doing the same. As I aimed my pistol and touched the trigger, my horse...jumped back and jerked me with the rope with which I was holding him and caused me to miss my aim....

Young Cunningham's account was mirrored in the local press, of course. It had been a slow news day in Mariposa, but editor Reynolds had a paper to get out and he was scratching hard for something to fill it up. He had written up a funeral, a camping party in Cathey's Valley, a wedding, and one divorce when he received some startling news.

Mariposa Gazette, July 29, 1882:

...Still later about dusk the community was startled at the intelligence of a serious shooting affray that had occurred between two neighbors living within the radius of a few miles of Mariposa in which one was seriously wounded and the other had come in to surrender himself to the authorities. So much for the events of one day.

The neighbor, one William "Pink" Dodson, shot too fast and missed both times. Howard shot just once, the bullet ripping through the right side of Dodson's jaw and taking out many of his teeth before embedding itself in his neck. Making sure Delia had not been hit in the exchange, Howard rode over to the fallen man to see how badly he was injured. After doing what he could to stop the bleeding, Howard helped him back on his horse and the three riders headed for Mariposa and, after a physician was found, Howard turned himself in to the sheriff. Remaining in custody on a $1,000 bond, he was scheduled to appear in justice court on Monday.

Mariposa Gazette, July 29, 1882:

...For some time past ill feeling had been engendering itself in the breasts of both parties until it had reached the climax and for causes best known to themselves. The parties by chance met on the evening mentioned about a mile from Mormon Bar on the road leading to Bridgeport. Howard, in company with his daughter Delia, was on his return from the Yo Semite Valley, and Dodson was on his way to Mormon Bar; consequently there was no third person present to witness the affray except the daughter of Howard. So far as known, there was but one shot exchanged, being that of Howard, which was from a pistol ball entering the face of Dodson and running back along the side of the face tearing the upper jaw and teeth quite seriously. ... Although suffering considerably, he is considered out of danger.

A justice court hearing was held on August 5, 1882, before Justice Temple. Dodson and Mr. and Mrs. A. H. Young were the only witnesses and they were on the stand most of the day. Since there were no witnesses to the actual shooting, their testimony probably dealt with the origins of the trouble. Confident of their case, Howard's two attorneys waived any testimony in their client's defense and Justice Temple ordered the defendant held for trial before the superior court.

The *Gazette* had somehow overlooked an important bit of evidence that had no doubt resulted in the lack of testimony from the defense. A stage driver had brought news of the shooting to Merced, the story being picked up in the Bay press the next day.

San Francisco Morning Call, **July 24, 1882:**

> *Merced, July 23.—A shooting affair occurred yesterday, about 7 0'clock P.M., near Bridgeport, a few miles from Mariposa....On examining the wounded man, a revolver was found with two chambers empty, apparently but lately discharged....*

The trial took three days, ending on October 19, 1882, with District Attorney George Goucher and W. E. Turner arguing for the prosecution. The following morning the jury announced a verdict of acquittal. The real question was what took them so long? Howard's defense was simply that he had shot in self defense, but how could it have been otherwise? If Howard had shot first, it's likely that Dodson could not have returned fire with his jaw ripped apart!

Dodson was many months recovering from his painful wound. He suffered mainly from an inflammation of his left arm and hand, supposedly from the lead pistol ball that could not be located in his neck and was causing blood poisoning. Six months later, Dodson's medical condition was resolved in an extremely unusual manner.

Mariposa Gazette, **February 10, 1883:**

> *...Dodson experienced no inconvenience from the presence of the ball until about a month ago, when a pain and soreness commenced in his neck, which gradually grew worse. Knowing the cause, he was about to go below to have a surgical operation, when he was attacked with a severe spell of coughing. In the midst of this, greatly to his astonishment and relief, up came the leaden bullet which had so nearly ended his existence. The bullet is very much battered and presents the appearance of having met with hard resistance. It had lain imbedded in his neck just six months and two*

days.... Now, that the irritating cause is removed, we presume that the inflammation will gradually disappear.

Although a practicing attorney, as well as a rancher, Howard apparently was always looking for new experiences and adventures. He ran for the nomination for Mariposa County sheriff in the Democratic primary of September 1884, but lost out in a close race to his friend, John J. Mullery. After winning in the general election, however, Sheriff Mullery asked Captain Howard to be his undersheriff. Although fifty-eight years of age at this time, Howard accepted the post and soon proved he could still ride as hard as the younger officers.

Sheriff Mullery and Howard worked well together. *Author's Collection.*

Howard was well aware that Mariposa peace officers had much more to do with misdemeanors and minor felonies than with major crimes. An old man named William C. Gann was an inveterate thief. Although said to be sixty-five years old, Gann was known to be a hard character and reportedly had a loosely knit gang who helped out in his rustling activities as needed. When a plow was stolen from his field in early December 1883, farmer Henry McMillan followed the tracks of the thief to a nearby fence, where the plow apparently had been transferred to the back of a horse. Following the tracks of two horses some nine miles, McMillan was not surprised when they ended at the Gann ranch.

After obtaining a warrant and the services of a deputy sheriff, McMillan accompanied the officer to Gann's place, but the old man was not at home. They confronted Mrs. Gann and her son Budd, who both denied knowing anything of the missing plow. A brief search of the ranch, however, disclosed the missing plow under a pile of barley sacks in one of the outbuildings. Confronted with the purloined implement, Mrs. Gann was philosophical about the situation, telling the officer to "ask me no more questions and I would tell no more lies." Meanwhile, old man Gann had vanished.

Mariposa Gazette, **February 2, 1884:**

W. C. Gann, for whom a warrant was issued out of Justice Temple's Court, was recently arrested near Milton, Calaveras County, and brought to Stockton, where he is held awaiting the arrival of the Sheriff or one of his Deputies from Mariposa to escort him up. Gann is charged with stealing a plow.

31

A brief stint in the granite Mariposa jail did little to curb the old man's propensity for theft. A few months later, in late June, Gann was back in jail for driving off another rancher's hogs.

While her father was awaiting prosecution in the Mariposa jail, Gann's daughter managed to saw off the bars in the window of his cell, allowing the old man to escape and disappear. Naturally, he had stolen a horse to make his escape. The purloined animal was from Captain Howard's stable and Howard was furious.

Mariposa Gazette, July 12, 1884:

Old man Gann's family would have to get along without him for a while. *California State Archives.*

> *...Howard simply issued his edict and had it promulgated through the Gann region that he had a horse missing and unless it was returned forthwith, his Honor would decree a fate upon the thieves that would not be susceptible of a reprieve. Suffice it to say the horse was returned to Howard's home the following night.*

When wanted notices were sent out around the state for the fugitive Gann, Tulare County lawmen recognized the old man and contacted the Mariposa officers.

San Joaquin Valley Argus, March 28, 1885:

> *Capt. W. J. Howard and Constable Sterne, of Mariposa, arrived on the noon train from Visalia on Monday, having in charge an old man named Gann, who escaped from jail in that county about a year ago, and up to the present time had eluded arrest. He was captured near Visalia by officers of that place from information furnished them from Mariposa. Officers Howard and Sterne left in the afternoon with their prisoner by private conveyance for Mariposa. Several charges of felony are pending against Gann.*

But Gann had gone to the well once too often. He was convicted of injuring a public jail and grand larceny. He was sentenced to six years at San Quentin and was admitted on April 26, 1885.

Stagecoaches could not go all the way into Yosemite from the San Joaquin Valley until 1875. It had been a gradual progression. Roads from Madera, Fresno, and Merced were carved out of the mountains gradually, as the need dictated. Logging roads and trails to mining camps were necessary as travel and supply routes and early in the 1870s, it became clear

A posed stage robbery photograph taken on the Yosemite road. The robberies continued until after the turn of the century, one of the holdups actually being photographed. *Author's Collection.*

that the Yosemite Valley would be a tourist mecca. Even in those earliest times, visitors were taking stagecoaches to Mariposa and saddle horses from there into the valley. When the road was built through to Wawona, where a crude hotel and pack station were located, the stages advanced to that point. Finally, in July 1875, the road was completed into Yosemite.

But it was not merely civic boosters who gauged the increasing travel into the world-famous valley. Others saw another type of opportunity in these travelers. One of the earliest stage robberies on the road, perhaps the first, took place on August 13, 1883.

It was the height of the tourist season and the coach was moving up Grouse Hill, some eight miles from the valley. Suddenly, three men wielding shotguns stepped into the road. Six men and two women were ordered from the coach and robbed of money and valuables amounting to nearly $2,000. The horses were then unhitched and a volley of pistol shots chased them down the road and out of sight. The highwaymen disappeared and despite a prompt pursuit by lawmen, were not apprehended.

The next robbery took place on May 7, the following year. Milton Lee and John Herbert stopped a returning Yosemite coach near Bates Station, in the foothills. The two nervous highwaymen obtained three watches and some $200 from the passengers, then fled to their home territory in San Jose. Both robbers were quickly picked up and did time in San Quentin.

Later that same month, another stage was robbed and it seemed that yet another tourist event was being developed. At Mace's Yosemite Hotel in Madera, where the passengers waited for their coaches, the ticket agent was mightily amused by some of the antics taking place. A "portly gentleman" announced that he was ready for any robber he might meet. After first going through all his pockets to find a key, he opened his valise and removed an article wrapped up and tied with string. After wrestling with the knots for a time, he finally produced a tiny, silver-mounted der-ringer "which," commented the station agent, "would make a highway-man as mad as blazes if he were shot with it."

Women could be just as goofy. "Do you think they will rob us?" asked one smiling female traveler. "Oh, no, madam," responded the grin-ning clerk, "you need not be alarmed in the least."

"Oh," she said, "I do wish they would!"...and her face fairly beamed with optimism at the idea of a romantic encounter with real, live robbers.

Late on the evening of May 22, 1885, a double stage robbery oc-curred. Two coaches were stopped, one while proceeding to the valley from Madera and the other going in the opposite direction. The first coach contained a full load of tourists, both men and women, on their way to Yo-semite; only the men were robbed, however. The second coach contained just two passengers and a Wells Fargo box. The box contained nothing of value and after searching the two passengers, the highwaymen motioned the coach to go on. The road ran through both Mariposa and adjoining Fresno County, so both Sheriff Mullery and Fresno's sheriff O. J. Meade were alerted. Several local constables and Merced deputy sheriff Hiram Rapelje were informed of the robberies and joined the other officers in the field.

Mariposa Gazette, **May 30, 1885:**

> *Under-Sheriff Howard is still out in pursuit of the robbers. We wish he might be successful in securing a portion, or all, of the reward offered. Some say it is $1,200 and others $1,700, either would be a helper.*

Perhaps the reporter was making reference to Howard's large fam-ily. (The story of the robbers' capture and trials is told in the chapter on Hiram Rapelje.) A unique aspect of this particular robbery, however, is that one of the victims wrote to complain of the incident to his hometown paper. An English couple, Mr. W. Chance and wife, had been returning from a trip to Japan when they arrived at San Francisco. A visit to Yosemite was also in their itinerary, and the Chances were robbed in the incident related above and mentioned in the *Gazette* account.

After seeing Yosemite, Mr. Chance must have fumed all the way back to England. At home, he wrote a letter to the *London Times* complaining of the holdup and warning others who intended visiting the "Far West." The letter was picked up by a news service and published in a San Francisco newspaper. Deputy Howard must have chuckled if he saw the article.

San Francisco Morning Call, **August 30, 1885:**

> *...We were all completely taken by surprise. They threatened to shoot upon the slightest move on the part of any of us. "If any man moves I'll shoot him or women either," were the exact words used. We were none of us armed, nor, indeed, with ladies present, would resistance in either case have been justifiable. We were then ordered to alight, ranged in line, and made to hold up our hands under a threat to shoot, if we disobeyed. One of the robbers, revolver in hand, went down the line and relieved us of our watches and chains and money, while the other, standing a short distance behind, kept his gun leveled at us as he had been doing all along, ready to shoot if we made any show of resistance.*

> *The robber actually had the cowardice to hold his revolver to the face of each lady as he searched her. Our stage carried the box of the Wells, Fargo Express Company containing money and valuables. ...As long as the Wells, Fargo Company are allowed to send the treasure entrusted to them in an ordinary stage, the attacks will continue. But travelers can be warned what to expect. My advice to them is to leave behind valuable watches, not to take with them more money than they actually require... The tourist must not expect to hear anything of these robberies at any of the ticket offices or hotels....*

Mr. Chance was right, of course, but ticket agents could hardly be expected to alarm their customers concerning something that had only a slight chance of occurring. Besides, in the mountains, horseback or wagons were the only means of travel.

After the capture of the two stage robbers by Howard and several Fresno and Merced officers, the trial began in early September and dragged on for the next few years. The men were convicted, but after two appeals and two more trials, they were finally released when the third trial resulted in a hung jury. (The story is told in more detail in the chapter on Hi Rapelje.) Captain Howard was no longer undersheriff after 1885, but he was called to testify in all three trials.

In late July 1885, when Santa Clara County deputy sheriff Bennett broke up a rustling ring, Charles "Arizona Cowboy" Doughty headed across the valley on one of the stolen horses, a fine gray. Bennett, before continuing the chase, alerted Sheriff Mullery and his men to watch for the rustler, who seemed to be heading their way. Captain Howard spotted the fugitive on a Mariposa street and promptly took him into custody. When Bennett and a Merced officer arrived shortly thereafter, they found their quarry waiting for them at the sheriff's office. "When thieves escape from beyond the Coast Range with stolen property," reported the *Argus*, "they rarely succeed in eluding the vigilance of Merced and Mariposa officers."

The strangest incident of Captain Howard's days as a lawman had its beginning in the California mining town of Bodie. Situated just over the Nevada border, Bodie had boomed in the 1860s and 1870s, but by the 1880s its salad days were long gone. The mines were still working, however, and it was still a bustling place that often displayed its frontier heritage of violence.

Even in his later years, Captain Howard preferred traveling by horseback or buggies rather than by automobiles and trains. *California State Library.*

Little is known of the antecedents of Peter Savage and his wife. Reportedly he was Canadian, while his wife was French. They had operated a hotel at Virginia City, and after a son was born to them in 1876, they moved on to Bodie. Mrs. Thalma Savage was described as attractive and more forceful than her husband. "The woman," noted one account, "shows more firmness, strength of purpose and energy than her 'hubby.' Her eyes are black, piercing and full of concentrated lightning." In other words, she ruled the Savage family roost!

When Peter Savage was looking for his wife one June evening in 1880, he found her arguing in the store of a fellow named "Frenchy" Mace. After asking his wife what was going on, he listened for a few moments, then whirled with his pistol in hand and began shooting. Mace was hit in the lower back and chest, with the third round going astray, but he stayed on his feet. Luckily, he recovered from his wounds, and Savage was acquitted at a justice court hearing. The incident, however, displayed the man's quick temper and perhaps his wife's duplicity.

HIGHWAY ROBBERY.

The Yosemite Stage Robbed by Masked Robbers.

Monday morning about 11 o'clock, the Yosemite stage driven by Stevens, and carrying six passengers was stopped on the way from Big Tree Station to the Valley and robbed by three men, on foot and masked. The place was almost eight miles from Yosemite Valley, near Grouse Creek. The robbers, who were armed with shot-guns and revolvers suddenly appeared and compelled the driver to stop and unhitch his horses. They, then frightened away the loose horses by shooting at them, after which they proceeded to rob the four gentlemen, who were passengers. They obtained money and jewelry to the amount of $2,000. The two ladies on-board were not disturbed. The robbers then decamped with their booty; the horses were got together and hitched up, and Stevens

Mariposa Gazette,
June 6, 1885.

Thalma and her ten-year-old son, Alexander, appeared in Mariposa County in late 1885. Her husband was not with them. Calling herself Mrs. Savageau now, she rented a cottage in town where she lived with her son. One day, while shopping, she met a Frenchman named Louie Hebert. Small of stature, Hebert raised garden produce and grapes on his Buckeye Creek ranch about a mile east of Captain Howard's Bridgeport home. The lonely, sixty-five-year-old French farmer was delighted to meet someone of his own origins so far from home, and the two met frequently in town after that. Indications are that Mrs. Savageau was very vague about her husband, perhaps hinting that she was a widow. Whatever she told him, Hebert was soon infatuated with the younger woman, who began helping him out on his ranch.

Whatever was going on here, it was soon to reach fruition. Little Louie Hebert was enjoying Thalma's cooking by now and during their conversation one evening he asked if she would be interested in owning his ranch. When she asked what he meant, Louie explained that if she would take care of him for the rest of his life, he would have a document drawn up deeding his ranch to her when he died. The woman smiled. Yes, she might be interested…and the lightning was dancing in her black and piercing eyes. The document was prepared by a local attorney and Mrs. Savageau began spending her days at the Hebert ranch, cooking meals, gardening and doing other work around the place.

Mrs. Savageau seemed to have a fatal attraction for men. *San Francisco Call,* March 1, 1887.

37

Mariposa was just another mining camp to the Savageaus, but a little Frenchman was going to complicate their lives. *Author's Collection.*

In June 1886, Peter Savage arrived in town and visited with his wife. He was also calling himself "Savageau" now. Hebert was not sure just what was going on, but was no doubt relieved when Savageau obtained work at the Washington Mine. By the time Savageau quit the mine in November and showed up again at the Hebert farm, the little Frenchman began to wonder about his agreement with Mrs. Savageau. When the Savageaus began moving their possessions from town into the Hebert place, Louie was certain he had made a terrible mistake.

During the next few weeks the relationship between Louie and the Savageaus turned bitter. There were threats and warnings of shooting. Neighbors were concerned and when they missed seeing Hebert for several days they suspected the worst and contacted officials. Looking into the matter, Sheriff Mullery and Undersheriff Howard soon discovered circumstances enough to warrant the arrest of Mr. and Mrs. Savageau. They were locked up in town and interrogated separately.

In questioning the two suspects, the officers were told that Hebert had gone away, but would return later. When some bloodstains were found near the house, they was claimed to be "chicken blood." Other stories told by the couple had the distinct odor of fish about them, but the couple was allowed to go home.

When Howard returned home from the investigation late in the morning, he took a nap before dinner. Awakened by one of the children, the captain seated himself at the head of the table with a strange look on his face. The family all knew Little Louie Hebert, as did most Mariposans. He had been living in the area for nearly thirty years. Looking around the table, Howard said, "We will never see Louie alive again." Then he told them of a vivid dream he had just had while napping. What follows are the captain's own words as he related the incident to a biographer years later.

Jill L. Cossley-Batt, *The Last of the California Rangers*, 1928:

> *Suddenly I arrived at Louis' ranch, and saw him come out of the barn and make his way to the house. There stood a large tree by the side of the path leading to the house, and behind this crouched Savageau, pistol in hand, awaiting the approach of the unsuspecting man, while his wife Thalma stood at the kitchen door urging him to shoot. When Louis reached the tree he seemed to feel his danger, and turned toward Savageau, who quickly raised his weapon, fired, and Louis fell forward on his face. ... Savageau then dragged the body near to the piggery, where he cut the flesh from the bones and fed it to the hogs. Then he burnt the bones in a furnace, which was used for heating water to prepare the pigs' food. In his agitation and eagerness to destroy all the evidence of the crime, he scattered the ashes around, but left the bones of the head undisturbed.*

Howard's family merely smiled and kidded him. "Why, Papa, it was only a dream," said one of the smiling children. Howard was troubled by the vision, and when he told some of his colleagues at the courthouse of his deadly reverie, he was again laughed at for believing a dream. Sheriff Mullery joshed him also, but said it might be a good idea to take another look around.

A scene in the foothills of Mariposa County. The peaceful ranch life of Louis Hebert was changed forever when the Savageaus arrived. *Roy Radanovich Collection.*

39

Howard and the sheriff rode over and again looked around Hebert place. When a pistol and watch were discovered that appeared to be Hebert's property, the Savageaus were questioned carefully. The couple kept insisting that Hebert had taken his blankets and gone to herd sheep. That night, Howard took his son Willie along and again visited the Hebert place to look for evidence. Going straight to an outdoor fireplace where hog food was prepared, Howard sifted through the ashes and found what appeared to be human bones and buttons. Identifying the site where other evidence had been buried in his dream, Howard dug up more bones. There were blotches of blood in the house. After leaving the bone fragments with two local physicians, Howard camped out that night and watched the house to make sure the Savageaus made no attempt to leave. The following morning when the bones were identified as human, the two suspects were arrested and again taken to Mariposa.

Mariposa Gazette, **December 11, 1886:**

> *Supposed Murder—Within the last few days the town has been much excited by rumors, of a most wicked and atrocious murder, supposed to have been committed on Buckeye [creek]. …Sheriff Mullery and under-Sheriff Howard looked into the matter and soon discovered circumstances enough, in their judgment, to warrant the arrest of Mr. and Mrs. Savage [sic], which was carried into effect Wednesday morning. Savage is in jail and Mrs, Savage is confined at the hospital….*

There was a good deal of circumstantial evidence by now and Howard confronted Savageau in his cell. He told the suspect of the investigation and the community feeling against him. When the deputy described just how the murder had taken place, Savageau was stunned. "How did you know all that," he asked? Howard was careful about how he described his intimate knowledge of the crime, as reported in the press.

San Joaquin Valley Argus, **March 5, 1887:**

> *To the question how he came to the correct conclusion about the murder and cremation? [Howard] said he thought it over Sunday; that night had it all pictured to him; saw Savageau kill him; saw Louis burning, a woman in the case; next morning told his family. Soon as he heard Louis was missing, knew what had happened…*

Sketch of Captain Howard at the time of the Savageau investigation. San Francisco Call, *March 1, 1887.*

Savageau now claimed that the killing had been in self defense, and he showed the deputy a scratch on his arm which occurred when Hebert had shot at him. Howard, experienced in such matters, reported that the wound looked as if it were a scratch inflicted with a broken stick.

The Savageaus were arraigned on December 13, 1886, with a preliminary examination set for the 23rd. Sheriff Mullery, Howard, and Dr. W. J. Kearney were the only witnesses examined, and the couple was held to answer and remanded to the custody of the sheriff. The trial was scheduled for February 23, 1887, at the Mariposa courthouse. District Attorney Newman Jones prosecuted for the people, while R. B. Stolder and J. W. Congdon appeared for Peter Savageau and his wife.

Many witnesses testified to the causes of antagonism between Hebert and the Savageaus. It soon became clear that Mrs. Savageau was the cause of the murder, but she had carefully kept her skirts clean from a direct involvement in the killing. Howard spent much time on the witness stand carefully going over the details of the crime and the evidence that had been discovered. Peter Savageau had confessed to the crime, but pleaded self-defense. The

Peter Savageau had been goaded into the murder, but only he would pay the price. *John Boessenecker Collection.*

evidence was too strong, however, and there was no legitimate excuse for the attempt to dispose of the corpse in such a barbarous manner. Although Savageau was convicted of first-degree murder and sentenced to life in prison, his wife was acquitted. The all-male juries in the frontier West rarely convicted women of murder.

Sheriff Mullery was not re-elected, and in 1887 Captain Howard could devote full time to his farm and horse racing...and reminiscing. He particularly enjoyed telling the story of the California Rangers and how they tracked down and killed Joaquin Murrieta. He gave interviews to four newspapers over the years: the *Merced Sun* in 1890, the *San Francisco Examiner* in 1893, the *San Francisco Bulletin* in 1899, and the *San Francisco Chronicle* in 1907. In his later years, Howard was always good for a story as he sat on a bale of hay outside his stable at San Francisco's Bay District Track.

An estrangement developed between Howard and his wife, Belle, perhaps originating in his large family or the couple's own age differences. They had lost several of their nine children over the years, always a particular tragedy for parents. After their divorce, Belle married a man named Northrup, and the couple settled in Texas.

Howard received a letter from Galveston, Texas, in late 1899. His brother Thomas had long ago moved back to Texas to take care of their mother, building a house for her in her final years.

Mariposa Gazette, **December 2, 1899:**

> *Another Ranger Gone— Hon. W. J. Howard received a letter last week announcing the death of his brother, Thomas T. Howard, at his home near Galveston, Texas. The deceased was a resident of California years ago and was one of the band of rangers who captured and killed the famous California bandit, Joaquin Murrieta. Hon. W. J. Howard of our county was also a member of the band of rangers....Mr. Howard is now the sole survivor of the famous band of rangers.*

The old Ranger's daughter, now Mrs. Ida Desmond, lived in Oregon and around 1904 asked that her father come live with her so she could look after him. Over the years, Howard had been writing the story of his life and he now saw the opportunity of finishing his project. He moved north and in 1905 was close to completion of his manuscript when it was destroyed by a fire. Upset at the loss, Howard hesitated for some time before finally resuming his project. He was eighty years old when he resumed work on his story, putting himself on a daily writing schedule. It was many years before he was finished.

The Portland Morning Oregonian, **February 5, 1922:**

> *Author, 96, Ends Book—History of California Rangers Completed.*
>
> *Captain William J. Howard, 96, the last of the dauntless California Rangers of '53, but now a Portland resident, is about to realize the dream of a lifetime of literary labor....*

Publishers, however, were unenthusiastic about the old Ranger's work. Seeing value in his tale of early California, one publisher suggested Howard have a professional writer put the manuscript into a more readable form. About this time, the old Ranger met a young Englishwoman, a friend of his daughter, whom he persuaded to take on the job. Jill L. Cossley-Batt, despite research in California and the Howard's participation, managed to assemble an interesting manuscript, but it suffered from a lack of depth, perspective, and a grasp of California history. Still, we must be grateful that the effort was made. It is, at least, an outline of a colorful life. The book, titled *The Last of the California Rangers*, was published in 1928. Copies are relatively scarce today.

Captain Howard was ninety-six when he died in Portland on January 3, 1924. He was survived by four sons and the daughter with whom he lived. The *Mariposa Gazette* published an uninspired obituary, but the *Fresno Morning Republican* had it right in stating that "California loses a most distinguished citizen."

Although Howard had been only a sporadic lawman, he had probably seen more excitement than many career officers. And, if he exaggerated some of his experiences on occasion, as a neighbor once suggested, perhaps that is one of the privileges of an advanced age.

Even at an advanced age, Captain Howard still had that steely look in his eyes. *Newspaper sketch in Author's Collection.*

This highly illustrated reminiscence of Captain Howard appeared in the *San Francisco Chronicle*, April 21, 1907.

In one of his last interviews, the old captain impressed the reporter with his tales of a long, varied, and fascinating life that was now inevitably drawing to a close.

Duluth Sunday News-Tribune, **January 29, 1922:**

> *If in memory he sees the fields of the Argonauts and longs for the strains of the mad Spanish waltz in the fandango, he says no word. He has hung up his spurs, saddle and bridle for the last time, but he is still a soldier of fortune who believes fervently in the destiny of America.*

The End

Chapter Two

Lafayette "Punch" Choisser

"He held official positions with honor..."

Stockton *San Joaquin Republican,* **July 10, 1855:**

> *A man named Brown, commonly known as "Cherokee Brown," killed three men and wounded three others, at Calaveritas, the fore part of last night. Particulars not known, except that he shot one man on account of a gambling quarrel and the others were killed and wounded in attempting to arrest Brown. The stage is just starting. I will give you further particulars by next express.*

Now this was some slaughter, even for early Gold Rush California. The killer's full name was Samuel M. Brown and he came from sturdy, Kentucky stock. His father, a prominent Democrat, had been horribly carved up in a personal encounter before being blown to smithereens in a steam-

Young Lafayette Choisser got off to a bad start in Gold Rush California, but he had a second chance. *Trabucco Family Collection*

boat explosion. Sam's two brothers, William and George, had fought in the Mexican War, William afterwards joining in the great California Gold Rush with his brother Sam. The two brothers apparently separated when Sam killed a man on the trail, then fled to California where he quickly learned the rudiments of mining in Mariposa County.

After taking up gambling during the evening hours, Sam Brown showed up one day at the claim of miner R. G. Dean, who later recalled the incident.

The Grizzly Bear, **November 1913:**

> *Sam's personal appearance was anything but that of a desperado, when he came over and seated himself on a rock-pile on my claim in the Agua Frio in*

March, 1850, and genially chatted with me about the diggings, and the laborious and uncertain results in mining.

He told me he had "Just come through from Texas, and allowed he'd rather play keards than run a [gold] rocker"....

By April 1854, Brown had moved his mining operation to the mining camp of Carsons, four miles west of the town of Mariposa. Late that month, young Brown shot a gambler named Gray during a card game. The wounded man lingered for several weeks before dying, but fearing that Gray's pals might want to get even, Sam moved north. Several friends in his entourage traveled with him, including John Hicks, Hugh "Bunty" Owens, and various others. Two young brothers named Lafayette and Tallyrand Choisser were tagging along with this rough crowd, mining and perhaps watching the gambling in their spare time. The Choisser brothers could not have selected worse companions.

At this time Lafayette was nineteen and Tallyrand thirteen years old. The two brothers had grown up in a farming family of Saline County, Illinois. Their father, Jean Choisser, was a wild and hot-tempered French Canadian who skippered keelboats to New Orleans for a living. After meeting Nancy Sutton, Choisser purchased 240 acres in 1817 and began farming, settling down after

An early engraving of an Illinois settlement. *The History of Jo Daviess County, Illinois, etc. 1878.*

marriage to sire twelve sons and one daughter. He named his first four sons William, Joseph, Timothy, and Charles, while succeeding offspring were a reflection of his heritage—Napoleon, Voltaire, Attallas, Tallyrand and Lafayette. Rounding out his offspring were a second son named Charles, Edmund, John, and Mary Ann.

Bored with farming and with a great gold rush going on, Lafayette, Tallyrand, and several neighbors joined a wagon train to California sometime in 1850. After a difficult journey, they were soon prospecting for gold in Mariposa County.

Now, as they traveled north with Sam Brown and his men, the Choisser boys crossed the Merced, Tuolumne, and Stanislaus rivers, stopping to gamble along the way. When winning, they would stay in an area until their chips ran low. In good weather they would try their hands at prospecting. By late summer of 1855, they were operating from a tent in Calaveras County at a mining camp called Calaveritas. But, wherever Brown went, trouble was not far behind.

Calaveras Chronicle, July 16, 1855:

> *At Calaveritas a man named Brown was dealing monte, and a Chileno came to the table, picked up some of the money lying upon it, and demanded to bet it. Brown refused, and ordered the man to put back the money. Hard words ensued, which soon provoked a fight. Two of the Chilenos were killed with a knife, another was badly cut, and one was shot through the body with a rifle ball; he is not expected to recover. The Americans were not injured at all. On Monday two of the men named Samuel Brown and Hugh Owens, were arrested, brought before Justice Spencer, examined and committed for trial. They were brought here by Deputy Sheriff Thorn, and are now lodged in the county jail. Four of the Chilenos engaged in the fight were taken at San Andreas on Tuesday night, where they are still held to await examination.*

Brown's demoniac temper had flared when one of the gamblers pulled the blanket off his table, upsetting his monte layout. After killing two of the gamblers with his Bowie knife, Brown and Owens fled with a howling crowd of Chilenos at their back. During their flight, they fired on their pursuers, mortally wounding another of the Chilenos. Brown and "Bunty" Owens were taken prisoner at the cabin of John Hicks, one of Brown's entourage. The Choisser brothers were at the cabin and watched

Wherever crowds gathered in a mining camp or the streets of San Francisco, there was sure to be a gambling hall or tent. *Author's Collection.*

47

as Deputy Sheriff Ben Thorn walked, alone, up to the cabin and arrested Brown and Owens.

During the preliminary hearing at Justice Orrin Spencer's office, the room was crowded with Brown supporters and angry Chilenos. In the excitement and babble of voices, young Lafayette Choisser tried to hand Brown a loaded revolver, which Thorn snatched as he knocked Choisser down. It was a desperate situation, but Thorn maintained control and delivered his prisoners safely to jail.

Ben Thorn was a long-time lawman in Calaveras County, and one of the best. *John Boessenecker Collection.*

Sam Brown stood trial for manslaughter at Mokelumne Hill in early October 1855. When his appeal failed, Brown was shipped off to San Quentin where he arrived on October 18 to begin serving a two-year sentence. He was an exemplary prisoner, but upon release, he resumed his career of murder and mayhem and was shotgunned to death by a Nevada stage station operator in 1861.

Brown's gang apparently scattered after the Calaveritas bloodbath, the Choisser brothers continuing their prospecting efforts after heading back to Mariposa County. In 1856, they took up residence in Bear Valley, near the town of Mariposa. This was considered the southern end of the mining country, where the oak trees of the foothills began making way for pines, chaparral, and manzanita. Indications are that the boys found work with the Fremont mining interests and became involved in yet another kind of trouble.

After leading several government exploring expeditions for the army, officer John Charles Fremont had been an early arrival on the West Coast. Participating in the establishment of California as a U.S. territory, Major Fremont served briefly as military governor in 1846, then purchased the Mariposa Land Grant from Mexican Governor Juan Alvarado for $3,000. This was a huge grant of land, dominating much of what is today modern Mariposa County. Returning to the East, Fremont resigned his army commission, published his memoirs, then returned to California on a private exploring expedition.

Fremont arrived back on the coast just after the discovery of gold in 1849 and was delighted to find a rich vein of gold had been discovered on his Mariposa grant. Appointed the first U.S. senator from the new state of California, Fremont turned over his grant to subordinates and returned to the East to find himself very popular due to his travels and writings. He ran for president on the platform of the new Republican Party in 1856, but was defeated and settled in California to begin developing his mining property.

When Lafayette and his brother returned to Bear Valley, it is thought they both went to work for Fremont's mining company. Lafayette, who by now had acquired the nickname of "Punch," was a good worker and apparently made many friends.

Neither brother had much education so they probably teamed, dug, hauled dirt, and did other manual labor at Colonel Fremont's claims: the Pine Tree Mine, the Mount Ophir claim, the Josephine Mine, and the Princeton. Reportedly, the monthly payroll alone at these mines amounted to $10,000. Although he was making a fortune, Fremont had many serious, and costly, legal problems.

The Oso House in Bear Valley, Fremont's company town headquarters. The town was the Choisser brothers' home for many years. *California State Library.*

As on other land grants around California, squatters and claim jumpers had swarmed over his properties, which were scattered over 44,386 acres. Although he had paid for the grant in good faith, the actual boundaries were not known, as the grant had never been surveyed. When Fremont leased his Mount Ophir mine, he found it already occupied by the Merced Mining Company, a company that also was working the Pine Tree and Josephine mines and had erected expensive machinery on the sites.

Fremont went to court to prove his title, but when he won, it made no difference to the Merced people, who refused to vacate the property and their investment. Although a shooting war was somehow avoided, there were nasty notices in the local *Mariposa Gazette,* as well as frequent skirmishes between employees

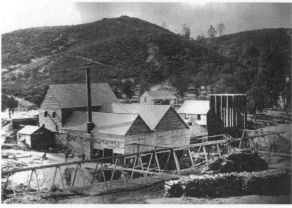

Fremont's Mount Ophir mine. Fremont's properties contributed much to the local economy. *Roy Radanovich Collection.*

of the two companies when they met in a saloon or on the street.

Margaret Bigler was one of the early settlers in Bear Valley. Joseph, her husband, worked for the Merced Mining Company and, being a thrifty soul, managed to save enough of his wages to open a saloon. There were at least two other saloons in Bear Valley—Fremont's Oso House hotel and a provisions store which also featured a bar. Punch Choisser frequented the two latter emporiums, but on occasion, with a few too many drinks under his belt, he and his pals might drift into Bigler's place looking for trouble.

Fremont had won the recent trial against the Merced Mining Company in July, but the case was under appeal and many were bitter that the situation continued to remain unresolved. It was after midnight when Punch and a friend entered Bigler's saloon on October 26, 1857.

Mariposa Democrat, **October 29, 1857:**

> *Fatal Shooting Affair — Again it becomes our melancholy duty to detail the occurrence of one of those unfortunate collisions which are becoming, we are happy to state, much less frequent than formerly. From the best information received by us, the following are the particulars: On Sunday last, a man named Punch entered a saloon kept by a man named Joseph Bigler and asked for liquor, which was served to him. After drinking, he was walking away from the bar without paying for the liquor, when Bigler asked him for the money. Some angry words then passed between Bigler and Punch, when the later struck the former on the head with his pistol. After some further altercation, Punch went out, in a moment returned, and in a scuffle which ensued, Bigler was shot with a pistol in the hand of Punch. The ball entered the right breast, and passed out at the left side,*

causing death in about twenty minutes. Bigler is reputed to have been a very quiet, inoffensive man. He leaves a wife and two children.

The *Mariposa Gazette* reported that as they were leaving the house, the proprietor asked who was paying for the drinks and Choisser replied that he would. At the same time, he asked if his credit was not good. Some words passed, and Choisser drew a pistol and struck Bigler on the head. Bigler, standing behind the bar, picked up a gun. Choisser was at the door with his pistol drawn, when someone present told him not to shoot. He replied that he would not, if Bigler would put up his gun. Bigler immediately set his gun aside. Choisser then rushed in and seized him, striking him another blow with his pistol, and then shooting him through the breast.

Sheriff Joshua Crippen was a good officer and had Punch in custody within a month after his flight. *Mariposa County Sheriff's Office.*

Other accounts add no more details to the shooting, but considering the bitterness between the Fremont people and the Merced Mining Company, it is likely that the controversy initiated the seemingly senseless murder. After telling Tallyrand what had happened, a disheartened and sober Punch disappeared into the cold, dark night.

Punch headed for his old stamping grounds in Calaveras County, perhaps hoping one of the old Sam Brown crowd would shelter him. Mariposa sheriff Joshua Crippen tracked the fugitive to Calaveras, but then lost the trail. Before returning to Mariposa, he alerted the local officers to keep an eye out for the fugitive. On November 9, Constable Lecky, of Independence Flat, spotted Punch and soon had him locked up at Mokelumne Hill. Sheriff Crippen was promptly on his way north.

Mariposa Democrat, **November 26, 1857:**

> *Murderer Arrested—Sheriff Crippen on Friday last passed through Hornitos on his way to the county seat, having in charge the man known as "Punch," who it will be remembered, shot Bigler at Bear Valley, last month. Much praise is due the sheriff for his exertions in procuring the arrest of the man, as well as for the discreet manner in which he was conveyed to the county jail; as we are informed that without the precautions taken, the prisoner would probably not have reached it.*

The Choisser brothers were reunited when Tallyrand visited Punch in the granite stone jail in the county seat at Mariposa. Henry G. Worthington was retained as Punch's attorney. At the arraignment in mid-December, he filed a demurrer which was overruled and the trial date of July 24, 1858, was set.

Perhaps Worthington felt sympathetic to these two brothers, since his own brother had led an outlaw's life and would die in a gunfight in Tulare County in 1864. Later, Henry Worthington would build a career as a very prominent attorney and politician. When he died in 1909, he was the last survivor of the pallbearers at Abraham Lincoln's funeral.

The trial records have not survived, but the judge would later state there was "conflicting testimony" in the case. When Punch was convicted of manslaughter, his lawyer filed the appeal to the state supreme court as soon as possible. Indications are that the prisoner was allowed bail and went back to work. Several of his friends urged him to leave the area, but he insisted on staying to protect his bondsmen. When the appeal was denied, Punch surrendered to the sheriff and was sentenced to five years in state prison. He was admitted to San Quentin on November 7, 1858, to begin serving his term.

While Punch tried to adjust to prison life, Tallyrand, Worthington, and other friends began collecting signatures to solicit the governor for a pardon. After his capture in Calaveras County, Punch was surprised by an old family friend who had recognized the name and visited him in the Mokelumne Hill jail. James Hardy had known the Choisser family in Illinois and now he was agreeable to writing a letter to Governor John B. Weller in support of a pardon for Lafayette.

"I knew Choisser at home," wrote Hardy, "knew his parents, brothers and sisters, all including the applicant bore excellent characters and

San Quentin State Prison as it looked in 1859 when Punch Choisser was doing his time there. *California State Library.*

were honest industrious people. I trust that you will treat this matter kindly and as the offense does not involve that moral turpitude attaching to other felonies... I think the ends of justice could be better observed by releasing the prisoner from his present contact with men of bad spirit...."

A long list of prominent Mariposa County names accompanied the Hardy letter, along with letters from the trial judge, County Clerk William Guard,s and others. Another plea was signed by the sheriff, prosecuting attorney, and various county officers. A letter from San Quentin attested to

San Quentin prison cell of the early days. *California State Archives.*

the good conduct of Choisser and was signed by the warden, the captain of the guard, the lieutenant of the guard, the turnkey, and other officers. It was also suggested that Punch be "requested" to leave the state upon his release and return home to Illinois where there would be no "improper associations" to tempt him.

San Quentin had been constructed slowly over the years, but it was fairly complete now, with the prisoners making bricks used in building the prison and to sell in San Francisco. The surrounding wall was finally finished, but it was out of square and built mostly with saltwater sand for mortar. If the food was bad, at least all holidays were observed. The prison population constantly fluctuated, but there were 500 prisoners now, mostly foreigners and some 200 native Indians. Punch made the best of his situation and Tallyrand may have been able to visit him briefly, although generally only visitors in groups were allowed.

One day Punch was summoned to the warden's office and told he had been pardoned by the governor. Perhaps Tallyrand met him at the gate on May 3, 1861, and the two brothers had a grand reunion and celebratory dinner in San Francisco.

A condition of the pardon, however, was that Punch leave the state and return home to Illinois. It is not known whether the family was apprised in some way of the tragedy in California. Modern descendants, contacted by the author, knew nothing about it, however, and certainly neither Punch or Tallyrand would have mentioned it. Chances are Tallyrand had borrowed, or saved, enough for the journey and had ushered Punch aboard one of the coastal steamers for Panama. Whatever the arrangements, Punch was going home.

Shortly after his brother left the state, Tallyrand showed that he had the same quick temper that had gotten Punch into trouble.

Mariposa Gazette, July 9, 1861:

> *A fight occurred in the town of Bear Valley, Friday evening last, over a game of cards between Tallyrand Choisser and a person whose name we could not learn, in which the former was slightly stabbed in the side. The party stabbing was knocked down and jumped upon before inflicting the wound. He was arrested and lodged in jail Saturday evening.*

Returning to the village of Eldorado in Saline County, Illinois, Punch must have had a touching reunion with his mother. The teenager who had left home more than ten years earlier had returned as a man. His father had died the previous year, however. Just which children were still in the area is not known, although several were serving in the Union Army, as was Mary Ann's husband, William Parrish. Timothy was still on the farm and may have looked after his mother, Nancy, who often went off to visit her married children in neighboring areas.

Punch seems to have learned the error of his ways and was determined to curb the wild temper inherited from his father and to make up for his past misdeeds. For a time he apparently helped out on the family farm, but when a traveling photographer came to Eldorado, Punch made his acquaintance and asked if he could learn the business. The photographer was agreeable, and in time Punch learned the delicate art of the cheap ambrotypes, tintypes, the newer Albumen prints, and the novelty Cartes de Visites.

Meanwhile, in California, Tallyrand became acquainted with Josiah Lovejoy, who had made a trip to the west side of the San Joaquin Valley in 1862. When Lovejoy discovered some oil and asphaltum deposits and seepages, he thought there was a good opportunity to develop them as a source of kerosene. In Bear Valley, Lovejoy organized the Buena Vista Petroleum Company, but it was not until the spring of 1864 that enough investors could be enrolled to begin operations. Among the first to invest was Maurice Newman, the new husband of Margaret Bigler, whom Punch had made a widow in 1857. Another was Tallyrand Choisser. Tallyrand and four other men were the first crew sent over to stake claims and begin work in Tulare County, now western Kern County, along the edge of the Coast Range.

Back in Illinois, Punch had met a girl. A teenager when she was courted by the handsome wanderer, Julia Aldridge married Punch on July 30, 1865. In time, Punch told her that he yearned to return to California, but he had to save up enough money to provide for a good start. He told her all about Bear Valley and his travels in the mining country, leaving out his troubles generated by the Bigler shooting. He wrote cheerfully to Tallyrand and told him of his new wife. Tallyrand's response to Punch's letter announcing his marriage has survived.

Frank F. Latta, *Black Gold in the Joaquin*, 1949:

> *Tulary Co Call   March the 18-1866*
>
> *Dear brother and Sister I seate myself to let you know that I am well at present hoping that when this comes to hand that it will find you injoying the same blesing. I received yore leter of the 1 ov Feb which gave mee much pleasure to her from you and family and the rest ove the conexions I recived yore wifes potograph which I think is very butiful I think you aught to bee hapy with her I will take good care ove the photograph…*
>
> *I have bin grately disipointed in regards to the Selling ove oure claims all thow I am in good spirits. I think that it is only a matter ove time. I have got a nuff grownd to make twenty men rich if it was in pensylvany wher oil lands is rody sale … You said Something a bout coming to this contry asking my advise I think that you had beter stay wher you ar if you can make a good living for yore self and wife. If I am lucy I will divide with you aslong as I have a dolar. Oinge to the uncertainty ove things I cood not ad vise you to cum to this contry I think ove coming home some time al thow I canot say when… Well Punch I cant think ove enymore Stuff to right to you You must excuse my bad spelling for I have lost my dictionary. Give my love to all…*
>
> *Tallyrand Choisser*

Punch was seemingly testing the waters for another sojourn in California, but he must have been concerned about any official or legal objections to his returning. For now he would stay put.

It had been reported in the short-lived *Fresno Times* a year earlier that "Since Tallyrand Choisser and two others…sold their claim to a company in New York for the sum of $20,000 in greenbacks" there had been a stampede to the area. It may have been, however, that this big sale was a newspaper rumor. Although the era of "Black Gold" was thirty years in the future, at this time the black gunk had to be refined into kerosene, or used as lubricating or roofing material. With no railroads in the valley yet, transportation to market from the isolated area was the real problem.

Apparently, Punch and Julia's first child, John, died in infancy. Their second child, daughter Nancy, was born in 1867, and Phillip two years later. In 1869, with the completion of the great transcontinental railroad, Punch finally decided that he had been exiled long enough and he told Julia they were going to California. There would not be any wagons or boats involved this time, however. Steel rails now linked the continent from the Atlantic to the Pacific. The Choissers looked forward to a vacation in the form of a comfortable train ride to the California coast.

The journey was planned for early 1870, when the new baby would be old enough to travel. Depending on weather, track problems, and any emergencies that might arise, the trip would take less than a week. They would take their own food, being aware that they could also have meals at stops along the way. As Punch pointed out, landmarks along the way that he had seen in 1850, the family must have thoroughly enjoyed the journey.

Bear Valley, as it appeared about 1860 in a photograph by Carleton Watkins. *Roy Radanovich Collection.*

In Sacramento, Tallyrand may have met them at the station with a wagon, and they made their way south to Mariposa and their new home.

Punch and his family are listed in the 1870 Mariposa census, but Tallyrand is missing. By 1867, the Buena Vista Petroleum Company had finally dissolved in the face of growing stockholder delinquent assessments. Tallyrand may have been working somewhere else during this period, his previously quoted letter indicating he was in Tulare County. Punch found work as a laborer, probably at one of the Fremont mines. He missed his brother greatly, but the two men were leading their own lives now, no longer the rootless boys of the Gold Rush days. They tried to get together for holidays but sometimes it was difficult to contact each other. Ironically, Tallyrand was actually nearby when Punch received final word of his brother.

Fresno Expositor, July 31, 1872:

> *Fatal Accident—On Friday the 19th last, as Mr. T. Choisser was riding on a high seated lumber wagon near Plainsburg, one of the wheels running into a rut, precipitated him to the ground. The fall was a very peculiar one, he lighted directly on his face, his feet and legs swung over backward, thus throwing the force of the fall upon his back and causing a dislocation of the spinal vertebrae. He was immediately taken up and conveyed in a senseless condition to the hotel at Plainsburg, where he was attended by Dr. Rucker of that place, who immediately pronounced his injuries to be of a fatal character....He lived until Saturday then died.*

Punch must have been shattered. After the burial, he wrote and informed his mother of the accident and then all went sadly on with their lives. Punch and Julia's fourth child had been born the previous February—a girl they christened Sara Emma. When their fifth child was born the following year, he was named Joseph Tallyrand Choisser.

It is not known if the Choisser brothers had arrived in Mariposa County at the time of the Indian troubles of 1850–51. Certainly they had heard of the "war" that had erupted in those first years of the Gold Rush, and of the resulting clash between militia and the Chukchansi and other local Indians. In the course of the conflict, the great Yosemite Valley had been discovered and the defeated Indians were forced onto reservations and into facing the grim reality of having to depend for subsistence on the invaders who had taken their lands. For the natives of the Mariposa hills, it was a harsh and bitter time. The grim scenario was repeated all over California.

Unable to either successfully fight back or comprehend the newcomers, some of the natives did what they could to get along in a white man's world. Many made a place for themselves working as laborers, while others could not. Liquor helped some forget the humiliation of villages plagued by drunkenness and venereal and other diseases. Whenever there was trouble, good Indians suffered along with the bad.

In the 1860s, when the reservation system failed due to the duplicity of the government and its agents, the natives returned to their ancestral lands. They established their Indian rancherias in remote areas so as to have minmal contact with the white man. While many of the white settlers appreciated the availability of Indian labor for their mines, ranches, and farms, others could only discern them with a jaundiced eye. And, as there are bad men in any society, so there were bad Indians—made worse by ill-treatment, liquor, and a white society mostly intolerant of those whose skin was of a different color.

In the 1870s, in the hills above the neighboring villages of Millerton and Mariposa, there was a steady, if sporadic, series of incidents, often in-

An Indian council on the Merced River, shown here in a photograph taken about 1872. *Bancroft Library.*

volving liquor. In late August 1870, the *Fresno Expositor* reported: "The Indians are certainly acting strangely. They have abandoned their camps at all points, and with their women and children have gone far back into the mountains. The course usually pursued, we learn from those versed in Indian matters, is when they contemplate an uprising, to send their squaws and children out of the way of danger...."

Militia groups were formed at various ranches, but it was soon learned that the rumors had been started by ranchers with stock in the mountains trying to scare other ranchers from taking their animals to the mountains to compete for feed. Actually, when they talked to the Indians they were told there were no plans for an uprising, but if there was one, they would stand by the whites. Another brief newspaper item reported one of many incidents during this period.

Fresno Expositor, May 31, 1871:

> *Indian killed—A few days since an Indian stole a horse from Mr. John Hughes of Upper Kings River. The owner discovering his loss went in quest of his property. He discovered it in the possession of the Indian who, finding that he was caught, showed fight. The Indians took charge of the body and buried it with the usual ceremonies of his race.*

On August 12, 1875, at a waterfall called the Cascades some seven miles below Yosemite Valley, a toll house on the Coulterville Road was burned down. It had been operated by George Boston, whose body was found in the smoldering ruins. Evidence suggested the house was broken into and the operator murdered.

Mariposa Gazette, August 21, 1875:

> *...On the evening of that night, a notorious Indian scoundrel, Piute George, the companion of another Indian called Zip, who is known to have committed two or three murders, was seen standing at the door of the toll house talking to Boston, with a six-shooter in his belt. Suspicion is strong against him as the murderer and incendiary, and his after movements seem to confirm those suspicions. Men are after him, and it is hardly possible that he will escape arrest.*

The following September, the chief suspect in the murder was captured by Deputy Sheriff Westfall. Paiute George was taken when several other Indians decoyed him into an ambush engineered by the deputy. "He

resisted capture," noted a report in the *Mariposa Gazette*, "and was dangerously shot, a charge of buckshot entering low down on each side of the
back-bone, coming out just below the groin, in the front part of each thigh.
In addition to this his breast and shoulders are riddled with shot. He is an
athletic Indian, not more than 21 years of age, and must be possessed of
extraordinary vitality to survive his injuries."

A five-hundred-dollar reward was offered for the Boston killers and
when two other Indian suspects named Lame George and Indian Tom
were captured, trials were scheduled in the district court for late April
1876. Paiute George was tried first. On the second day he was convicted
and sentenced to life in prison.

Lame George and another Indian named Colorado George were
tried next and were acquitted. Indian Tom and another Indian named Zip
had their cases dismissed amid groans of surprise and resentment among
many of the courtroom spectators, who felt a great injustice had occurred.
But, the evidence was just not there.

Punch and others living in the mountains must have wondered just
what would happen next.

During this period there were other incidents—horses being stolen
and nearly run to death, then turned loose. Other times they would be
found butchered for food. Houses had been broken into and plundered
and lone women threatened if they did not give up items of property. In
August 1877, rancher Samuel Wilson disappeared from his home on Pea
Ridge and could not be located. Another rancher, John Hale, returned
home after a trip to find his cabin on the Chowchilla River had been broken into and thoroughly trashed. The door had been forced and the inside
was a shambles with crockery broken, chairs smashed and heaved into the
fireplace, and blankets and clothes cut into ribbons. Hale and others were
convinced that Indians were the culprits.

Then on May 9, 1878, there was another killing in the mountains. A
young son of Eleazar G. Laird, a prominent rancher in the Chowchilla Valley, stopped by the cabin of farmer Jonas Thompson, who lived on Striped
Rock Creek. It was warm and he wanted a drink of water, but saw no one
about. The cabin door was closed, but young Laird heard Thompson call
for him to come in. Entering, the boy saw bloodstains and Thompson lying

on a mattress with his rifle beside him. When Laird asked if he were sick, Thompson replied, "No, but I am shot!" Young Laird rode to the nearby Whitley ranch and asked that someone go aid Thompson, while he rode to Mariposa for a physician. It was mid-afternoon when Doctors Ward and Kavanaugh arrived and rendered all the aid possible. Later, Dr. Ward related events to editor Reynolds of the *Gazette*.

Mariposa Gazette, May 11, 1878:

> The doctors arrived at the place about three o'clock, and found Thompson very weak, and suffering great pain. They administered stimulants and opium, which gave him some relief. Thompson told them that at about eight o'clock in the morning he had gone out into his garden and was stooping or kneeling by a small walnut tree, for the purpose of examining it, when he was shot in the back from a pile of rocks near by; that he walked to his house as quickly as possible for fear of another shot, went inside, took down his gun and then pulled a mattress onto the floor and laid down on it with his gun by his side. An examination of his wound showed that he had been shot in the back, the ball entering on the left side of the backbone, passing through the left lung, and coming out under the pelvic bone; thence it passed into the right thigh, from where it was extracted by the doctors.

The fifty-three-year-old rancher said he did not think he had an enemy in the world just before he died. Robbery was thought to have been the motive for the shooting, but when Thompson walked quickly back to his cabin, the assassin apparently thought his shot had missed and fled the scene.

Suspicion was immediately directed against local Indians as the culprits. A posse of neighboring ranchers followed tracks to the vicinity of Pea Ridge, but there the trail was lost. "If it should so happen," noted the *Gazette*, "that the murderer ever is found in this vicinity we think that the services of courts and officers would be dispensed with." In late May, a $500 reward was offered by Governor William Irwin.

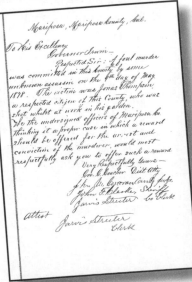

Letter from Mariposa officials to the governor seeking a reward for the killer of Jonas Thompson. *California State Archives.*

Suddenly, on June 11, there was a break—or what seemed to be a break—in the case. Jimmy Butler, a popular Chowchilla River rancher, noticed a gray horse being staked out for the night near his home. The rider, whom Butler thought he recognized, crawled under a bush for his evening slumber. With his rifle in hand, the rancher watched the site all

The granite Mariposa jail stands on a hill behind the town and would be difficult to break into even today. *Author's Collection.*

night and captured a young Indian when he was untying his mount. He surrendered quietly and Butler took him to town where he was lodged in the county jail. At his justice court hearing on June 13, young Willie Ross was charged with the killing of Jonas Thompson.

In Mariposa, a local election was held on June 19 and the count was going to take all night. About 2 A.M. the following morning, a tremendous racket woke up the town and sent startled residents running into the streets. The din of the noise led the crowd up a slight hill to the county jail, where a mob was shouting encouragement to several men with sledge hammers, crowbars, and chisels trying to break down the heavy iron jail door. The ranchers of the Chowchilla River area were certain that Willie Ross was Jonas Thompson's killer and were not going to wait for the law this time.

Mariposa Gazette, **June 22, 1878:**

> *…These people have become alarmed—their lives, their homes and families are in great danger; they know not what moment they are to be shot down or disposed of in some summary manner by the hand of the assassin, who has been lurking in their midst for some time in the past. And they have reasons to believe the Indian to be the bloody and high-handed assassin, since the murder of Thompson, which occurred on the 9th of May—these people have, as we are informed, been diligently inquiring into and searching for evidence by which to perfect the chain of circumstances brought to bear against this Indian, and have carefully and calmly considered the subject with which their lives are kept in continued jeopardy….*

In short, they would wait no longer for justice! Sheriff John F. Clarke and District Attorney George G. Goucher pushed their way through the crowd and had a conference with Eleazar G. Laird, a local rancher and leader of the raid. In a few minutes the throng broke up and began leaving town.

"It looks to an outsider," opined the *Gazette*, "as if the stubborn resistance made by the door has had more to do with the Indian's present general good health than all the arguments and promises of the Sheriff and District Attorney."

It was mid-December before Willie Ross's trial was scheduled for January 5, 1879. The courtroom was always crowded, often with the ranchers of the Chowchilla district, who nodded their heads grimly when each bit of circumstantial evidence was introduced. They had not forgotten the Boston murder and how Lame George and Colorado George had been acquitted and Zip and Tom dismissed for lack of evidence. It was true that Paiute George was convicted, but the others were probably just as guilty. This must not happen again! The assault on the jail had failed, but they were going to settle with Indian Willie, one way or an-

Built in 1854, the Mariposa County Courthouse is the oldest in the state still in use. It was from here that Punch Choisser's desperate ride began. *Author's Collection.*

other, as a lesson to any of the malcontents and killers roaming the mountains! When the jury announced its verdict on January 15, it was "Guilty!" With the agreement of the defendant, Willie's counsel waived time for sentencing and the judge sentenced the eighteen-year-old Indian to life in prison. As the courtroom was being cleared, Sheriff Clarke took charge of Willie and quickly ushered him into a back room where he explained the plan to get him safely out of town.

Sheriff Clarke was a wise man. He was well acquainted with many of the Chowchilla River ranchers and knew they had been extremely worried about their families during the past few years of Indian troubles. He also remembered the recent assault on the jail. For the past few days, there had been too many ranchers in town calling themselves the "Chowchilla

Lafayette Choisser proved to be the right man for the job of getting Willie Ross safely to San Quentin. *Author's Collection.*

Rangers." Clarke was sure a lynching was planned and would be implemented unless he could prevent it. He had sworn in several extra deputies who were stationed in the crowd outside. The sheriff had already put a plan into place that would get the prisoner out of town, and out of harm's way, as soon as the sentence had been pronounced.

He swore in Punch Choisser as a special deputy during the last days of the trial. Sheriff Clarke had told him of his plan and made him aware of how vital timing and speed were to avoid a vigilante lynching. When the verdict was announced in court, Punch was quietly waiting outside a side window of the courthouse, mounted on his spirited horse, Black Bess. The animal was a beautiful dark mare with a white star on her forehead. Punch loved the horse and he looked anxiously at the saddled prisoner's mount, wondering if it would be able to keep up.

Nothing is known of the reasons Punch was chosen for this job. He was mentioned as serving as a constable in Bear Valley, and constables were officially utilized as allies of other lawmen in troublesome times. Clarke and Choisser must have been well acquainted indeed for the sheriff to trust him with such an important and desperate plan.

Sheriff Clarke led Willie to the designated window and helped him through it and onto his horse. "Good luck," said the sheriff as Punch spurred his horse out onto the road that led to Mount Bullion, the trail to Hornitos and the railroad at Merced. It was cold, with an inch or so of snow on the ground, while a fog bank eased down off nearby Mount Bullion.

Mariposa Gazette, **January 18, 1879:**

> *...In charge of Deputy Sheriff Lafayette Choiser (sic), who was well mounted, and in less time than it takes to write it, the Deputy with his prisoner galloped away toward Merced....Then commenced a rustling and running in all directions, some to convey the intelligence, others for the horses of those who were bent upon pursuit and shedding the blood of the Indian.*

The Chowchilla Rangers took some twenty minutes to get organized and gallop past the courthouse in pursuit of their quarry. It was a Wednesday afternoon in Mariposa, and in the saloons and on the streets an unusual number of people were talking about the exciting events.

Mariposa Gazette, **January 18, 1879:**

> *After a few hours the suspense of the community was partially abated by news brought in by Mr. Snyder, who had met the deputy and his prisoner about twelve miles out, on the lower end of Slattery's toll road; they were going as fast as their horses could carry them, Choisser urging the Indian to do his best riding, but telling him that his pursuers were gaining ground. Snyder had heard several guns fired before and after meeting them. He did not meet the pursuing party, they having taken a by-trail as it is supposed, with a view to a cut-off.*

More waiting ensued, as the citizens listened for news and discussed their views on the subject. The *Gazette* account continues:

> *...Later in the evening, came another dispatch. The Deputy with his prisoner had arrived in Hornitos, hotly pursued by the enemy. They only halted a moment, to order fresh horses to be sent after them, and at the same time requesting that no fresh horses be given to the enemy. This was a strategic move on the part of the deputy, for which he is entitled to great credit. It was with much difficulty that the principal pursuer obtained a fresh animal, but after some delay he succeeded in obtaining one, and took up the chase with the speed of a hurricane. Choisser had been overtaken in the mean time and mounted on fresh horses, and with a start of about three miles set out on a twenty-six mile race to Merced.*

It was only later discovered that the pursuing posse of Chowchilla Rangers had begun to lose interest early in the chase and began dropping out in the foothills along the way. Perhaps this was because Sheriff Clarke and several deputies were spotted closing in on them from the rear. In any

Street scene in the old Gold Rush town of Hornitos, where Punch obtained fresh horses during his desperate ride. *Author's Collection.*

case, only one man reached the old mining town of Hornitos. This was most likely Eleazar Laird, the outspoken leader of the Rangers who was not going to give up the chase.

Late that evening, the Merced stage arrived in Mariposa. *Gazette* editor Angevine Reynolds was at the depot with his notepad and questioned the driver as the coach was being unloaded:

> *Great anxiety was manifested to learn the result of this ride for life, as nothing was heard from the parties after the deputy received his fresh horses until the stage arrived Wednesday evening. The deputy and "Lo, the poor Indian," arrived in Merced at 5:30 p.m. just fifteen minutes ahead, and had the prisoner safe in the jail before the enemy arrived. This is perhaps the best time ever made between this place and Merced—a distance of forty-five miles via Hornitos—they having left here about half-past one o'clock.*

Punch slept in the Merced jail that night. At six the following morning, the lawman and his prisoner warily climbed aboard the train for San Francisco. Now, he could relax. In the Bay City, Punch went to the city jail, where convicts were kept overnight before the trip to San Quentin. When Punch was asked for the prison commitment papers, the officer gave them a blank stare. He had forgotten the papers! The documents were forwarded and Willie Ross was admitted to San Quentin on January 18, 1879, as prisoner No. 8636. He died in the prison hospital in January 1888.

Back in Mariposa, everyone was relieved that the episode seemed to be over. But this was wishful thinking. The worst was yet to come.

Situated on Mariposa Creek, in the foothills some five miles below Mariposa, was what was left of the old mining camp of Mariposita. The camp dated back to the

The commitment papers of Willie Ross, shown here, had to be forwarded when Deputy Choisser left without them. *California State Archives.*

early 1850s, but when the small camp had worked out its placer deposits, the miners moved on. The few buildings there were cannibalized over the years for the lumber and by the 1870s the area was home to a small settlement of local Indians. Their shelters were constructed of lumber scraps, old canvas, heavy tree limbs, and brush. There were also some native huts, brush or tule mat-covered pole frameworks, the origins of which dated back to ancient times.

An Indian village in early Mariposa County. Just such a settlement was the scene of a murderous attack by local ranchers in late January 1879. *California Department of Parks and Recreation.*

These native inhabitants, like other Indians who found themselves in contact with the whites, were still suffering from the disruptions of the 1850s. In the Mariposa area, the native groups were Chawchila, Chukchansi, and other foothill Yokuts groups, with complements of others who had been pushed out of their own territory, or were simply looking for a land where they could live in their old ways. Paiute George was probably a Paiute from Nevada who had come over the Sierra for these reasons. The great majority of these In-

San Quentin was a death sentence to many of the Indians within its walls, who were used to a life of freedom in the open. *California State Library.*

dians worked for the local farmers and ranchers, few of whom stopped to think that they were living on land that had belonged to the Indians. That some of the Indians took property and committed other crimes against the isolated settlers is undeniable, however. That they were on a collision course with their white neighbors seemed inevitable.

January 26, 1879, was a Sunday. Early in the morning, two young Indians, named Jack and Jeff, staggered into Mariposa shouting that their village had been attacked by some white men. Both boys were exhausted from their flight and were so excited it was hard to get the gist of their stories. They finally gave a coherent account of the tragedy to someone who then rode to the scene and reported back to editor Reynolds.

Mariposa Gazette, **February 1, 1879:**

> *...Our informant who was upon the ground on Sunday soon after the slaughter, gathered the following from Indian Jeff who with another, Indian Jack, escaped from the assassins. Early in the morning Sam, who occupied the cabin with his family, was awakened by a knock and call at the door. He responded to his name and requested the outsider to wait till he put on his shoes and he would come out. As he opened the door he was seized and his hands tied behind him. At the same moment, the other Indians who were sleeping in another wig-wam, were seized and likewise tied in the same manner. All five were then required to stand or sit down together with a guard over them, while the old Indian was being executed by hanging.*

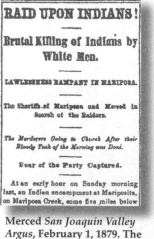

> *Just at this moment a break was made, Sam ran into his own house when he was followed and killed. Jack and Jeff made good their escape. Charlie was shot in the forehead and in the neck, Amos in the eye and in the back—Sam in the head. A favorite old washerwoman about the town was shot in the side of the face inflicting a severe wound considered dangerous...*
>
> *...It was, as described to us, a scene of carnage never before witnessed in this region of the country. There lay promiscuously upon the ground dead, three stalwart young Indian men, each shot through the head; close by was an old decrepit Indian about seventy years of age, who had been hung up by a rope till dead, and afterwards cut down—said to be the father of Willie Ross, convicted for the murder of Thompson, and sent to prison for life....*

Merced *San Joaquin Valley Argus,* **February 1, 1879. The** terrible story made front page news around the state. *Author's Collection.*

The three young Indians all worked for local farmers to support their families. The older Indian, known
as Teacha, called Old Teacher by the whites, had been
hanged and then shot to to make sure he was dead. His
wife had been shot in the face, the wound being painful,
but not mortal. "Never," opined editor Angevine Reynolds, "since the organization of Mariposa County, or the
existence of the *Gazette*… has its editor been called upon
to chronicle such a dastardly, infamous, and inhuman
massacre."

**Merced County sheriff
Anthony Meany.** *From
Elliott & Moore's, History
of Merced County, 1881.*

Sheriff Clarke investigated the scene and from
talking to the survivors verified what he already knew.
The Chowchilla Rangers had exacted their revenge. A coroner's jury examined witnesses and concluded that the vigilantes responsible for the Mariposita massacre were Eleazar G. Laird, his two sons, Samuel and Robert,
Fred Holt, Charles Hendricks, Charles Groves, Nathaniel Green, and John
Hale. After the slaughter, Laird and others had gone from Mariposita to
attend services at a Mariposa church, apparently to establish alibis.

Laird owned ranches in both Merced County and Mariposa County.
Since Laird's Cathey's Valley ranch was in Merced County, Sheriff Clarke
contacted Merced County sheriff Anthony J. Meany about a joint roundup
of the suspects. Deputies Choisser and Barnett joined Sheriff Meany and
his deputy, and the four officers rode over to Laird's place, known as the
Barber ranch. Laird's wife reported that her husband and three sons were
driving a herd of hogs to Mormon Bar. A search of the house turned up
none of the wanted parties and the lawmen proceeded to follow the wagon tracks of their quarry.

It was midnight when Punch and his party reached Mormon Bar,
about two miles below the town of Mariposa. They found the two younger
Laird boys at Newman's store-hotel and learned that Eleazar Laird and his
son Sam would be returning for them in the morning after visiting some
friends on the Chowchilla. The following morning, Meany and his posse
were waiting.

Mariposa Gazette, **February 1, 1879:**

> At the moment Laird and Sam were seen approaching the store, out
> steps Sheriff Meany who confronted them with a salute of, "Good morn-

ing, Mr. Laird," which attracted his attention to Sheriff Meany; he [Laird] appeared bewildered and turned as if to make off in another direction, but upon hearing Meany's command to stop, and observing one or more of the deputies rapidly closing in with guns pointed toward him, he bethought himself at once that prudence was the better part of valor, and surrendered.

In Mariposa, Laird refused to go into the jail until convinced by the lawmen he was going in, one way or another. Inside, he sulked in the corner of his cell for a time, then in a sudden violent rage broke out the glass in a barred window.

In a Hornitos justice court on February 14, Laird and his fellow rangers were admitted to bail in the sum of $25,000. District Attorney George Goucher and Merced lawyer Russell Ward appeared for the prosecution, while W. E. Turner represented the defendants. By the time the trial was commenced, on April 24, the famed attorney David S. Terry had been added to the defense.

David S. Terry, ex-state supreme court justice, for the defense. *Author's Collection.*

Two of the defendants were still at large, but the jury was selected and trial commenced, dragging on for several days with the interminable reading of the longhand indictments. When the prosecution introduced its various Indian witnesses—"Jeff, Minerva, Willie's Mother, etc."—the defense offered its ace in the hole and objected on the basis that the Indians did not understand the nature of an "oath." Prior to 1863, Indians had not been allowed to testify against white men in court. Now, their testimony was acceptable, but it was probably David Terry who had come up with this zinger, and the prosecution, in the words of the *Gazette*, "was left like a ship at sea without sail or a rudder." It was late in the day and the judge proposed adjourning until the following morning, which was done.

Court docket showing murder charges against the Chowchilla vigilantes. *Mariposa County Archives.*

The court was convened again in the morning when spectators, counsels, and clients assembled. The defense had done its homework well and offered "indisputable authorities" to back up their objection. The Indian testimony was the whole case and there was nowhere

A modern view of the old courtroom where Punch was tried in 1857 and where the ranchers were tried for the murder of the Indians. *Photo by Ernie Hoge.*

to go but to give the case to the jury, which was done. When they returned a short time later, it was with a verdict of "not guilty."

Far from being outraged at the verdict, editor Reynolds declared that "there appeared to be a unanimous congratulation to see and to know that the grand farcical drama…was ended. It is to be hoped… that no more bills of indictment will be found in the future founded upon Indian evidence alone, as appears in these cases."

Laird and his co-defendants were released, but the leader of the Rangers was not to have a happy life. Laird's increasingly erratic behavior resulted in his family consulting with a physician. An examination indicated that, for the safety of his family, Laird be admitted to the asylum at Stockton. The *San Joaquin Valley Argus*, February 9, 1884, reported "E. G. Laird, of Mariposa County, passed through Merced on Monday last, in charge of officers, who were taking him to the Stockton Insane Asylum, to which he has been committed." There was little doubt among his family and friends that his mental state was largely responsible for his involvement in the appalling Indian tragedy.

In time, Laird appeared to respond to his treatment and he was released to his family. He led a normal life for a time, but the demons that plagued his consciousness returned again. Although the family watched him carefully, in late June 1891, he slipped out of the house at three o'clock in the morning and in a nearby field fatally stabbed himself. "He leaves a wife, and large family of grown children," noted the *Gazette*, "who are among our most respected citizens, and who have the sympathy of all who know them in this dreadful calamity."

Sheriff Clarke's temporary deputies were no longer needed, and Punch and the others went back to their regular lives. Sometime in the early 1880s, Punch was promoted to assistant superintendent of the Mariposa Grant under Judge O'Connor. He was pleased to get the extra money, since by 1883 there were six children in the Choisser household: three girls and three boys. Nancy, his oldest daughter, was sixteen when she agreed to marry John Trabucco, son of neighbors Louis and Elenor Trabucco, Bear Valley merchants. The couple were married at the Choisser home on February 23, 1884, with many guests from around the county.

Daisy was the baby of Punch's family. She was born in 1882 and before she passed away in May 1972, she was the last survivor of Lafayette Choisser's family.

Punch's work in the Willie Ross case was not forgotten when Democratic candidates were being sought to run for sheriff in the spring of 1884. Editor Reynolds stuck his toe in the water for Punch when the time came.

Mariposa Gazette, **March 29, 1884:**

> *Lafayette Choisser of Bear Valley, is spoken of for Sheriff. He has had experience as Deputy Sheriff and Constable, and is conceded to be a brave and efficient officer. Had it been Choisser who was close upon Greely the other day, that $900 would have been left in this county. He is popular with the foreign element of the county and would poll a strong vote.*

Stage robber Burton Greeley had recently been captured locally by a Calaveras County lawman, and editor Reynolds was irritated that the reward money would now be spent elsewhere than in Mariposa. Punch must have smiled at the compliment, but he was concerned about how his prison record would reflect on his family. He could only hope he had perhaps removed a blot on his good name in Mariposa. As it turned out, Punch decided to run in the August 30 Democratic primary. Unfortunately, he came in last in a field of five candidates. John J. Mullery won a close race with William J. Howard, a veteran of Harry Love's California Rangers. It was stiff competition, indeed. Mullery won the general election and later picked Howard as his undersheriff. Punch still had his job as assistant superintendent of the Mariposa Grant.

On the morning of November 17, 1884, Punch left his Bear Valley home, saddled Black Bess and stopped at Pearl's saloon for an eye-opener. Inside he met Antone De Silva, a friend, and after a drink the two men rode down to Benton's Mills on the Merced River to look at some scrap metal in which de Silva was interested.

Afterward, they rode over to De Silva's house for a light dinner of crackers, cheese, and homemade wine. Before going to the basement for the wine, De Silva opened a bottle of brandy, which Punch had sampled by the time he returned. A man named Evans stopped by for a time and after visiting with the two men, left.

When Choisser stood up to leave, he realized he had had too much to drink. De Silva suggested he lie down for a while, but it was four o'clock in the afternoon and he was anxious to get home. After some help getting into the saddle, Punch directed Black Bess toward home.

When Punch failed to return that evening, Julia was concerned, but assumed he had been busy and would be back sometime during the night. When Punch still had not returned the following morning, the family became concerned. Fifteen-year-old Phillip told his mother he was going to look for his father and rushed over to the stable where Black Bess was kept.

Saddling a mule, Phillip rode down to Benton's Mill on the Merced River. Here, he was told his father had left with Antone de Silva the previous morning. De Silva's house was farther down the river and Phillip rode over there next, but was told that De Silva had not seen the elder Choisser since he had left about four o'clock the previous day. Retracing his route

back to Benton's Mill, Phil was crossing a part of the trail built over a rock shelf when he noticed something five or six feet below the trail. Looking closer, he saw it was his father. Dismounting and scrambling down the slope, his worst fears were quickly realized. "I soon saw and

Benton's Mill was one of the old Fremont properties on the Mariposa Grant. It was near here where Punch's body was found by his son. *Author's Collection.*

satisfied myself that he was dead," Phil later recalled. "I went back to Antone's and told him my father was dead. He said, 'No! It could not be!'"

The boy stopped again at Benton's Mill and told the man in charge where the body was and asked him to watch over it while he took the news back to Bear Valley. Strangely enough, it was Maurice Newman, the widow Bigler's second husband, who carried the news to Mariposa and brought back a physician for the inquest.

The inquest was held at the site and testimony taken by the last men who had seen him. Henry Peard, the local justice of the peace who had officiated at the Nancy Choisser–John Trabucco marriage, conducted the proceedings. There were two wounds, one in the forehead and one on the back of the head. Either could have produced death. Doctor Bell stated that both wounds were from "violence of some kind." After all the testimony had been taken, the coroner's verdict stated that "they were unable to say how the immediate cause of the death of said Lafayette Choisser was produced."

Today, few people know the story of the brave man who lies here in the Mariposa Cemetery. His wife, Julia, rests just a few feet away. *Photo by Jim Secrest.*

No speculation as to how the death occurred was discussed, apparently. Neither the witnesses nor the doctor could see how two mortal wounds, one in front, the other in back, could take place at the same time. It seemed clear to all, however, that he had fallen from his horse and received one of the deadly wounds. It seems not to have occurred to them that he could have fallen from his horse and received one of the wounds from a sharp rock on the trail, then rolled over the edge and fallen down the six or eight feet onto another sharp rock, producing the second head wound.

But there is a second scenario. Bill Evans, one of the witnesses who had lunched that day with Punch and De Silva, testified that he had seen a man named Domingo Azevedo in the area that day. Reportedly a hard character, Azevedo (or someone else) could have stopped to talk to Punch on the trail. Seeing he was drunk, the stranger may have distracted him by pointing out something across the river, then struck Choisser's head with the butt or barrel of his six-shooter. Falling from his horse, Punch would then have tumbled down the slope, acquiring the frontal wound when he hit the ground again.

When Phillip returned home that day, he found Black Bess waiting at the Bear Valley stable. The funeral was attended by many friends from around the county.

"This is a sad blow," commented the *Gazette*, "to a helpless wife and six children, who are deserving of the deepest sympathy of the community in which they live....He was an early settler, and during his residence here he held official positions with credit and honor to himself and to the people....He was honest, industrious and a good citizen."

To which might be added, Punch must have earned some amount of redemption for that long-ago prison stain on his colorful past.

The End

Chapter Three

Emil Harris

"One of the greatest detectives in the West."

On the evening of May 3, 1927, Major Frederick R. Burnham gave a talk to the Historical Society of Southern California. Burnham, at this time sixty-seven years of age, was famous for his experiences during South Africa's Matabele Wars and as Chief of Scouts under Lord Roberts during the Boer War. He had grown up in Los Angeles, however, and on this evening he was speaking of the adobe village of his youth as he remembered it.

In the course of his talk, one of the guests asked how crime was handled in those days of vast open spaces and widely separated towns. Burnham's response was most interesting.

Historical Society of Southern California, Annual Publications, 1927:

Emil Harris, pioneer detective of old Los Angeles. *Author's Collection.*

> *An incident concerning this may shed some light on the problem. [Emil] Harris was one of the men who afterwards took part in the capture of Vasquez and was looked upon as one of the greatest detectives in the West. A murder was committed in San Francisco and they sent for him. After he returned, a few of us were together one night, when the conversation drifted along that line, and we asked him how he found it possible to locate a murderer in a great cosmopolitan city like San Francisco. In those days, San Francisco was looked upon as an enormous city. Its population was about 70,000 and contained representatives of all classes, sailors, trappers, hunters, miners and a sample of nearly every nation in the world. It seemed impossible to us that he could find a criminal in a city like San Francisco.*

Harris told us this was accomplished by the use of a little common sense. In the first place, when a crime is committed, it is by either a man or a woman. Almost surely there will be some mark to show which it is. Immediately you cut the world in half. Half the population need not be considered from that time on. You next naturally eliminate the very old and very young. It is not likely that they would commit a crime. Perhaps the latter would not apply to these days, but it did then. So, by a very quick process of elimination, it only takes a moment or two to narrow that crime down to one of a very few people. In this particular instance it was a woman that was killed. There had been a fight in the room. The man had reached up and put his hand on a shelf. Harris was clever enough to note that mark of the hand in the dust on the shelf, and saw it was not the print of a man's hand which had been reaching up on the shelf, but had clutched the shelf to support himself, showing there had been a struggle.

Then he discovered that the man wore a number ten shoe. The number of men who wear a number ten shoe is rather limited. By careful examination he soon narrowed it down to a few men, and soon he found a strand of hair and realized it was a white man. Then he discovered where the man had taken a wide, rolling step on leaving the premises, and he knew the man was a sailor. Had he been a miner or plainsman he would have walked more as an Indian walks. The number of white sailors wearing a number ten shoe, even in a great port like San Francisco, was quite limited, so in a very few days Harris, with the assistance of local police, caught the murderer in San Francisco.

Major Burnham was speaking of Emil Harris, a far-famed Los Angeles lawman and detective during the second half of the nineteenth century. Burnham's tale well illustrated the way lawmen worked in a day before scientific technology had evolved. Was Harris's

Major Frederick R. Burnham, scout, soldier, and explorer. *From* Scouting on Two Continents.

story, filtered through Burnham, exaggerated to any degree? Maybe. Time does that. What we do know is that in nineteenth-century San Francisco, the city's detective force was headed by Captain Isaiah W. Lees. One of the more noted sleuths of his time, Lees was captain of detectives for most of his career, until appointed chief in April 1897. The time frame of Burnham's Harris story is not known, but if there was a Los Angeles connection to the victim, Lees would have telegraphed the proper authorities concerning the murder. Sent north to look into the matter, Officer Harris would have helped in the investigation, but Lees and his men had jurisdiction and it would have been a joint effort.

Born to Jewish parents in Prussia on December 29, 1839, young Harris accompanied an aunt to New York, where in 1853 they joined other immigrant family members. Harris had heard a good deal about California from his uncle who lived on the West Coast, and the boy decided to join him there. In late 1856, he boarded the steamer *North Star* for Panama. Crossing the isthmus, young Emil boarded the steamer *John L. Stevens* and landed in San Francisco in March 1857. He went to work in the city as an apprentice in a local print shop.

Not caring for his new vocation, Harris next tried waiting tables in a Kearny Street restaurant, but this too quickly palled on him. After discussing matters with his uncle, Harris accepted a position in his relative's Stockton billiard hall.

A supply center for the mining country to the east, Stockton was also a gateway to the vast San Joaquin Valley. It was a lively town and good experience for the boy and he quickly learned the rudiments of bartending, as well. When his uncle acquired an eight-table billiard hall in the growing village of Visalia on the edge of the Sierra Nevada Mountains, Emil was sent across the plains to manage it.

Brought up in the Jewish religion, young Harris was also a physical fitness enthusiast and had been active in the German Turnverein Society in the past. Open to Jew and Gentile alike, the society stressed keeping fit through gymnastics and fencing. In Visalia, Harris was instrumental in establishing the Visalia Gymnasium Club in late May 1865. It was good public relations and a pleasant way to meet people while also promoting

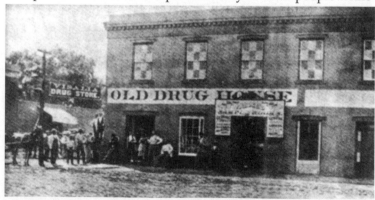

An undated street scene in old Visalia, where Emil briefly became part of the community. *Author's Collection.*

his saloon and billiard hall. Emil was put in charge of the new club's property and appointed gymnast instructor for the organization.

When his uncle sold the Visalia billiard hall, Emil returned to San Francisco where he became a naturalized citizen on March 18, 1867. It was sometime during this Visalia–San Francisco sojourn that Emil met a young Jewish girl of his same age, named Leda. The two had much in common and were married in late 1866 or early 1867. The following year their son was born. They named him Busta, a Jewish name, probably with a family history. Emil was likely working as a bartender at this time, but he was soon restless again. When he heard that the Southern California village of Los Angeles contained a large colony of German and Jewish immigrants, he packed up and made what turned out to be his final move.

The Harris family probably took the coastal steamer *Orizaba* down the coast to the scraggly port at San Pedro. The trip from there to Los Angeles was some twenty miles by the recently constructed railroad, and the family probably took a room at a local hotel or boarding house until a more permanent address could be secured. It was early April 1869, and after seeing to his family's comfort, Emil took a stroll around town. He liked what he saw.

The village of Nuestra Senora la Reina de Los Angeles had been founded in September 1781 by a group of colonists from Mexico. In time, the city's name was shortened to "Los Angeles." Established near a Yangna Indian village, the town was laid out with tule huts constructed for shelter. These soon evolved into adobe dwellings with thatched roofs of reeds, and later of brea (tar), or red tiles. At the time Emil Harris looked around the town, there were still a great many adobe buildings and homes, although larger, wooden frame houses and commercial brick buildings were now scattered up and down Main Street. The Pico House was under construction, a vast stone and brick hotel across from the plaza church. A theater was to be next door, while southwest on Main Street, or Calle Principal, the more modern Bella Union Hotel faced the Lafayette Hotel across the street. The mostly adobe dwellings of old Sonoratown, where many of the Hispanics resided, was northeast and across the street from the town plaza. Brushy mountains surrounded the town.

In the heart of the town, Emil noticed that the large public square, fronting the Catholic church, had recently been planted with small trees.

This was a good sign of progress, although the town was one of the oldest in the state. He also noticed that Bath Street, which stopped just short of fronting the church, was lined with the bordellos and cribs of Sonoratown. As Harris walked around the plaza with an acquaintance, Nigger Alley, politely referred to as the Calle de los Negros, was pointed out to him. It was originally the home of various early Negro, mulatto, and dark-skinned Mexican families, but now was a rundown adobe alley filled with Chinese gambling dens, bordellos, saloons and shops. It was also an eyesore and a constant source of trouble.

The old Catholic Church overlooks the town plaza at right, with Sonoratown at the center. Main Street curves around the church, while Bath Street runs into Sonora town off Main. Despite the slums and old adobes, Emil was charmed by the growing town. *Author's Collection.*

Enjoying a drink in a nearby saloon, Harris learned that although there seemed to be good local job opportunities, he had brought his family to a tough frontier town filled with drunken Indians, wild Californio vaqueros, ranchers, miners, teamsters, and assorted desperadoes. With a population of between five and six thousand people, there were one hundred and five saloons in town, not counting the dozens of hotels, grocery stores, and boarding houses that also offered a bar.

Although Harris had sojourned in frontier towns before, some of the local Los Angeles tales often defied belief. Like the time in 1854 when Mayor Stephen C. Foster had resigned his office to lead a lynch mob, then was voted back into office after the lynching had taken place. Or the local

Indian slave trade, whereby Indians were paid off for farm work with a few coins and cheap brandy so they could get blind drunk at the end of the week. They would then be picked up, thrown in jail, and re-hired by a farmer who paid their bail, and the inexorable routine would begin again. The system was not conducive to a long life and the local Yang-na were disappearing rapidly.

Los Angeles Daily News, **February 12, 1871:**

> *Arrested—An Indian, two squaws and a child were arrested on the 12th for drunkenness. The fines levied were paid by parties desiring to secure their services.*

The numerous adobe buildings in Los Angeles were the reason there was, as yet, no fire department in the town. When insurance companies became aware of this, of course few of the town merchants and property owners could obtain policies with which to protect themselves. The owners of various new brick and stone buildings going up along Main Street assumed they were not in need of fire insurance, but a few serious fires changed this attitude. Adobe buildings were no longer practical, however, and between and along Fort and Spring streets all new construction was wooden, framed structures and brick.

Emil found work tending bar in a saloon called the Wine Rooms, on Main Street. It was a good place to meet people and he was soon well-versed in the burgeoning problems of the not-so-angelic city.

After he saw a notice in the local press announcing a meeting being held in Buffum's Saloon on the evening of November 6, 1869, Emil was in attendance. The meeting concerned formation of a new fire company, and local merchant Henry Wartenberg was elected president of the temporary organization. A vice-president, treasurer, and secretary were also elected and an initiation fee of two-and-a-half dollars was decided on for membership. Monthly dues of twenty-five cents were also assessed. Emil promptly signed up as a charter member, as did a half-dozen or more others.

A committee formed to seek further subscriptions had little luck, but when Rowan's American Bakery burned down in December, the City of Angels knew it was time to get serious. Until some hydrants were established around town, firefighting would remain an extremely difficult business, however. The first wooden pipes had burst and had been replaced with iron pipes. Very interested in the origination of a fire department, Emil was an active member and enjoyed the socializing and politicking which were an integral part of firehouses in nineteenth-century America.

It was probably at this time that he met young George Gard. After arriving in California in 1859 from Ohio, Gard had engaged in mining, sawmill operation, and horse and cattle ranching, before establishing the first ice plant in Southern California. During the Civil War, he was instrumental in organizing Company H, Seventh California Infantry, which served in Arizona and New Mexico. Up to this point, the two young men were very dissimilar.

What they had in common was working as bartenders and both being married with a young child. They enjoyed each other's company and worked hard to establish the new fire company. Harris was elected first assistant foreman the following year.

In discussing their long term vocational concerns, the two men expressed an interest in the local police force. Both also knew several of the local officers and enjoyed listening to their stories while tending bar. Los Angeles had been hard on its lawmen. Sheriff James R. Barton had been killed, along with two of his posse, in a pitched battle with a gang of bandits led by ex-convict Juan Flores in 1857. Sheriff Billy Getman was killed the following year while trying to arrest a gunman on the street.

The second city marshal, Jack Whalen, had been stabbed to death in December 1853, while trying to arrest a murder suspect. Both Harris and Gard were living in town when City Marshal William C. Warren was gunned down in the street by his own deputy in late 1870. The two had

Contemporary sketch of a vigilante lynching of five thugs and thieves outside the Los Angeles County jail in 1863. *UCLA Special Collections.*

quarreled over a reward. Warren, one of the most effective lawmen in the state, had drawn his weapon first, and at a hearing Joe Dye, his killer, was easily acquitted.

Street gunfights occurred almost weekly, as did drunken brawls of every description. The *Los Angeles Star* listed fourteen fatalities from gunshot wounds in 1870. These were only the casualties upon whom autopsies had been performed in the city. There were many others shot, wounded, and killed around the county who were not included. The town also had a bad reputation for lynching. Five prisoners were taken from the city jail in November 1863 and hanged on the porch rafters of the building. A murderer named Lachenais was hanged by vigilantes in late December 1870. The small police force could not control the huge mobs involved in the affair. The vigilantes warned, in a letter to the local press, that they would no longer ignore the light sentences handed down by the county's courts.

Aside from his vocational interests, Harris believed in keeping fit, and he saw the large Jewish and German population in Los Angeles as another opportunity for forming a Turnverein Society.

Los Angeles Daily News, **May 19, 1870:**

> *The Gymnasium is now open at Mrs. Wiebeck's* [beer] *garden, Alameda Street, near the depot. Application for membership or admission must be made to Emil Harris at Wine Rooms on Main Street or F. Morsch at Heinisch's on Commercial Street.*

Harris and Gard must have discussed the police force often. Samuel Whiting, the first city marshal in 1851, had authority to hire deputies only as needed. He did have the sheriff and his one deputy to rely on, as well as local justice court constables and their deputies. By late 1870, there were a few more deputies for the marshal. When Marshal Warren was mortally wounded by Dye, however, officer Jose Redona received a shot in the arm during the gunplay. The city police were then short two officers.

Officer Frank Baker assumed the marshal's job when Warren died. After talking to several of his friends in the fire company, Emil obtained their endorsements, then applied to Marshal Baker for the job of deputy city marshal. Gard did the same thing. The local press announced the new deputies on New Year's day.

Los Angeles Daily News, **January 1, 1871:**

> The following were nominated and upon the part of the Council, confirmed as policemen: Jesus Bilderain, William Sands, S. Bryant, Geo. Gard and Emil Harris.

Among the new officers on the police force were Emil Harris (left), Sam Bryant (middle), and George Gard (right). *Author's Collection.*

Thomas Mulligan was retained on the force, but resigned in May and was replaced by Esteban Sanchez. Baker remained in the marshal's position until the next election the following year. Harris and Gard were put on patrol as a team, with Jesus Bilderain, a Californio, on horseback. The trio worked out a system of police whistlesignals in order to summon the mounted officer for use in a chase. Officers Sands and Sanchez, with Sam Bryant mounted, formed the other watch. The two teams alternated their night and day watches.

Police officers were expected to enforce all city ordinances and watch secondhand shops for stolen goods. Merchants were monitored to assure sidewalks were kept clear in front of their shops and that they were following the rules concerning fire hazards. On night patrol, officers were to check doors and windows and be particularly watchful for fires.

With so many saloons in town, the new officers had no illusions as to what would be a large part of their job. There was a steady string of drinking-related arrests, drunken brawls in saloons and on the street, as well as property damage claims. These were run through the justice courts as quickly as possible; the city could use the money and the jail was neither large, nor all that secure.

The home-wrecking results of the many saloons were often made evident, as the new officers promptly discovered. In early February 1871, a man named Harmon concluded a tour of village drinking establishments by returning home and beating his wife, then chasing her out of the house. "Not content with thus summarily controlling his own household," reported the *News*, "he invaded that of a neighbor and came to speedy grief, a report of the affair coming to the ears of Officer Harris. His case will come up for trial today before one of the justice courts."

A week later, the *News* reported another drink-induced row. "Arrested—Yesterday morning officers Gard and Harris arrested a rowdy for breaking dishes and raising a row generally at McDaniel's hotel, or lodging house, near the depot."

In early March, a crowd of boys playing baseball near the plaza were interrupted by three drunken Indians who, grabbing the bat, took over the game. "One young American," noted the *News*, "with true Caucasian instinct shied a stone at one of the invaders, and a battle-royal was likely to ensue when officers Harris and Gard appeared on the scene, and marched the Indians, who were very drunk, off to jail."

With no street lights in town yet, the night patrols were proving to be hazardous to the new officers. The main streets had saloons open until all hours and helped illuminate the area in the front, but alleys and back streets were usually filled with holes, stacks of lumber, garbage, and other impediments to chasing fleeing burglars. When Marshal Baker appeared before the city council and requested lanterns for his night patrols, he was told to purchase them. Night patrols then became much safer.

In mid-April, Harris interrupted a fight near Negro

The new Pico House (left) and Merced Theater gave the town a metropolitan look. *From* La Reina. Los Angeles in Three Centuries.

Alley between several "cholos," a Californio term for lower class thieves and rowdies. When he released one of the brawlers for a moment to grab another, the freed one bolted. The fellow ran away, up Sanchez Street, Harris right behind him. A short time later, the officer returned with his man.

The recently completed Merced Theater was set to open on April 20, featuring "Professor Silvestre, the greatest Illusionist and Magician in the World." Emil and Leda Harris enjoyed social events and were certainly in attendance, if he was not on duty.

There were nine public schools and five or six private institutions in the city now. Los Angeles, however, had grown in a haphazard fashion, as need demanded, and with little planning. The result was that several adobe schools were located along Bath Street, near a row of bordellos. In late April 1871, a principal of the schools protested to the city common council, in session, about the noise and bawdy language being used by the strumpets across the street. Principal Rose suggested either the women be quieted or the schools be moved. The council ordered Marshal Baker to look into the matter, and he acted promptly.

Los Angeles Daily News, **April 28, 1871:**

> *To Keep within—The police yesterday in obedience to orders from their chief, the City Marshal, notified the troublesome dames in Bath Street to keep within their doors during the day, and to refrain from the use of disorderly language. This is the result of Dr. Rose's remonstrance to the City Council, which should, perhaps, have been made months earlier.*

The next day, as Harris and Gard were walking in front of the *Los Angeles News* office, a span of mules up the street was spooked and broke into a run. The team was rushing down the street when the two officers jumped in front of it, separating so that the mules would have to run between them. Grabbing the harness and reins of the two lead mules, the lawmen managed to halt the plunging animals. The scene caught the attention of someone in the newspaper office and a brief article noted that "Had the team escaped the officers attention but one moment more, some children crossing the street would have received serious injuries."

County Jailor Frank J. Carpenter. *From* Sixty Years in Southern California.

A few days later a thug named Bell wound up a tour of the local saloons by creating a disturbance in a Requena Street restaurant. After paying a justice court fine for his actions, he resumed his tour the following day. Winding up at the same restaurant, he recommenced operations on a larger scale, vowing his intention of "going through" the establishment, which he proceeded to do. When Harris and Gard were summoned, Bell resisted their efforts all the way to the city jail. The jailor, one Frank Carpenter, received the same treatment and was as patient as the officers had been until he was struck by the prisoner. The jailor responded in kind and heaved him into a cell. "Soon after," reported the *News*, "Bell inquired plaintively for a basin of water, and all became quiet." Probably, a split lip needed repairing.

The redlight district stirred the local pot again when an over-sized harlot named May Merritt, with the nom de plume of "The Fenian," was hauled into justice court by a constable. She was charged with breaking a decanter over the head of a patron during a late-night supper in a restaurant next to the Blue Wing Saloon. Her cursing was shut down by a stern look from the constable, but when she requested a witness who looked "just like you, Judge," the court could hardly contain himself and quickly gaveled for a hearing the following day. She was acquitted when the witness corroborated her story of being called "a vile name" by her accuser prior to her attack. She left court accompanied by a large black dog, "the absence of which, at the time of the difficulty, Mr. Short probably owes his life." The girls made for lively times.

The local demimonde was a constant source of such scenes in justice courts.

Los Angeles Daily News, May 4, 1871:

> *Maria quarreled with her lover yesterday evening; that was natural, but in so doing she raised her voice to an unnatural pitch, and he pitched into her. The affair resolved itself into a vigorous row, and ended by both parties being arrested by the officers on duty and conveyed to jail, where they remain. Maria is a member of the demi-monde, or of a monde somewhat lower. Her lover (?) is lower than any monde at all.*

When "The Fenian" again showed up in jail a few weeks later, the *News* just could not resist some colorful comment and published this item.

Los Angeles Daily News, **May 31, 1871:**

 To Jail — Two soiled doves went fluttering and somewhat wrathfully cooing down Main Street under the protecting wing of officer Gard. They roosted last night in [jailor] Carpenter's poultry yard, and will be plucked by the Mayor this morning. In other words, the English of the above is, the Fenian and one of her companions had a difficulty and went off to settle it according to the womanly art of self defense. Law interfered before other damage had been done than such as four finger nails could execute upon the Fenian's visage.

To promote an upcoming Turnverein program at its hall, Officer Harris invited a *News* reporter to attend one of its semi-weekly meetings. The newsman was particularly impressed with the gymnastic skills of the young boys. Emil, who was chief instructor of the group, was quite proud of his youngest students. "The skill of the pupils does great honor to the ability of the leader," the reporter later wrote, "and to his activity as well, as he must set the example on each new movement."

A flurry of counterfeit bills was found circulating in late May. A Lafayette Hotel clerk named A. W. Bell, who had lately taught a course in identifying bogus currency, kept a supply of counterfeit bills on hand as examples with which to compare real notes in his class. One night a burglar broke into Bell's room and, not knowing the stack of currency he found were bogus, grabbed them and escaped. A few days later the bills started showing up in town and Gard and Harris were soon on the trail of the thief.

Obtaining a description of the man from various establishments where he had variously passed, or tried to pass, the counterfeit bills, the two officers soon spotted him on the street and had him in jail. Joseph Merchant, a twenty-year-old Frenchman, had no sooner been booked into the city jail than more counterfeit bills began showing up. These were $10 and $20 notes on the Bank of Utica, New York. Again, Harris and Gard sallied forth, tracking and arresting a young man named W. A. Ford at the Lafayette Hotel. In searching Ford, he was found to be wearing a buckskin vest in which was found some fourteen hundred and eighty dollars in counterfeit ten and twenty dollar bills. Young Ford insisted that the money was payment he had received from a cousin in Arizona. He could prove his story by "creditable witnesses." Ford, a former resident of the nearby village of Los Nietos, did indeed have an excellent reputation according to several "reliable parties" from that town, as reported in the press.

Ford's preliminary hearing was held before U.S. commissioner Lander on June 4, 1871. Several witnesses were examined, the case was continued until the 19th, and Ford was released on $1,000 bail. He promptly disappeared. Enlisting the services of Harris and Gard, Deputy U.S. Marshal Jonathan D. Dunlap prepared for a horseback desert chase.

Dunlap's posse headed for San Diego, then rode east toward Arizona. They searched around western Arizona looking for signs of the counterfeiters, but without any luck. Finally, they got on the trail of one of Ford's party. Dunlap stayed behind to see what he could find, while Harris and Gard followed the trail back into California. They were not surprised when the trail led straight to the Ford gang's origins, Los Nietos. Seeking out the homes of several witnesses who had testified as to Ford's good character, the two lawmen found they had been trailing L. E. Chilson, and he was quickly taken into custody.

After returning to Los Angeles, Chilson said he was not with the Ford party. He claimed to have been offered $300 by Ford's bondsmen to bring him back, but no one believed him. Chilson was accused of abetting a counterfeiting operation, as well as perjury for giving false testimony as to Ford's good character. By July 15, Chilson was on his way to San Francisco and a grand jury hearing, while Marshal Dunlap returned from Arizona with no further news of Ford's gang.

The Chilson capture was the main prize of the Arizona expedition, but there was yet another bonus to the affair. While in the border town of Arizona City, Harris and Gard noticed everyone in town was suspicious of—or feared—a white man employed as a waiter in a Chinese restaurant. Ira W. Raymond, when questioned by the two detectives, claimed he too was a detective employed by the government in covertly watching several government officials in town. Raymond left town the next day, stating he had finished up his tour of Arizona.

Upon returning to Los Angeles, Harris and Gard found Raymond registered at the Pico House as a "Detective, Secret Service Department." He had been poking around government offices in town, questioning the small amount fixed for the bond in the Ford case and government operations generally. By now Harris and Gard were becoming increasingly aware of the strong and distinctive aroma of fish, and they began snooping around.

Raymond, apparently as dumb as he was fraudulent, next called at Deputy U.S. Marshal Dunlap's office and began foolishly throwing his weight around. Fortunately, a real government detective named Henry Finnegass was present and immediately questioned Raymond's authority. When the con man showed a bogus telegram and offered various other phony stories, he was turned over to Harris and Gard, who clapped him into jailor John Clancy's "hotel," and then headed for the Pico House to search his room.

Los Angeles Daily News, July 23, 1871:

> *He spent the night in jail and his papers were searched with a view to finding out what manner of man he really might be. Among them were found what purported to be the naturalization papers of a Chinaman, the offender's employer at Arizona City. Upon the person of the delinquent was found a paper purporting to be another railroad transfer in the shape of a deed from Leland Stanford to Ira W. Raymond, granting in consideration of the sum of $1,500, "all real estate donated by Congress for railroad purposes and situated in the town of Arizona, county of Yuma, and Territory of Arizona." The document was duly signed, and was also attested by the signatures of Lloyd Tevis, Chas. Crocker, and M. S. Latham, all three gentlemen having subscribed themselves in a wonderfully similar style of penmanship.*

"The wild goose chase after Ford," concluded the *News*, "set on foot by Mr. Dunlap has been productive of good leading to the discovery of an imposter." Of course, the officers involved were all praised lavishly. Raymond soon found himself escorted aboard the coastal steamer *Orizaba*, heading north for a San Francisco grand jury appearance. Not caring to risk a trial, Raymond pleaded guilty to a felony and was admitted to San Quentin on October 17, 1871, to serve his one-year term.

Back on regular duty, Harris and Gard received word that a Chinese girl had been badly beaten by one Sing Lee, a "boss" in one of the Chinese companies. Among his other business concerns, Lee dealt in women. When the two officers arrived at Negro Alley, they found the girl had received a severe beating from her master and they took her immediately under their protection. When the lawmen told Lee he was under arrest and must accompany them to jail, he adamantly refused. A pistol under his nose convinced him otherwise, however.

Los Angeles Star, July 22, 1871:

> The woman, when Sing was arrested, begged protection from the officers, and asked to be put in jail where the Chinamen could not get to her, declaring that she belonged to Sing, that he wanted to sell her for $500 to another Chinaman for use as a prostitute, and that when she refused to agree to the sale, Sing attacked and beat her, swearing that she should go or die. She begged to be allowed to stay in jail, stating that Sing was "a big Chinaman," and that, because she had been the cause of his going to jail, the other Chinamen would kill her, cut her body into little pieces, and conceal the murder so effectually that the "Melican man" would never find it out. She remains in jail, but as her owner is rich, and able to fee a lawyer, she will probably be taken out on a writ of habeus corpus, and turned over to his tender mercies.

In concluding the article, the *Star* voiced its racist opinion, and to some extent the growing opinion of the country, on the Chinese presence in America:

> We venture the assertion, that many a dark and terrible deed has been perpetrated by these heathen in their secret dens, which will never come to the knowledge of the Christians whose places they are usurping.

Further illustrating the local feelings on the subject, the *Los Angeles News*, July 19, 1871, went even further in editorializing on the Sing Lee case; "The Chinese have no business here, and never can form part of our people; but being here, they must not be suffered to carry out their heathenish customs."

Adding to the perceived infamy of the case, Sing Lee was fined a mere $10 by the mayor's court. Although many were outraged at this slap on the wrist for such a brutal crime, the true feeling against the Chinese was anything but sympathetic. The Chinese had arrived in the earliest days of the great Gold Rush. Times were very unstable at home. The reports of the fabulous Gum Shan, the "Mountain of Gold," in far off California electrified the Orient, as it did much of the world. A few thousand dollars in gold would allow a Chinese coolie to retire in comfort with his family when he returned to his homeland.

In 1851, some 2,716 Chinese immigrants were tallied at the San Francisco customs house. The first census of the Chinese taken the following year recorded 25,000 in the state—with more still arriving. Most headed for the mines, but soon Chinatowns were springing up, both in the mining camps and the major cities.

The Chinese themselves were exclusionary. They wanted to live with their old customs and their own kind. When a Chinese man died, his bones were shipped home to be buried in his homeland. He could not understand the "Melican man," and for years did not want to. The Americans felt the same. They were frustrated at the customs, funny clothes, and strange language, but were soon accepting Chinese rent payments on tenements in the worst sections of towns, money for stagecoach and steamer tickets, and taking advantage of the very low wages paid to Asians in the work force.

The Chinese form of self government, the vice-controlling Tongs that fought their feuds, and the squalor of the Chinatowns also contributed to a growing schism between the races.

After the Gold Rush was over, the transcontinental railroad was inaugurated and began building West. On the coast, the Southern Pacific constructed the line from Sacramento eastward. With mountains of rock to carve through and a timetable to fulfill with the government, the railroad builders looked to the Far East. Hordes of Chinese tunnel and bridge builders were imported from Kwangtung Province, and they performed magnificently, much to the disgust of the Anglo workers. This, and the low wages for which the Chinese would work, was the genesis of a growing bitterness toward the Asians. This animosity was apparent, even to an Eastern newspaper a continent away.

New Hampshire Sentinel, **March 10, 1870:**

> *The Chinese in California—It is said that the hard times now prevailing in California are creating a bitter feeling against the Chinese, and evil consequences are feared. In San Francisco a riot is greatly feared, as the consequences would be most terrible, resulting in the massacre of all the Chinese.*

That summer of 1870, there was an incident in China itself that was published in newspapers around the world. Even at this early time, China was awash in foreigners—merchants from around the world looking for advantages, missionaries, miners, and others, all trying to capitalize on China's perceived opportunities. At this same time there was a series of child kidnappings by traders who sold their victims and blamed the crimes on "foreigners."

The "literary class" in China had long advocated ridding their land of these hordes of Europeans and others. They now blamed foreigners, particularly missionaries, for the kidnappings. At an acrimonious meeting between the French consul and Chinese officials at Tientsen, matters got out of control and French soldiers opened fire on a threatening Chinese mob. The crowd ran amuck, killing three Russians and nineteen Frenchmen, including nine Catholic nuns of the Sisters of Charity—who were horribly mutilated. Thirty or forty Chinese children were murdered, also, simply because they were pupils in a mission school. Catholic and Protestant churches, alike, were looted and destroyed. Ominously, stories of the "Tientsen Massacre" were published extensively in the U.S. press, including in California.

On October 20, 1871, Emil Harris returned from a business trip to San Francisco. He had testified against Ira W. Raymond, the bogus U.S. detective who was accused of multiple counts of forgery and sentenced to a year in prison. L. E. Chilson, one of the Ford counterfeiting gang, was also in the Bay City for his appearance before the next federal grand jury.

Three days later, on the morning of October 23, Harris arrested one Ah Choy in Los Angeles and took him before William H. Gray's justice court. The complainant was one Yo Hing, a member of the Hong Chow Company, a rival of Ah Choy's Nin Yung Company. Those familiar with the Chinese community knew well of the feud between these two groups. Originally both companies belonged to the See Yups, but disagreements among members resulted in a split into three companies the previous year.

An early sketch of the Calle de los Negros, the Chinese Quarter in old Los Angeles. *California State Library.*

There had been trouble ever since.

On this morning, Yo Hing charged that Ah Choy had tried to shoot him, resulting in bail for Choy being set at one thousand dollars. When Sam Yueng offered to post bail, Judge Gray denied it, saying that he did not believe Yueng had that kind of money. When Yueng insisted he did have it, officer Harris was sent back with him to be shown the disputed funds. They returned a short time later, Harris verifying Yueng's claim of having seven thousand dollars in his possession.

Of course, there was a woman involved in the case. Yit Ho had been the property of Ah Choy's Nin Yung Company, but Yo Hing reportedly kidnapped her for his own purposes. At five-thirty in the evening of October 24, Ah Choy and some others showed up in Negro Alley looking for Yo Hing, with blood in their eyes. When Hing and several companions showed up, there was shooting, and Ah Choy dropped with a bullet in the neck.

Officer Jesus Bilderrain, enjoying a drink in Higby's saloon, heard the shots, leaped on his horse and rushed over to the alley. Seeing Ah Choy down and his armed friends about to attack, Bilderrain ran into Sam Yuen's shop, where he met a series of pistol explosions and powder smoke from Yuen and some cohorts. Robert Thompson, a bystander, rushed in to aid him, but collapsed with a mortal wound, as Bilderrain stumbled backward with bullets in the shoulder and legs. Word that "officers had been killed by Chinamen" quickly spread around town, and saloon crowds emptied into the streets. Gunsmoke filled Negro Alley and there were periodic shots as crowds began to gather.

The first rush was of men anxious to help the police, but soon the riffraff, drifters, and vagabonds began swelling the ranks of a shouting mob that was quickly out of control.

City Marshal Frank Baker heard the first shots while on patrol near the corner of Requena and Los Angeles streets, southeast of the plaza. Running down the street, he heard a police whistle and arrived at Negro Alley as Officer Bilderrain staggered out of the building holding his bloodied shoulder. In another minute, Thompson had been shot by Chinese men shooting from the doorway. Baker shouted for the firing to stop.

Harris was on his Commercial Street beat when he heard the first gunshots. They came from the area of the plaza and he sprinted to Los Angeles Street, where he saw crowds gathering ahead of him at the entrance to Negro Alley. Harris later recalled that bloody night in testimony published in the local press.

Los Angeles Star, **October 28, 1871:**

> *Found the sheriff there; he requested me and all citizens…to stand alongside of him; a great number volunteered, and others more excited, wanted to force their own way into the houses, and [Sheriff] Burns requested them to stand still, that he would make disposition to guard the house until morning…the excited multitude got the upper hand; after this all efforts to prevail upon the citizens to cease firing and keep quiet, were unsuccessful; I and Officer Gard prevented those on Los Angeles Street from firing for fear they would kill some white person accidently, and succeeded in keeping order until a crowd of men on the roof of Coronel's building chopped through the roof…and began firing rapidly at objects on the inside of the house. While standing on Los Angeles Street, one Chinaman came running out of one of the buildings opposite Caswell & Ellis, one of the Yo Hing houses. Heard a cry by some white persons, "Here is one! Here is one!" and I succeeded in capturing him and started to jail with him, got as far as Mr. Burdick's store on Main and Spring streets, when some parties unbeknown to me, about 100 or more, took him from me, held me, and took him up Temple street. They cried "Hang him!" That was the last I saw of him….*

Negro Alley was a hotbed of vice and violence that crouched and waited for the right moment to erupt. On the evening of October 24, 1871, it erupted. *Los Angeles Public Library.*

Returning to Los Angeles Street and the head of Negro Alley, Emil was attempting to prevent anyone from entering the houses when he heard the shout of "fire." Officer George Gard had joined him by now and, climbing up on the roof with several citizens, the officers shouted for the arsonists put the fire out, which they did.

Back in the street, Harris and Gard saw several Chinese shot down by the gathering mob as they left the alley buildings. The yelling of the crowd was interspersed with the sporadic explosions of gunfire as a mob now burst into the adobe structures and began looting the shops. As they left, some Chinese were herded with them, while all the time Harris and Gard were shouting to take any captives to the jail as these were innocent men whom they knew. The officers did what they could to stop the looting, most of the crowd being saloon loafers whom Emil did not recognize. Guarding the area for the rest of the evening, Harris was relieved by Sheriff James Burns at midnight.

Edward Wright was returning home from the racetrack about eight o'clock that bloody evening when he heard gunshots and saw a mob in the distance on the street:

"...Went to the hay scales on Los Angeles Street; saw the crowd taking Chinamen up Main Street; saw the crowd put ropes around the necks of four Chinamen, and string them up; don't know the names of any of the parties who used the ropes, but can lay my hand on any of them; see them every day around town.... Saw him make a knot, put the rope around the Chinaman's neck and say, 'Boys, hoist him up'; he had a rifle in his hand; I see him nearly every day on Main Street...."

Robert Widney, a local attorney, was walking down the street when the trouble began. Following the crowds to Negro Alley, Widney quickly saw and heard what was happening and determined to prevent any innocent Chinese from being lynched. Following the mob to the corner of Temple and Buena Vista streets, the lawyer saw ropes being tossed over the crossbeam of the gate at Tomlinson's corral. Obtaining a pistol from his brother, Widney pushed his way

Robert Widney and others bravely supported the efforts of Harris and the officers.
Security First National Bank.

toward the Chinese prisoners, grabbing one of the lynchers. Widney would later recall the terrible scenes of that night in a magazine article.

The Grizzly Bear, **January, 1921:**

> …*"Get out, or I will kill you!" I said, in a low tone of voice. He understood…he turned and fled to the sidewalk, without a moment's hesitation. No human being ever mistakes the tone of voice that has irrevocably decided to kill.*
>
> *I then took hold of the next rioter in the same manner and did the same to him as to the first one….*

In this manner, Widney and others saved nearly two dozen Chinese, but despite their desperate actions, the lynching and killings went on.

When the long night ended, people began cautiously prowling the debris-ridden streets of the Chinese Quarter. They were startled at the bodies—four hanged to wagon trees on Los Angeles Street and more to Tomlinson's corral gate at Temple and Buena Vista streets. The dead were already being taken down—some nine had been hung and others shot or stabbed to death. Most of the corpses had been robbed. Eighteen bodies were recovered, but it was known that some had been taken away by Chinese families. The corpses were arranged in rows in the jailyard for the benefit of the coroner's jury.

THE NIGHT OF HORRORS!

NAMES OF THE KILLED

$10,000 ALLEGED TO HAVE BEEN STOLEN.

ADDITIONAL CAPTURES AND FURTHER PARTICULARS.

THE CORONER'S INQUEST.

BURIAL OF THE DEAD.

From the Daily Star of Thursday.
In our paper of yesterday, we published a very full and complete account of the outrages of the night previous, their cause and extent. This account we now continue as

Los Angeles Star, *October 28, 1871.*

The tragedy was headlined around the country, repeated from the Los Angeles press and presented fairly accurately, although there was some exaggeration.

The Indiana Progress, **November 9, 1871:**

> …*In addition to the 16 persons hanged, two men and one woman were found dead, and another man was discovered in jail in an insensible condition. Only one of those who were hanged has been identified as having shot at the officers. The others are supposed to be innocent, the guilty ones having escaped before the mob assaulted their houses. The old Vigilance Committee has been reorganized to prevent a repetition of the rioting.*

Nine men were eventually tried on manslaughter charges for what has became known as the "Chinese Massacre." Two were found to be not

Bodies of dead Chinese in the jailyard after the lynchings. Reparations were later paid to China. *From* On the Old West Coast.

guilty, while the remaining seven were sentenced to ten years in state prison. An appeal resulted in a reversal of the verdict, and the men were released after a year. Sam Yuen, charged with killing Robert Thompson, was tried, but found not guilty for lack of evidence. The occasion remains one of the bloodiest incidents of mob violence in Western history.

The month following the riots, a suit against the city was commenced for the damage done to one of the principal structures in Negro Alley. Known as the Coronel Adobe, the building was owned by Antonio Coronel, a former mayor and now California state treasurer. The suit was for $5,000 for damages to his property, outraging a letter writer who asked why such a prominent man would rent to prostitutes and gamblers in the first place.

Los Angeles Star, **November 25, 1871:**

> *Instead of the city paying a cent, their claim, in equity and justice, should be against him for $100,000....Mr. Coronel now humbly asks this city to pay him $5,000 for damages, when the last assessment told the Assessor of this county that the entire property was not worth more than $1,500.*

The *Star* later reported that instead of "$1,500," the Coronel property was only assessed at $300. When Coronel announced that if he was to rebuild, it would be for the purpose of (again) renting to Chinamen, the newspaper was shocked. "It is almost impossible," not-

Don Antonio Coronel, the venerable Los Angeles pioneer. *La Reina,* Los Angeles in Three Centuries.

ed the *Star*, "that Mr. Coronel should wish evil to the city and people who have given him political preference and support."

Apparently, aside from plugging up a good many bullet holes, little was done to the property and Negro Alley lasted well into the 1880s. But history can be revealing. Apart from his deserved renown as a politician and historian of early Mexican days, Don Coronel was apparently also a slumlord. The United States government, however, ended up paying a heavy indemnity to China for the deaths of its citizens.

The New York Chamber of Commerce voiced an immediate concern for the safety of any Americans in China, while the *San Francisco Examiner* wailed that it was the "beginning of the end." And so, Los Angeles moved on.

The police department and other local lawmen had done the best they could, but they had been overwhelmed by the size of the mob. The police were undoubtedly relieved to resume their usual routines.

Los Angeles Star, February 3, 1872:

> *A Lively Chase—Officers Gard, Harris and Bilderrain had a lively chase after two Frenchmen, who got "obstreperous," and commenced firing off six-shooters. When the officers "went for them," they made a break, and waded across the river, where, after crossing it, they commenced firing again. The officers returned to town, got a hack, and after a little strategy, overhauled the gents near the brandy-refinery, brought them to town, and lodged them in jail.*

The receptacle for such rascals, the county jail or calabozo, was also referred to as "Clancy's Hotel," after the current jailor, John Clancy. Lo-

The two-story, brick jail is shown at center right, surrounded by the ten or twelve foot high board fence. The one-story city hall, on Main Street, is partially hidden by the jail. Photo taken in 1869. *Los Angeles Public Library.*

99

cated just south of the plaza church, the jailhouse lot was enclosed on three sides by a high plank fence about ten or twelve feet tall. A row of adobe buildings housing the jailor's family, the city marshal's office, and other county offices occupied the remaining side of the enclosure.

Near the center of the lot was the jail, a thirty-three-foot-square, two-story structure of brick and stone. Downstairs were an office and sleeping quarters for the jailor. The upstairs area had four windows "with the usual iron gratings" and four eight-foot-square cells. The floor consisted of two layers of wood flooring, sandwiching a layer of sheet-iron between them. Meals were served twice a day—at seven o'clock in the morning and at one o'clock in the afternoon. Bread and coffee, or tea, was breakfast, with bread, soup, meat, and vegetables for dinner. A Chinese cook prepared the meals. Even given such first-rate quarters and sumptuous meals, inmates still occasionally tried to break out.

During the afternoon of March 8, 1872, prisoners Jim Downey and Andronico Sepulveda were released from their cells to empty the "slop" buckets. Downey was a street thug and Sepulveda an accomplished horse thief. As Jailor John Clancy relocked their cells, the two prisoners entered the yard, dropped their buckets, and ran for the wall. Support braces on the surrounding fence aided them in getting up and over, and they promptly disappeared into the city. By the time Clancy went to the door to see what was keeping them, he found that the two birds had flown his "hotel."

The police force was promptly alerted and an unsuccessful search was initiated. Harris and Gard recaptured Downey a few nights later in a local boarding house, but Sepulveda made a successful escape.

Only a month later, another break was attempted when some prisoners converted a small knife into a saw. This was discovered and the men were put into heavier irons. "These prisoners," commented the *Star*, "with several other like notorious characters were captured by Officers Gard and Harris, who by their vigilance and energy, have in this city become a 'terror to evil doers, and a praise to those that do well.'"

Los Angeles Star, March 30, 1872:

> *Birthday Gift—Officer Harris yesterday filed a deed of a lot fronting on Main Street, valued at five hundred dollars, which he will present to his wife today as a birthday present, and no doubt agreeably surprise her.*

We can only hope that Mrs. Harris received her gift before obtaining a copy of the *Star* which contained the premature announcement. Emil's eighty-dollars-a-month salary would not allow such extravagances, of course, but his extra pay for serving papers, government service such as the recent Arizona manhunt, along with rewards for recovering stolen property bolstered the family budget nicely.

On April 26, an earthquake centered in the Owens Valley rocked and rattled buildings in Los Angeles, but no damage was reported. However, the town of Lone Pine was almost totally destroyed, with more than twenty-three people reported dead and many injured. Los Angeles merchants, who derived much business from the Owens Valley mines, promptly called public meetings to solicit aid for the area. "In extending relief to them," lectured the *News*, "we are aiding ourselves."

With all the trials of frontier life, Los Angeles was, this same month, enjoying the introduction of gas streetlights to certain areas in town. At last there was a modicum of safety in walking the streets at night—certainly the police were more comfortable on their beats in the lighted areas of town.

On May 3, 1872, two Mexicans, fired up by a jug of aguardiente in the confines of Negro Alley, got into a shouting altercation. Lomar, one of the combatants, seized his two-foot-long brush-cutting knife and began chopping on his unarmed opponent, slashing him in the head, face, and wrists in a shocking manner. "After the cutting," reported the *Star*, "Lomar fled and secreted himself in a house on Alameda Street, where he was soon after arrested by Officer Harris and Captain Turner." Captain William Turner was a popular Mexican War veteran.

It had been a long, hard pull, but a fire department for the city was finally going to be realized. At this early day, many in the city still felt that it was a frivolous quest, that cities like San Francisco perhaps needed such things as a fire engine, but with insurance and the many brick buildings in town now, Los Angeles was just fine. Aided by several destructive fires, Harris and his comrades successfully persevered, however.

After consulting with San Francisco firemen, it was decided to order the best engine made, an Amoskeag Steam Fire Engine manufactured in New Hampshire. After many delays, the engine finally arrived and on

June 21, 1872, it was wheeled down Main Street with its accompanying hose cart and a line of firemen on each side. The procession stopped at Ducommun's corner, a few doors down from the Bella Union Hotel, where the firefighters hooked up their new steam engine to one of the few hydrants in the city. Crowds lined the streets and several nearby hotel balconies. Foreman Emil Harris was in charge of the demonstration, assisted by George Gard and R. J. Wolf.

Los Angeles Star, June 22, 1872:

> *Steam was raised in a very few minutes and soon a full stream of water was spouting at least seventy-five feet above the roof of the Temple Block. So effectively was this block drenched in a few moments that the water flowed in through Wolfensteins Gallery and down through the law office of O'Melveny & Hazard.*
>
> *...The Fire Company evinced great proficiency in managing the Engine and hose, and we believe them to be equal in efficiency and general skill to any company in the State.*

Late on the afternoon of September 6, Emil was heading home after going off duty. As he walked down Arcadia Street, a man rushed out of a saloon shouting that three drunks had chased out the two bartenders and were now breaking up the place. Stepping into the doorway, the officer shouted for the men to stop, but instead they began moving toward him.

The police did not yet wear uniforms for identification, but, backing into the street, Harris showed his badge as one of the drunks, with a knife in his hand, kept closing in on him. The knife wielder, Richard Stillman, took a swipe at the officer, who stepped back, drew his pistol and called out again for him to surrender. When Stillman again lunged at him, Harris fired, the bullet striking him in the fleshy part of his arm and continuing into his side. Stillman was taken to a nearby drugstore where he was treated and taken to the county hospital.

After arresting Stillwell's two companions, Harris lodged them in jail, then surrendered to Police Officer Billy Sands. In a hearing before Justice William Trafford the following day, Harris was easily acquitted due to the testimony of the many witnesses of the incident. "We understand," reported the *Star*, "that he (Stillwell) still intends to kill Harris, when he can get a chance, and that he stated so yesterday to some of his friends."

Emil considered this just talk and fortunately, nothing came of the threat. The incident must have horrified Leda Harris, however.

Despite his police duties and participation in the new fire department, Harris still devoted time to the Turnverein organization he had helped establish. The temporary rented quarters of the "Turners" had long since become inadequate and a new hall had been built on Spring Street. There was to be a grand ball, festival, and dedication held on September 22, 1872. The "Turners" would assemble at the old hall and parade through the streets to the new hall, which featured a basement restaurant that served meals at any hour for fifty cents.

Emil and his wife also immensely enjoyed the masquerade parties of the "Turners" and attended many over the years. It must have been difficult sometimes for Harris to keep up with his social obligations and his police workload.

Joe Dye had kept a low profile lately. He had come to California in the early 1860s, by way of Texas, New Mexico, and Arizona. A miner and teamster in the Southwest, along the way Joe had learned to handle a gun. When the Los Angeles

Harris helped establish Turnverein in Los Angeles and built a hall, shown here, for activities. *From* Sixty Years in Southern California.

police force was organized under City Marshal William C. Warren, Joe was a member of the small group. Dye made a good officer, but he had been a Southern sympathizer during the Civil War and had a vicious temper.

In early November 1870, Joe quarreled with Marshal Warren over a reward for a Chinese girl who had fled a brothel. The two men had been at odds previously over other matters and both now refused to back down. Following Warren out of a justice court, Joe kept insisting that he deserved part of a reward Warren had been paid for the retrieval of the Chinese girl. Warren had palmed a derringer in the courtroom and in the street he turned on Dye and fired, just grazing his face. Both men then drew their pistols and shot it out, Dye making a mortal shot, then delivering the coup de grâce by biting a chunk out of the dying marshal's ear.

At the following hearing, all the witnesses testified that Warren had fired first and despite the marshal's popularity, Dye was released. The local vigilantes, however, were very active at this time and Dye was concerned about his safety. Leaving Los Angeles, Joe took up prospecting in the Santa Clara Valley, east of the burgeoning village of Ventura. He occasionally returned to Los Angeles on business or to see friends and he was in town on the late afternoon of July 29, 1873.

William R. Rowland, a large rancher and a member of a prominent family, had been elected sheriff in March 1873. Only twenty-seven years old at this time, the young sheriff had just been in office a few months when he had a confrontation with the most feared gunman in Southern California.

Los Angeles Weekly Star, **August 2, 1873:**

> *A brace of excitements took place in our generally quiet city last Tuesday...*
>
> *The first one took place in the front of Downey's Block, about half past 5 o'clock between Sheriff Rowland and Capt. Dye. We know nothing of the cause of the meeting, nor of its commencement. We only know that we ran with the crowd, and saw Dye with one hand holding Rowland's beard, and with the latter he held a pistol in close proximity to the latter's breast. That's all we saw...*

Sheriff Rowland was young, but he had nerve.
California State Library.

That was all the reporter saw because, fearing a shootout was about to transpire, he ran like blazes in the opposite direction.

Sheriff Rowland had ridden into town from his ranch that late afternoon. Meeting several friends on the street, he was informed that Dye had told them that Rowland had gone into a recent political convention and pledged himself to support the entire People's Party ticket. Since he had done no such thing, Rowland immediately set out to find Dye and straighten the matter out. The two men were not on good terms due to a previous argument, and Rowland felt it was necessary to confront the badman immediately. One friend suggested he merely explain the matter in a card in the newspaper. The young sheriff, however, was not afraid of Dye, or anyone else.

Walking down the street, Rowland spotted Dye in front of the Orient Saloon talking to Charles Beane, editor of the *Los Angeles News*. After greeting them, the sheriff asked point blank who was Dye's authority for what he had said. Dye replied that the source was a local politician named Higbie. Rowland now asked for Dye to accompany him to Higbie's to see what he had to say. Dye refused, asking that Rowland bring Higbie to him. When Rowland called the badman a liar and threw a punch, Dye whipped out his pistol and demanded he take it back. "I have nothing to take back," responded the sheriff. Dye now grabbed Rowland by the beard and again demanded that he take his words back, and the two men clinched.

Joe Dye was quick on the trigger and had a temper to match. *Author's Collection.*

Constable J. R. McMurray was standing nearby and tried to blow his police whistle, but it had become fouled by some tobacco in his pocket and made no sound. At this point, Emil Harris and Constable M. D. Hare rushed up. Harris related what happened next.

Los Angeles Weekly Star, **August 9, 1873:**

> *When I arrived in front of the Orient saloon, I saw Dye have hold of Rowland with his left hand, and Rowland had hold of his sleeve, to the best of my knowledge, and Dye had his pistol in his right hand; I grabbed hold of one with my right hand and the other with my left, and separated them. I took Dye away and told him I had to do my duty as an officer, and told him to give me that pistol, which he did when I got upstairs; we took him upstairs; his clothes were torn, and he wanted to dress himself, as his clothes were torn so as to expose his under garments....*

It had been a close call, as Dye's mercurial temper was likely to erupt at any moment, but Harris's separating the two men successfully concluded the incident. It was later learned that Rowland had his hand wrapped around a cocked derringer in his pocket.

A hearing was held the following day in Justice Trafford's court. Dye himself examined all the witnesses, including the sheriff. "I never asked to have Mr. Dye arrested," stated Rowland, "and as far as I am concerned, I want this prosecution to stop." The young sheriff was not about to start a feud with someone like Dye, who had a long memory. Dye was held for trial, but was released in a few days. Years later, in 1891, Dye was shot and killed from ambush as he walked down a Los Angeles street. He had again tried to bully the wrong man.

By late September 1872, various apartments in Negro Alley had been re-occupied. "It is presumed," noted a dogmatic article in the *Star*, "that the priests of Confucius, who were here a few weeks ago, succeeded in driving off the devils from these houses." At this time, the dreaded area had pretty much reverted to its previous state of crime, gambling and prostitution.

In early September 1873, the Chinese pastime of one company stealing women from another company blossomed again. At eleven o'clock one morning, it was learned there had been a shooting in Negro Alley. Ah Sam, a Chinese cook, had been shot three times by two residents of the alley — Mah See, a storekeeper, and his employee Ah Cum. Sam had tried to steal a young woman and been filled with lead by her protectors. He later died in the jail.

Officers were promptly on the scene, with Billy Sands chasing the fleeing Ah Cum into a vineyard, where he was captured with the aid of several Hispanics. Harris arrested Mah See and both suspects were in jail within a half hour of the shooting.

A stagecoach delivers lodgers to the Lafayette Hotel, while Negro Alley simmers and boils in the background. *California State Library.*

In late October, a San Gabriel resident named James Howard had his horse stolen from in front of the Pico House. Detective Harris was put on the case and with his usual diligence, he soon had the horse thief in custody. The jail was nearby and the lawman, not thinking handcuffs necessary, began walking down Main Street with his prisoner.

Los Angeles Herald, October 25, 1873:

Suddenly, however, when opposite the jail, the prisoner turned round and struck Detective Harris a violent blow on the nose and mouth. These little ebullitions of feeling always please Mr. Harris who went for his man, and in less than a minute had him single handed in safe custody. The thief was half choked, and will probably regret physically for a long time the effects of his rashness. Mr. Harris used neither his club nor revolver, but he made that man sicker in two minutes than he ever was before.... The horse was also recovered through the same officer's exertions.

One of Harris' fellow officers was Benjamin Franklin Hartlee, a forty-three-year-old native of Missouri who had joined the police force shortly after Gard and Harris. He was regarded as a good officer.

Officer Benjamin Hartlee was a good officer and later served as a guard at Arizona's Yuma Prison. *Yuma Prison Museum.*

On the night of January 9, 1874, there was a robbery in the Dexter Saloon. Working on the case with Officer Hartlee, Emil pointed out that Dave Cunningham, who had been released from jail, penniless, a few days prior to the robbery, was now freely spending money in the city. Hartlee began shadowing Dave and when he saw him talking to "Seven-up Joe" in an alley, he edged up closer, attempting to hear what they were saying. He heard enough to convince him that Dave was their burglar and both men were escorted to police headquarters.

Seventy-six dollars was found on Cunningham and he was locked up. The officers then grilled Joe, who finally confessed that he had been the lookout man while Dave went in and stole the money. That night the officers accompanied Joe to a field near the Los Angeles River where the balance of the loot was buried. Realizing the jig was up, Cunningham declared that he had spent $50 and that, with the recovered loot, was all that was taken. "Officer Hartlee," reported the *Herald,* "is entitled to great credit for energy and sagacity in working up this case."

The next morning, the *Herald* saw fit to modify its account of the investigation with the following statement: "Detective Harris is entitled to great credit also in the discovery of the Dexter Saloon robbery. He is an active and energetic detective, and has discovered many criminals in this county." Emil was constantly recognized in the press as a detective, and it is likely he was not happy about being ignored in the *Herald's* original account. Hartlee, on the other hand, was always referred to as "officer" Hartlee. It seems likely that "Detective Harris" did not like credit for his work going to "Officer Hartlee." A detective's ego is always a potent portion of his methodology and personality. Besides, his constant good press and detective work had made Harris a rising star on the police force.

But much more serious troubles were brewing, troubles with a genesis in Southern California. A young Californio named Tiburcio Vasquez had grown up in Monterey during the early days of the Gold Rush. After becoming involved with a bad crowd, Vasquez was mixed up in a saloon brawl in 1854, during which a local constable was killed. A companion of Vasquez was lynched for this killing, while Vasquez and Anastacio Garcia fled. It was the beginning of one of the more audacious bandit careers in California history.

In 1857, Vasquez was sentenced to state prison from Los Angeles for horse theft. He later served several terms in San Quentin, which was a veritable "school for crime" in those days. He participated in several desperate escape attempts and upon his release in June 1870, he was soon in trouble again after a shootout over a woman.

A young and dashing Tiburcio Vasquez. *Author's Collection.*

The following year, Vasquez and two compadres held up a stagecoach and several travelers on the road south of San Jose. While hiding out near Santa Cruz, the bandits were discovered by the local sheriff, who shot and killed one outlaw and badly wounded Vasquez. The other bandit, Narciso Rodriguez, was captured the next day, although Vasquez managed to escape.

After lying low for a time in the Coast Range, Vasquez assembled a new gang and planned more ambitious raids. In late February 1873, Ti-

Tres Pinos as it looked in 1900, after the the name had been changed to Paicines.
Author's Collection.

burcio and four others robbed the store and a stagecoach at Firebaugh's Ferry. When a planned train robbery fell through in July, Vasquez and his men plundered a hotel and restaurant on the railroad line. In August, they swooped into the village of Tres Pinos and robbed Snyder's Store, killing three men in the process. Fleeing with stolen loot packed on nearly a dozen stolen horses, the outlaws fled south with posses hard on their heels. There were close calls and gunfights in the hills north of Los Angeles, but the bandidos were magnificent horsemen who stole fresh horses as they were needed and rode like "el Diablo" himself.

Doubling back, Vasquez and his men next appeared in late November, far to the north, at Jones' Store and ferry on the San Joaquin. They burst into the store and saloon at six o'clock in the evening, tying up a dozen patrons, then robbing both the captives and the store safe. Riding away into the bitter cold evening, the bandits vanished and soon lost themselves to the sheriff's posse on their trail.

This brazen series of robberies culminated the day after Christmas 1873, when Vasquez, his lieutenant, Clodoveo Chavez, and nearly a dozen bandits attacked the isolated village of Kingston, on the Kings River. Concealing their horses in some brush along the river, the bandits crossed a toll bridge and worked their way through the shops and hotel, tying up and robbing some thirty-five victims in the process.

Rancher John Sutherland, who lived nearby, received word of what was happening. Grabbing his Henry rifle and several of his men, they rushed into Kingston and opened fire on the bandits, driving them back across the bridge. Several of the outlaws were badly wounded and others captured as Vasquez again leaped into the saddle and disappeared.

Hiding out for a time in Southern California, Tiburcio met up with his lieutenant, Chavez, and in late February 1874, the two robbed a stagecoach at Coyote Holes Station in the Mojave Desert. The outlaws now headed south to lie low for a time. Besides the large rewards being offered for Vasquez, a formidable posse under the direction of Sheriff Harry Morse, of Alameda County, was preparing to take the field.

Vasquez never had a regular gang, but instead recruited members as were needed. While he and Chavez were staying with a local rancher

Abdon Leiva rode with Vasquez on several raids.
Author's Collection.

ten miles from Los Angeles, Vasquez enticed three young Hispanics to join him. He had in mind a raid on a wealthy ranchero who was known to have sold a large amount of wool recently. The bandits rode to the ranch of Alessandro Repetto, tied him to a tree, and demanded $800 for his release. When Repetto insisted he had no money in his home at this time, Vasquez told him he must make out a check and send someone into town to cash it. A nephew was sent off immediately, while the desperadoes lounged about the house, indulging in their host's wine.

In town, the young messenger was such a nervous wreck that the Temple & Workman Bank manager summoned Sheriff Rowland, who quickly got to the bottom of the boy's agitation. The sheriff, certain the robbers were Vasquez and his men, hastily assembled a posse consisting of police officers Emil Harris, Billy Sands and Marshal Frank Hartlee, who was now chief of police. Several constables and volunteers filled out the posse. Within a half hour, Rowland's party was headed for Repetto's, while a second posse hastened to cut them off if possible at Tejunga Canyon.

The boy had been kept at the bank, but he pleaded so earnestly for his uncle's safety that he was released, and he immediately rode hard for Repetto's via a shortcut.

Fourteen horses were captured by Los Angeles officers from Vasquez and his men.
Los Angeles Herald, October 5, 1873.

Vasquez was not to be captured easily. Spotting the posse in the distance by their dust, the bandits leaped into their saddles and were off. The outlaws' animals were fresh, while the posse's horses had been pushed hard in hopes of catching Vasquez off-guard.

Despite all the lawmen on their trail, Vasquez and his men kept well ahead of them. The fleeing desperadoes even managed to stop a wagonload of irrigation pipes being delivered to local orange groves by Charles Miles and several friends. The outlaws took everything of value from their victims before galloping off. Sheriff Rowland returned to town that afternoon and put together yet another posse, but the bandits had disappeared again.

Los Angeles Star, April 25, 1874:

>*Most of the officers and others who went in pursuit of Vasquez have arrived, the latter having managed to make his escape. It is fervently hoped that Morse and his party may take the desperate bandit in out of the wet.*

It was a bitter pill for the young sheriff, but he had learned much from the episode. He was convinced that Vasquez would remain in the area where he had many friends. Rowland's mother was Hispanic and a native of New Mexico. The sheriff spoke Spanish and had many friends in the Californio community. Borrowing money and using it freely, he carefully sought information from the Hispanic friends he could trust. In his quest for information, he also employed private detectives in surrounding counties to contact him immediately with any news of Vasquez.

In the midst of all this, while at El Tejon on April 27, Sheriff Harry Morse received word of Vasquez's whereabouts and caught the first stage for Los Angeles. The next day he consulted in secret with Sheriff Rowland and gave him the information he had acquired about the outlaw's location. Rowland told Morse he knew the informant and considered him unreliable. It was Morse's hope that he and Sheriff Rowland could form a posse and share in the capture of Vasquez, but Rowland thought otherwise. Indications are that he took Morse's information, checked it out, then went into action. Giving Rowland the benefit of the doubt, however, he may have already had the information from another source. In either case, the Los Angeles sheriff could hardly be blamed for not wanting to share capturing the notorious bandit with some "big city" sheriff from the San Francisco Bay Area.

The reported hiding place of Vasquez was the cabin of Greek George, a native of Cyprus, who was brought to the United States in 1855. Known now as "George Allen," Greek George had been brought to the area to be a camel driver in an ill-fated government camel experiment in the Mojave Desert and Arizona. Sheriff Rowland now sent Deputy D. K. Smith some ten miles due west to the San Gabriel Mountains, in the shadow of which was the crude adobe cabin of Greek George. Posing as a drifter looking for work, Smith returned to the city two weeks later and reported that the bandit was indeed staying with Greek George.

Rowland had meanwhile been secretly assembling another posse. His own deputies, Undersheriff Albert Johnston, deputies Henry Mitchell and D. K. Smith were, of course, included. The balance of the team consisted of police detective Emil Harris, city marshal Frank Hartlee, Constable Sam Bryant, Walter E. Rogers, proprietor of the Palace Saloon, and George Beers, correspondent for the *San Francisco Chronicle*. The men all must have been prepared to respond to the sheriff's call on a moment's notice. This could not turn into another Repetto fiasco.

Undersheriff Albert Johnston would command the posse to go after Vasquez. *California State Library*

Frank Hartlee had recently been appointed acting marshal when the prior officer had resigned. Hartlee had friends in high places and when a newly established police commission was created later in the year, he was appointed chief of police.

After hearing from Smith, Rowland alerted his posse to meet him immediately at the law office of Deputy Henry Mitchell. They were told to meet just after midnight at John Jones' corral on the corner of Spring and Fifth streets in the southern part of town. Each was directed to arrive by a different route and at separate times. Their horses, guns, and other supplies would be waiting for them. Aware that Vasquez had spies watching him, Rowland reluctantly would stay behind.

The party left at two A.M., May 14, 1874. It was dark and very foggy and they were careful to detour widely around farm houses to avoid barking dogs. The trip took most of the night and sometime before morning they stopped at a local bee farm in Nichols Canyon. Johnston took Mitchell and Smith to a nearby mountain from where the adobe of Greek George could be watched with a pair of field glasses. Harris was put in charge at the bee farm. He had sent Bryant, Hartlee, and Beers down to a neighboring farm for breakfast when, about ten o'clock that morning, a two-horse wood wagon came along. Two young Mexicans were driving and they were startled when Emil stepped out from behind a tree and stopped them. Harris later related the unfolding events.

Los Angeles Express, **July 25, 1874:**

I had instructions from Johnston to permit nobody to pass in either direction, so emerged from behind a tree and ordered them to halt, which they did in a reluctant way after considerable expostulation. They eventually laid down in the bottom of the wagon, which was empty, and went to sleep, while I stood guard over them. About 11:30 a.m. Bryant, Hartlee and Beers returned from Knowlton's and I asked Bryant to go up and learn what Johnston had discovered. Leaving Hartlee and Beers in charge of the two Mexicans, Rogers and I went to Knowlton's for breakfast, which consisted of black coffee and bread hard enough to knock down tenpins with, but I think we enjoyed the repast more than if we had dined at the Van Nuys or Angelus.

...Johnston and Bryant returned to our camp and sent word for me to come immediately, as we were about to start. Johnston, Rogers, Hartlee, Beers, and myself, besides the younger of the two Mexican boys, then laid down in the bed of the wagon, at Johnston's suggestion, while Bryant, who was rather dark and resembled a Mexican at a distance, got up on the seat with the driver to prevent any treachery. We were completely concealed from view by the sideboards of the wagon and were as closely packed as sardines. The driver was ordered to proceed to a point near Greek George's house, and not to attempt to betray our presence in any manner, either by word or sign, under penalty of death.

Johnston, Bryant, Rogers, Hartlee, and Beers were armed with double barreled, muzzle loading shotguns loaded with buckshot, while I had an old style sixteen shot Henry rifle. All of us carried revolvers in addition—powder and ball, of the Colt's Navy pattern. When within one hundred yards of the house we stopped the wagon and all jumped out and threw themselves face downwards on the ground, while the wagon turned and was driven rapidly back in the direction of Nichols Canyon. As soon as we saw the coast was clear, we arose in a body and made a dash for the house. My intention was to kill Vasquez's horse in the event of his coming out and trying to escape in that way. The house was constructed in the form of an "L." I ran to the northeast corner of the structure, followed by Johnston, Bryant, and Rogers, while Hartlee and Beers took up a position in a mustard patch on the southwest side of the building.

I looked through an open door into the living room and beheld a young woman of rather comely appearance with some plates in her arms, in the act of waiting upon a man seated at the table, who was in his shirt sleeves and wore overalls. Both had their backs toward me. I turned and beckoned our men to close in. The woman's attention seemed to have been attracted in some way, and she made haste to close the door, but I rushed up and thrust my gun between the sill and forced it open. As I entered the room the man had arisen hurriedly and made a break for a small window, and was partially through when I raised my rifle quickly, without taking deliberate aim, and fired. The ball struck him in the fleshy part of his left arm, underneath, entered his body immediately over his heart, ran around under the skin and came out at his right breast, making a superficial wound. I did not know this at the time, however, as he bled profusely. He plunged through the window, and I turned and hurried around the house to head him off, when I saw Johnston, Bryant, and Rogers outside, and one of them—either Johnston or Bryant—fired at him as he was making for his horse.

At this juncture Hartlee also fired upon him at close range with both barrels of his gun, but when captured only two buckshot were found to have struck him, one having lodged in the back of his head and the other in his right arm. I thereupon leveled my rifle at him, when he turned and threw up his hands, exclaiming, "Don't shoot! I give up!"

When I reached him he was covered with blood and I took him by the arm and led him toward an enclosure, at the same time asking him why he ran. He replied that he was afraid we wanted to kill everybody in sight. At that time none of us knew it was Vasquez, but I told him we were hunting for criminals, and the fact of his trying to get away had led us to assume that he was some guilty party. Upon being asked his name he replied, "Alejandro Martinez." I had in my possession a photograph of Vasquez taken when he was about twenty-five years of age. Upon referring to it, immediately I saw the resemblance, and said, "Yes, Alejandro Martinez sometimes, and sometimes something else."

"Oh, no," was his answer. "I came here to shear sheep."

By this time we had reached the enclosure, where Johnston, Bryant, and Rogers were, and I said, "Boys, I think we have got the chief." I told him to sit down in the enclosure until the whole of us were together, when Beers was placed over him as a guard while the rest of us returned to search the house, as we had been led to believe from our information that he would be accompanied by four others, comprising his entire gang. Johnston, Hartlee, and Rogers stood guard outside, while I proceeded to investigate matters on the inside of the house.

At this time a young Mexican [Librado Corona] emerged with an infant in his arms, followed by the Mexican woman whom we had first observed, and she implored us not to kill the man. We assured her it was not our intention to harm anybody if we could avoid it, and endeavored in other ways to calm her fears, whereupon she took the baby from him, and we handcuffed him to a post, telling Beers to keep a close watch upon both prisoners. We then continued our search, and by the side of the chair at the table...was found a long-bladed Bowie knife sticking in the floor. The wife of Greek George had only recently been confined, and underneath her bed we resurrected a vest, in one of the pockets of which was a stopwatch which I at once recognized as having been taken from Charley Miles in the Arroyo Seco affair. In the room from whence the man had come with the baby we found six revolvers, two Winchester rifles of the model of 1873, then considered the best weapon made, and a Spencer seven-shooter [rifle], besides another dangerous looking knife and some saddles, bridles, etc.

We afterwards found out that Greek George's premises were one of the regular headquarters for the gang. Upon searching Vasquez we found a silver watch chain belonging to John Osbourne, which was likewise one of the proceeds of the Miles holdup in the Arroyo Seco. Then I said, "Now I am certain we have got the chief. Your name is Tiburcio Vasquez."

For a moment he hesitated, but finally made a clean breast of it in the following language. "Yes, once I was a gentleman, but now I am guilty."

I then inquired, "Are you hurt very badly?"

"Yes," was his reply. "I think I am."

"Do you think you will die?"

"Yes, I think I shall."

At our suggestion the young woman brought a basin of water and we dressed his wounds as well as possible under the circumstances. Then I inquired if he wished to make any statement in view of his probable death, and he asked, "Who is your captain?"

I referred him to Undersheriff Johnston, and he requested the latter to bring a small memorandum book from one of the pockets of his coat. I got the book, and upon opening it found clippings from the Los Angeles papers of the day previous, giving detailed accounts of our movements. I handed it to Johnston, and Vasquez continued, "I have two children living in Monterey, although I am not married."

A spring wagon was borrowed from a neighbor and the wounded man was made as comfortable as circumstances would permit. Mounting their horses, the lawmen now lined up on each side of the wagon. Harris continued:

Before starting, however, I took a flask of whiskey from my saddle-bags and offered Vasquez a drink. He responded, "I like to drink with brave men, and you are all brave, like myself."

...Mitchell then rode on ahead to apprise Sheriff Rowland of the capture, and the news spread like wildfire, so that when we arrived at First and Spring streets, which was then the outskirts of the business portion of Los Angeles, we were met by an immense concourse of people, rendering it necessary for some of us to ride on ahead and clear a pathway for the vehicle. We reached the county jail between four and five o'clock in the afternoon...

Young Fred Burnham and a friend were walking to their local swimming hole that late afternoon, Burnham later recalling the excitement:

"The day was hot; the dust deep. We saw a farm wagon jogging slowly along. On either side of it rode armed men so covered with dust

The cabin of Greek George was an old adobe with several rooms tacked on, located at the foot of the San Gabriel Mountains. *California State Library.*

that we could not recognize anyone. Inside the wagon, on some straw, lay a man with bloody clothes. Another knelt, fanning the wounded man.

"Arthur exclaimed, 'I'll bet they have caught Vasquez!' The officers would not tell us, whereat our suspicions increased...."

In Los Angeles, the clerk of the city council was preparing to read a communication to the group when a rising commotion in the street interrupted the meeting. As the noise increased, there was a general rush to the front door and windows. Ben Truman, editor of the *Star*, immediately thought Vasquez "had something to do with the fuss," and he was right. In a light wagon at the street entrance to the jail lay the bandit chieftain, "pale and bloody."

Sheriff Rowland immediately placed the bandido under the care of doctors and it was soon established that despite all the blood, he was not severely wounded. In a few days, Vasquez was eager to respond to the calls that the public be allowed to see the famous outlaw. There was a steady stream of visitors for the next few days.

The dreaded Tiburcio Vasquez, captured at last, and Emil Harris was there.
California State Library.

"Everybody who could, visited him and I was no exception," wrote prominent local businessman Harris Newmark. "I was disgusted, however, when I found Vasquez's cell filled with flowers, sent by some white women of Los Angeles who had been carried away by the picturesque career of the bandido; but Sheriff Rowland soon stopped all such foolish exuberance."

Harris had managed to grab Vasquez's knife, saddlebags and rifle during the capture and kept them for many years as trophies.

Although minimized at the time, Marshal Hartlee had a disagreement with Detective Harris, but the cause of the squabble did not become public immediately. When Rowland's secret deputies met at Jones' corral for the assembling of the posse, the marshal and Harris realized for the first time that they both had been selected.

Dr. Joseph P. Widney was the principal physician who tended the wounded bandit. *La Reina. Los Angeles in Three Centuries.*

Hartlee apparently saw no reason for them both to go and he told Harris he had better stay on duty in town. Harris had been selected for his detective abilities, his courage, and his skill with a rifle, and he refused to be left behind. The following month Hartlee preferred charges against Harris for leaving his post as a city police officer. Before the city council's Committee on Police, Marshal Hartlee recommended removal of Harris from the police force and the appointment of a Mr. E. Ryan to fill Harris's place. Of course, Hartlee had every right to do this, depending on the circumstances.

Speaking out against the dismissal, councilman Dockweiler defended Harris, stating that the detective had materially aided in the capture of Vasquez, "and for leaving the city for this purpose he should not be discharged." Harris Newmark, one of the more prominent Los Angeles pioneers, inadvertently weighed in on the controversy in his later reminiscences.

Harris Newmark, *Sixty Years in Southern California*, 1916:

> *...Rowland then concluded to make up a posse, but inasmuch as a certain element kept Vasquez posted regarding the sheriff's movements, Rowland had to use great precaution. Anticipating this emergency, City Detective Emil Harris had been quietly transferred to the Sheriff's office....*

Newmark, a careful historian, has probably given us the answer to Hartlee's pique over Harris' refusal to stay behind. Due to the secrecy of the whole matter, the marshal was probably not told that his subordinate had been "quietly transferred to the Sheriff's office." Hartlee may, or may not, have been secretly transferred to the sheriff's office, also, although as city marshal he could probably come and go as he pleased. It is likely, then, that neither man knew the other was part of the posse, until they rendezvoused at Jones' corral that early May morning.

The old one-story adobe that was the Los Angeles City Hall. The door on the left probably led to the back yard and the two story jail where Vasquez was held. The porch rafters were the gallows from which five outlaws were hung in 1863. *From La Reina. Los Angeles in three Centuries*

118

As valuable an officer as Harris was, the charge certainly smacks of politics, and when the dust settled, the detective was docked half of his monthly salary. Later, this was restored. The secrecy of the mission seems to have been forgotten during all this. Speaking of Harris at the time, the *Los Angeles Herald* noted that "his efficiency both as a detective and tireless officer is attested by Sheriff Rowland and his deputies." This should have calmed Hartlee down, but there was no love lost between Harris and the marshal from then on and the real reason for Hartlee's city council stunt would soon become clear.

Another incident continued to feed Marshal Hartlee's bitter resentment of Harris. A few days after the Vasquez capture, Sheriff Rowland called his secret posse together once again at the photographic studio of Tuttle & Lee. A photo of Greek George's cabin had been taken and now portraits of the possemen were made and placed around the cabin image and re-photographed to be sold as souvenirs for the public. Of course, it also immortalized the lawmen and captors of Vasquez. Whether it was an oversight or deliberate, is not known, but Marshal Hartlee's visage is not on the card!

As soon as he was pronounced able to travel by the physicians, Vasquez was shipped north and tried for his crimes in San Jose. In November, word was received that Vasquez was suing all the members of the posse that had captured him. He wanted to recover "sundry rifles, revolvers, saddles, bowie knives, riatas, saddle blankets, etc., which those gentlemen took from him by 'force of arms'" at the time of his capture. He further claimed he could prove that he bought them in Los Angeles and the "capturing party" had no right to divide the "booty." Nothing more was heard about the lawsuit and the most famous outlaw since Joaquin Murrieta was hanged on March 18, 1875.

That fall of 1874, four men announced themselves candidates for city marshal: Jacob F. Gerkins, John J. Carrillo, Emil Harris, and Benjamin F. Hartlee. It was an imposing field of candidates, all of whom were quite popular. The squabble between Harris and Hartlee now suddenly made sense. Because of his skilled detective work, Emil had always gotten much more press than Hartlee, and the burly officer had no doubt resented it. When the city's oldest newspaper, the *Star*, came out for Harris with some glowing editorials, it was assumed the detective was all but elected.

Los Angeles Star, November 28, 1874:

> *The San Francisco Alta says such a good thing of that excellent officer, Mr. Emil Harris, and says it so neatly, that we cannot resist copying it, thus: "We observe by the Los Angeles papers that Emil Harris is up for the office of City Marshal of that flourishing city. Harris was one of the Vasquez captors, and stood his hand with coolness and courage, ready to go for that notorious bandit on 'a short call.' He took, with the others, strong chances for his life; but strategy secured the robber without loss of blood. The fact that he was there and ready with his rifle to do his part, redounds to Harris' credit. Los Angeles cannot do better than reward him with the office of Marshal."*

Marshal Hartlee must have ground his teeth over that one.

Major Ben C. Truman had come to Southern California in 1867. As a government representative, his job was to set up post offices in the Los Angeles area, as well as in Arizona. By the time he had accomplished his mission, he had decided to stay. In July 1873, he purchased the *Star* and assumed the editorial chair as well. Like so many others, he had learned to greatly admire Emil Harris and now cheerfully endorsed the veteran officer.

Los Angeles Star, December 5, 1874:

> *...We have yet to meet a business man or property owner who has not openly expressed a preference for this honest and efficient officer. It may not only be said of him that he is seemingly always on duty, but successfully so; for hardly a day passes that he does not capture a pickpocket, a burglar, a robber or a horse thief....We have heard a great many people say they would turn out next Monday if it was only to vote for Harris, and thus contribute to the elevation of a model and praiseworthy officer.*

When candidate Jacob Gerkins withdrew in favor of Harris, it seemed the election was all but decided. "It would not surprise us," reported the *Star*, "if others withdrew in Mr. Harris' favor, as his election is a foregone conclusion." But there was a powerful voting block that was not being considered. First reports indicated Harris enjoying a comfortable lead, but the gap was soon being closed. In the end, Harris had a total of 546 votes, to Hartlee's 430. John Carrillo, however, had successfully rallied the Hispanic population to a vote totaling 569. Emil had been beaten by twenty-three votes!

It was tough to lose by so slight a margin, but Emil's vote-getting proclivities insured that there would be other opportunities. At least he thought Carrillo, who assumed his duties on December 18, would make a good marshal.

J. Ross Browne had been in Los Angeles recently and was startled at the progress of the town he had first seen in 1849.

San Francisco *Daily Evening Bulletin,* December 10, 1874:

> *Los Angeles is no longer a straggling village, composed of adobe cabins, ox-hides, grape vines and prickly pears. It is now a full-fledged city, with numerous public buildings in the latest style of architecture, railroad and freight depots, large and spacious brick stores, reasonably good hotels, the usual compliment of churches and billiard saloons, and a street railway.*

> *...One of the best signs of the times is the subdivisions of large ranches into farms and small particles of land for the cultivation of semi-tropical fruits. The owners are beginning to see that men and women are more profitable than cattle; that a small number of thoroughbred cows and sheep is better than a large stock of worthless animals; that a thousand acres of land well cultivated is more profitable than 10,000 lying waste....*

This was all true, but the original owners of those thousands of acres of land, the Californio rancheros, had mostly lost everything to the Americans marrying into the families, or acquiring land grants declared invalid by the new laws and court systems. Taxes also gobbled up many of the old properties. The Californios would have to learn the new ways to survive, and many did.

Many of the old adobes of Sonoratown were still around when this 1880s photograph was taken, but there were many frame houses now, also, amid the still-barren hills. *Author's Collection.*

No matter how much the old pueblo had grown, Emil was still deal-ing with the darker side of Los Angeles that was growing, also. About six o'clock on the evening of June 9, 1874, Gabriel Mendiaroy met one Jaime Fernandez in front of the Palanconi House in Sonoratown, just north of the plaza. Mendiaroy was in poor health and was considered a quiet, inof-fensive man. Fernandez, on the other hand, was considered a "bad and quarrelsome character." There was trouble between relatives of the two men and Fernandez had been verbally maligning the other's family. When the two men met, Mendiaroy was out of patience. "Stop abusing them," he pleaded, "abuse me!"

Los Angeles Herald, **June 10, 1874:**

> *Upon this the other drew his revolver, and fired, Mendiaroy was shot near the heart, and expired in about ten minutes. After the deed was committed, Fernandez rushed down a narrow alley beyond the house and succeeded for the time in making his escape.*

When the news reached the marshal's office, Emil and officer Frank Carpenter rushed to the scene and began to search for the killer. Surpris-ingly, they found him close by the scene of his crime, hiding in the Los Angeles River. A crowd continued to grow, many threatening to hang the killer. Suddenly, a son of the victim pushed through the crowd and thrust a pistol at Fernandez's chest. Before he could fire, one of the officers grabbed the weapon and there was a fierce struggle to subdue the young assailant. The son was held by officer Thomas as Harris and Carpenter fought through a yelling mob that was trying to work up the courage for a lynching on the spot. It was a close call. The glowering Fernandez was heaved into a carriage and was soon safe in the Calabozo.

Los Angeles Herald, **June 10, 1874:**

> *These demonstrations by lawless persons are becoming painfully frequent, and it is to be seriously hoped, that such an example will be made of the perpetrators that an effectual check may be placed upon them. If the authorities would hang one a day for a month or so we might hope for a material improvement in the law and order of the country.*

Lately there had been a rash of wife murders in and around the city. "Of all the wickedness of which man is guilty," lamented the *Herald*, "this is the most beastly and damning." The description was particularly apt for an incident that took place in late June in a back room of a boarding house on Commercial Street. The place was operated by John McDonald and his wife, Elizabeth, a thirty-five-year-old woman from Northern Ireland. The couple had worked hard and owned enough property to be considered well-to-do. They had been married about eight years and had four children. For some time McDonald had been treating his wife brutally. He had been arrested several times, paid his fines, then went home and returned to his cruel ways.

Just after five o'clock on the evening of June 29, McDonald was slicing some cheese in a back room of his lodging house. When his wife entered the room, he asked her where she had been. She gave the name of a neighbor, to which he replied that he had just been down there and had the door slammed in his face. Saying this, he punched his wife in the face and kicked her. Staggered, the woman rushed upstairs and returned in a few minutes with a baby at her breast. Apparently she thought the baby would circumvent a further attack. A waiter in the room, Jose Tamorine, witnessed what happened next.

Los Angeles Herald, **June 30, 1874:**

> *Mrs. McDonald went up stairs and got her baby, and coming back sat down by the table and was nursing it. McDonald, after saying some words to her, struck her twice with his fist, when Fernandez (a waiter) took hold of him and prevented him from striking her again. When Fernandez let him loose he (McDonald) commenced cutting up some cheese on the table, and in about three minutes he said something else to her and then threw the knife at her, striking her in the side and inflicting the wound. She drew the knife out and said, "I'm dead!" and told me to take the baby, which she held in her arms. I did not take it quickly enough, and she laid it down on the table and ran out of the room....*

Running a short distance up the street, the bleeding woman staggered into a small grocery store and collapsed. McDonald had followed her and seeing his wife on the floor in a spreading pool of her lifeblood, fell on his knees sobbing as he realized what he had done. A horrified crowd was standing around asking what had happened, but all McDonald could do was blubber, "I did it!"

By the time Emil and another officer arrived, the growing crowd was getting ugly. Grabbing the killer between them, the policemen pushed their way through the mob and soon had the hysterical prisoner in a cell.

"After being placed in jail," reported the *Herald*, "McDonald acted like a mad-man, throwing himself about the cell and calling down imprecations on his own head for the crime which he committed. "

But it was far too late for that. A suicide watch was put on him, and when vigilantes were rumored to be forming, twenty-five members of the Los Angeles Guard were called out to protect the jail. At his trial on October 3, 1874, the indictment was found faulty when it was discovered that Mrs. McDonald's name was "Eliza," and not "Louisa." The defendant's attorney asked for a dismissal, but the judge ruled that a new and corrected indictment would be the basis for a new trial, after which McDonald was sentenced to life in San Quentin State Prison. Granted a new trial in June 1876, McDonald, along with three other criminals, was brought back to Los Angeles by Emil Harris.

The editor of the *Star* was thoroughly disgusted. "The trial of McDonald, the wife murderer," he howled, "has already cost this county over seven thousand dollars and the end is not yet." This time McDonald was convicted of second-degree murder and again sentenced to life. He had probably convinced himself his heinous crime was a mistake by now, but in any case he managed to secure a pardon in 1889.

Harris arrested a thief named John Beegan in early February 1875. Beegan was accused of robbing a Chinese peddler, but after being arraigned before Justice William H. Gray, Harris found a circular on him from Salt Lake City. It seems he had been convicted of murder the previous December, and while being conveyed to court for sentencing, he managed to shoot his two guards and flee to California. The fugitive was clapped in jail and the Salt Lake authorities were notified. A deputy U.S. marshal picked him up a week later to face the Utah charges.

The annual masquerade ball of the Los Angeles Turnverein Germania was held on Friday evening, March 13, 1875. The Harrises were active in the preparation for the festivities and also kept busy making their costumes. It was always one of the grand social events of the year. The *Star* reported a long list of participants, noting "Mrs. Emil Harris as Semi-Tropical California — very richly and elegantly dressed; her costume was adorned with tropical fruits and flowers. Emil Harris as Boss Tweed, a candidate for the Presidency — rich, striped suit." The Harrises were noted for their imaginative costumes and they seldom disappointed.

A few days later Harris arrested another fugitive, this time from Santa Barbara. He was a forger, to the amount of ninety dollars, and within a few days he was picked up and returned for prosecution.

Late on the evening of May 16, city marshal Carrillo received word of a murder at the La Ballona rancho, some ten miles southwest of town. A man had shot his wife and since no details of the incident were known, Detective Harris went along to investigate the scene. With the Hartlee–city council embroglio still fresh in his mind, Emil insisted on being sworn in as a deputy sheriff before he and Marshal Carrillo rode off toward the ranch. Apparently no one in the sheriff's office was available that night.

Arriving at the ranch about nine-thirty, the two lawmen found a terrible scene. Mrs. John Vohle lay dead in her bed, shot through the heart. Her farmer husband lay on the floor, nearby, holding a towel to a bullet wound in his forehead. Neighbors were in the room and standing around outside. Vohle had already told them what happened and now he reported events to the two officers. The marriage had been in trouble for some time, but the farmer had thought he could resolve things, one way or the other. It seems he had chosen "the other."

Vohle's story was that his wife had told him in the early evening that "this night I am going to sleep with my lover. This is the last night I will sleep with you." The farmer was so distraught at this declaration, he seized his pistol and shot her through the heart. Horrified at what he had done, Vohle put the pistol to his forehead and fired, but the bullet just ripped a bloody crease along his forehead and scalp. Dazed, he had run to a neighbor who had taken him back home and sent for an officer. When the gathering crowd heard what had happened, they started discussing a necktie party, but Carrillo and Harris told them in no uncertain terms that Vohle was under their protection.

After looking around, Emil determined that the murder had occurred pretty much as Vohle had described it. The two officers took the killer back to town and jail, then sent for a physician. The wound looked worse than it was and Vohle would live to be tried for his crime. He was sentenced to ten years for manslaughter, and Detective Harris escorted him and another prisoner to San Quentin in early September 1875.

George Gard lost his position on the police force when Marshal Carrillo was elected. Gard found a job as manager of the Orient Saloon, but the law was in his blood and he kept an eye open for a position with the sheriff's office.

Early on the morning of May 27, 1875, the cry of "Fire!" went up in the Angelic City. Emil quickly rushed toward the glow in the sky that turned out to be the Dotter & Bradley furniture showrooms on Main Street. The fire company arrived promptly and soon had the fire under control. This was no sooner accomplished when another fire broke out in the city stables. The fire company rushed over and were able to quickly extinguish that blaze, when flames again shot up by a nearby haystack.

It seemed clear that incendiaries were at work, and Harris kept busy interviewing witnesses and looking for clues. The man who had turned in the first alarm said he saw a heavily-bearded man rushing down the alley at the back of the store just as the first fire flared up. Also, just prior to that first fire, three men knocked at the door of Hurd's Stable on Aliso Street. They demanded saddle horses. On being told there were none to be had, they pushed their way in and announced they were going to take whatever was there. "They were persuaded to retire," reported the *Star*, "by the free exhibition of a Henry rifle." An hour or so later, there was a second and similar visit and demand, with like results.

There had been a great deal of fire damage, but it might have been worse if not for the firemen. Much of the furniture and goods that survived the fire had heat and water damage. A citizen's committee was immediately established to look into the origins of the various blazes. Others made veiled threats.

Los Angeles Star, May 29, 1875:

> *Incendiaries will please bear in mind that this is generally a peaceful and law-abiding county; yet, sometimes their kind are "summoned to heaven or hell" without the presence of judge or jury. A good many people will sleep in their warehouses and stores and stables for awhile, and the first thing you know someone will get hurt.*

Emil had tracked down one of the suspects in early January, but there was not enough evidence to convict him and he was released.

The popular and effective Sheriff Rowland was still in office when a vacancy occurred on his staff in early 1876. Rowland liked the idea of having a detective in his department, and he offered Emil a deputy's badge.

Although "detectives" in the past had been seen as shady characters who bartered with thieves for stolen goods and the rewards, detectives were now increasingly considered a necessary arm of law enforcement. Detective Captain Isaiah W. Lees commanded a three- or four-man staff on the San Francisco Police Department. By 1872, Wells Fargo detectives were quickly at the scene of a stage or train robbery, while Alameda sheriff Harry Morse had long been utilizing his detective skills on the job, as had others in the field.

Type of badge worn by Deputy Sheriff Harris. *Collection of Jim Casey.*

Harris accepted the sheriff's offer. He undoubtedly looked on it as a broadening of his experiences as a lawman. He knew all of the other deputies and was kept busy right from the start. In mid-March, he received a warrant from San Diego ordering the arrest of two Chinese men for grand larceny. He spent nearly a week tracking his quarry, finally locating them in a house at the old Mission San Gabriel. Meanwhile, new sheriff David Alexander had taken office that month.

In mid-August 1876, a San Francisco detective arrived in town from San Pedro and called at the sheriff's office. He was on the trail of two con men who had sold a stock of goods worth $26,000 that did not belong to them, and then disappeared. The leader was named Hawver, while his pal was known as "the Count." Working with Deputy Bill Banning and new undersheriff Tom Rowan, Emil found that Hawver was in the city and requested the needed arrest warrants by telegraph. The two fugitives had been discovered in a sleazy boarding house in the outskirts of the city.

Undersheriff Tom Rowan was a well-liked, early pioneer who later served as mayor. *From* Sixty Years in Southern California.

Rowan was a bakery owner and had just served a term as county treasurer. He was also a volunteer fireman, but he wanted a more exciting occupation. He was a good friend of Sheriff Alexander, who must have been pleased at Harris and Rowan's good work.

Los Angeles Daily Star, **August 17, 1876:**

> *After the usual introductions in such cases, Mr. Hawver, who by the way, claimed entire innocence in the premises, was politely escorted to the*

127

Hotel de Clancy. Through papers in his possession, a clue was obtained to a large amount of money, and other articles of value, which will go a great way in lessening the present loss to creditors; or parties defrauded. Mr. Harris is now on his way to San Francisco with Hawver. The arrest and capture reflects great credit on our Sheriff's office, and particularly to the officers above-named.

Later that fall, there was a series of burglaries and holdups in the city. The first in the series of crimes took place early on the morning of October 29, 1876. Two pedestrians were stopped on Temple Street and relieved of all the change in their pockets. It was later discovered that one of the victims was in with the robbers, and the gang had thought the victim was carrying some $300.

At this time, Emil had recognized a man on the street whom he had previously suspected of being involved in the robbery of the Santa Monica Land Office the year before. Some $600 had been taken. Harris told Undersheriff Rowan of his suspicions and the officers decided to keep an eye on the suspect, who they now suspected of involvement in the Temple Street robbery.

Early on the morning of November 1, a house on the corner of Figueroa and Jefferson streets was entered by three masked robbers who tied up and gagged the five Chinese occupants. The place was then ransacked and some $500 in gold and silver coin was taken. "One Chinaman," reported a neighbor, "who offered some resistance on being tied was beaten on the head with a pistol until the blood flowed quite freely."

Harris and Rowan had been following their suspect earlier in the evening when he had joined two other men. The officers had lost their quarry just prior to the robbery, but before returning home they had placed a guard on their suspects' lodgings.

On November 9, another Chinese house was robbed, the occupants being burned and otherwise brutalized to obtain some $300 in loot. The thieves returned home about six o'clock that morning. From then on, the two officers never let the suspects out of their sight. The next night the officers watched as the trio tried their skeleton keys on a drugstore and the shop next door. When nothing worked, they moved on.

The following night, the robbers were seen hanging around the same shops again, waiting for them to close. When one of the suspects left the others and strolled toward the Commercial Street Bank building, the waiting detectives swung into action. As soon as he was out of sight of his pals, the suspect was quickly cuffed, disarmed, and escorted to the jail.

Harris and Rowan now returned to observe the other two suspects as they again tried their keys on the two shops. When they again failed, one walked through the hallway of the U.S. Hotel, while the other strolled down the street. Thinking one of them was now going to try the back door of the shops, Harris watched him, while Rowan shadowed the other.

When Harris's man did not show up, the detective checked the suspect's room several times to be sure he had not returned. Determined to stay on guard until daylight, Harris finally saw his man stroll into the hotel hallway and into the barroom. Walking up to him, the detective pulled his pistol and told the suspect to throw up his hands.

Los Angeles Weekly Star, **November 18, 1876:**

> *He hesitated at first, when Mr. Harris again said "Hold up your hands!" He at once threw up his hands, was handcuffed and searched, and sufficient evidence found upon his person to fasten upon him complicity in the two Chinese raids, the robberies of McDonalds and Slaneys and many other burglaries....*

Although Rowan had given up and gone home when his man did not show, it was a good night's work and many recent crimes had now been solved. The *Star* was euphoric over the arrests, reporting that "this is not only one of the most important, but one of the best managed arrests that has been made in this city for many years...." Emil and Rowan were both worn out, having been up most nights since the first Chinese robbery.

One of the robbers, John McCormic, was promptly tried, and then sentenced to San Quentin for ten years on November 25, 1876. He entered state prison on December 9, but managed to secure a pardon two years later. The fate of his pals is not known.

In late December, Deputy U.S. Marshal Dunlap dropped into the sheriff's office with a notice of two missing sailors. There was a standing reward for deserters. Dunlap asked Harris to come along and the two officers began searching the city and surrounding area. Realizing they could cover more ground if they split up, the officers separated. After a long search, Harris recognized the two seamen on Los Angeles Street and took them into custody. It was a routine enough search, but over twenty-two hours were involved in locating the sea-going fugitives.

This same month in Los Angeles, the *Star* announced that "Nigger Alley is no more!" Although widened and renamed Los Angeles Street, the squalid area would linger for a few more years.

At this time, Harris was assisting Deputy U.S. Marshal Dunlap, who was investigating a stage robbery in San Diego County. According to the press, the local knights of the road were becoming much too active.

Los Angeles Weekly Star, March 24, 1877:

> *Stage robberies are becoming alarmingly frequent in Southern California of late. An attempt was made Saturday night to capture the Wells Fargo & Co's box from the Coast Line stage near Santa Barbara, but the plucky driver refused to be bulldozed, and outran the mounted highwayman, who in his rage fired several harmless shots at the retreating stage.*

A robbery had occurred on the night of March 7, west of the San Bernardino Range near the desert village of Indian Wells. It was rough desert country, but the Southern Pacific Railroad was now building toward Yuma and the village was growing daily. "Every house is a saloon," wrote a correspondent to the *Herald*. It was more than one hundred miles to Indian Wells where Harris and Dunlap interviewed the stage driver, a man named Webster. He thought he would be able to recognize the robbers if he could see them again. Webster also filled the lawmen in on the local watering holes where the outlaws might be known.

It was soon discovered that a saloon owner at nearby Walker's stage station was a shady character with some equally seedy friends. Frank Gibson was known to be broke the day before the robbery, but the day after he was seen flourishing a fistful of greenbacks in a flagrant manner. A witness recalled that Gibson had frequently been seen in the company of Charles Bush and Jake Phillips.

San Bernardino as it appeared about the time Harris arrested his two stage robber suspects. *Author's Collection*

The two lawmen were convinced this was the trio that had stopped the stage.

Dunlap planned to pick up Gibson at his saloon, while Harris took a stage horse and headed back toward Los Angeles. The two other suspects had been seen heading in that direction and he would have to check every stop along the way. Harris found his quarry late at night in a San Bernardino boarding house and with the aid of the clerk quickly had the two suspects in handcuffs.

Dunlap had also successfully captured his man and the two officers rendezvoused in Los Angeles after a long, hard chase.

Los Angeles Weekly Star, **March 24, 1877:**

> *An examination was held before U.S. Commissioner Whiting, yesterday, in the case of Charles Bush, one of the highwaymen who robbed the stage near Indian Wells recently. Webster, the driver of the stage, recognized Bush as the man who was spokesman for the party and into whose hands he was compelled to deliver the mail bags and treasure box. Other evidence also pointed to Bush as the ringleader of the gang, and he was committed for trial in default of $5,000 bail. Today the examination of Frank Gibson comes up....*

"Messrs. Harris and Dunlap deserve great credit," reported the *Daily Star*, "for ferreting out this Indian Wells affair and bringing the perpetrators to speedy punishment." After the local hearing, the two officers escorted their prisoners to San Francisco for their trials in the U.S. district court. Jose Tapia, another stage robber, accompanied the group. Bush was convicted and given an eight-year sentence for robbing the U.S. mail. He entered San Quentin on August 15, 1877, but was pardoned in late 1880. His two partners were luckier. The evidence against them was primarily circumstantial and did not hold up in court.

There was an echo of the past when Yo Hing was attacked in the former Negro Alley by a hatchet-wielding Wong Chu Shut. Terribly mutilated, Yo Hing lingered for several days before dying.

Los Angeles Weekly Star, **May 26, 1877:**

> *The funeral of Yo Hing, the murdered Chinaman, took place Saturday afternoon, and was very largely attended, the deceased having during his ten years residence in Los Angeles made quite an extensive ac-*

quaintance. It may not be generally known that Yo Hing was the identical Chinaman in whose behalf the disturbance was raised which preceded the memorable Chinese riot of 1871. He was a prominent man in the company he affiliated with, and was the object of a deadly hate from the members of the opposition. There appears to be no question but a price was set on his head and his murderers were simply hired assassins....

Deputy Sheriff Harris had just returned from Bakersfield with a cow thief when he was given charge of three prisoners for San Quentin. Wong Chu Shut had been given a life sentence for the murder of Yo Hing, Horse thief Jose Montoy was given two years to reflect on his misguided past, while a highwayman named Morales had seven years in which to decide on a new vocation.

Wong Chu Shut's Tong and company connections resulted in a new trial the following year, but the first conviction was upheld. He was conditionally pardoned, however, in 1887.

Emil had been captain of the Turnverein Rifle Team for some time and always made a point of keeping up his practice. In a target shoot in early July, he shot against a Mr. Morsch who succeeded in making 36 points out of 60. Captain Harris was the last to shoot and had scored 26 out of 60 points on his fifth shot. He had to make a bull's-eye to win, which he did to the cheers of the crowd. It was his second silver medal.

Emil Harris is shown here with the Turnverein Rifle Club in 1885. Harris is middle row, center, wearing his shooting badges. *Special Collections, UCLA.*

Later that month Harris received word from San Joaquin County that two of their jailbirds had flown the coop. William Clifton and Thomas McKenna were thought to have passed through Los Angeles on the way to Yuma, and officers in the area were asked to keep an eye out for them. There was a reward offered, but without more specific information, Emil thought it was impractical to launch a search.

On August 16, 1877, Ventura County sheriff John R. Stone arrived in town. He was on the trail of a fugitive named William Fine. He consulted with Harris and the two lawmen decided that Fine might very well be in the same area as Clifton and McKenna, and a joint expedition was planned. Hoping to capture all three fugitives, Harris and Stone left the next day, getting off the train at Banning. Here, they learned that a man answer-

ing the description of Clifton was working on a road building crew at the head of nearby San Gorgonio Canyon under the name of George Talbot. McKenna had left some time before, heading toward San Jacinto. However, there was no sign or word of Fine, Sheriff Stone's man.

The desert town of San Jacinto. *Author's Collection.*

Obtaining horses, the two lawmen rode out to the pass where the workers were just sitting down to dinner. Quickly working out a plan, the officers stepped into the cook shack. Harris asked for a drink of water, and Sheriff Stone stood in the doorway. The three men seated at the table were now between the two officers. Harris asked to talk to the foreman, a Mr. Edmonson, who got up and walked over to him.

"Mr. Edmonson," said Harris, "the gentleman in the doorway has a letter for one of your men who I believe is named Talbot."

The men at the table had been watching all this and now one stood up and held out his hand for the letter. Tearing it open, the man read the following note:

Stockton, August 8, 1877

*William Clifton, alias George Talbot - Be kind enough
to throw up your hands and you will not be hurt.
Very truly, etc*

> *Thomas Cunningham,*
> *Sheriff, San Joaquin County*

> *By Emil Harris, Detective*

Clifton turned deadly pale, then looked around and saw both officers with their pistols trained on him. His hands shot up in the air and he was searched; then everyone sat down to dinner.

Los Angeles Weekly Star, August 18, 1877:

> *After the capture the officers...then rode back to Banning's Station, where they stayed all night, Harris sleeping with his prisoner, the two being handcuffed together. At Colton the officers got off the train and went over to San Bernardino, having obtained information that Fine had lately been seen in the vicinity. After a long search the officers came upon him in a restaurant, and his capture was easily affected. It had been a very productive trip and the fugitive McKenna was now being sought in the San Jacinto Mountains.*

On the morning of September 1, 1877, word was brought to the Los Angeles sheriff's office of a murder some miles to the west, on the road leading into the city. The victim was a farmer named Frederick Weitzel, who had been driving his wagon to town. Sheriff Alexander called in his undersheriff, Tom Rowan, and Detective Harris, detailing them to assemble a posse and get right out to the scene of the crime. Taking along Deputy Sheriff Bettis, the coroner, and two police officers, Harris found the scene about six miles from town. The detective later reported that Weitzel and a friend had been driving to town on a wagon and when opposite a clump of willows, suddenly two shots rang out in a cloud of powdersmoke. As his friend jumped from the wagon, Weitzel collapsed with a bullet through his heart and another near the right nipple that lodged in his back.

While an autopsy was being performed and several of the officers were sent in search of witnesses, Rowan and Harris probed the area around the ambush scene. A bullet and an empty cartridge case were found in the willows, narrowing down the weapon used to a Spencer or a Winchester rifle. The two assassins had immediately left the scene, one on horseback and the other on foot. The murder had all the characteristics of another land squabble.

A man named Jeff Gaines had attacked Weitzel with a knife the previous year and was still in jail awaiting trial. Two neighbors, Patrick Connolly and his wife, were also isolated as suspects in the murder and enough circumstantial evidence was gathered for an indictment. Both, however, were pronounced not guilty at their trials in December. Despite Harris's efforts, the murderer was apparently never caught.

Los Angeles had changed greatly during the previous ten years. Emil and others in the Old Pueblo looked around at the remarkable evolution of one-story adobes into three- and four-story brick and stone buildings along Main Street. Streetcars traversed the city now, while gas pipelines lit the streets, business houses, and homes. That December there was a demonstration in town of a new invention that was rapidly spreading across the country.

Los Angeles Weekly Star, **December 1, 1877:**

> *Through the courtesy of Lieut. Philip Reade, Acting signal Officer and Superintendent of military telegraph lines in California and Arizona, we formed one of a party yesterday afternoon to witness the workings of the mysterious telephone. The parlors of the St. Charles and Lafayette Hotels had been selected for the experiments, and both rooms were filled with members of the press, telegraphic operators and other interested spectators. For about two hours a running fire of conversation, piano playing, etc. was kept up, to the infinite amusement and most perfect satisfaction of every one present. ...The instruments used are Prof. Alex. Graham Bell's speaking telephones, which are very simple... .*

But crime was also evolving. A new type of criminal, "hoodlums," had developed in the tenements and slums of 1870s San Francisco. Gangs of these thugs, ranging in age from teenagers to young men in their twenties, wandered the streets of San Francisco crowding pedestrians off the sidewalks, engaging in petty larceny, initiating saloon brawls and shakedown rackets, even assaulting police officers when they could be caught alone on their beat. No one knew for sure how the term "hoodlum"originated, but one explanation was that the gang leader would yell "Huddle 'em" to his thugs when mischief was in the offing. Others insisted it derived from a Bavarian-German term, "hodalump," which means the same thing as hoodlum. In any case, the term invariably meant trouble.

By the late 1870s, hoodlum gangs were showing up in other major California cities, such as Sacramento and Stockton. In Los Angeles, Harris was well aware of the hoodlum problems in the Bay City and probably was not surprised when one showed up in the county jail. His name was John Caldwell and he was picked up attempting to steal a suit of clothes from a local tailor. He bragged that he was a hoodlum while being booked and when sentenced to the chain gang, refused to go.

Hustled into the newly built dark cell to ruminate on his lack of cooperation, Caldwell instead ripped off the rim of his slop bucket and began digging into the new brick wall. The mortar had not yet hardened and in a few hours he had gouged out a good- sized opening. He had just reached the outer tier of brick when jailor Clancy dropped by to see how his new occupant was getting along. "Mr. Caldwell," reported the *Star* on December 1, 1877, "now wears a pair of leggings which would seriously interfere with his locomotion even should he make a more successful attempt for freedom than that of Monday night."

With elections pending, the *Star* had earlier predicted that there would be a fight over Emil Harris becoming chief of police, but as it turned out he did not have to run again. For one thing, the title had evolved in the last few years, from city marshal to chief of police. Emil's friend, local merchant Bernard Cohn, was now on the city council and he proposed that the council should appoint the new chief, rather than elect him. Cohn made a good argument, and his proposal was adopted. The councilman now nominated Harris as the new chief, with another member proposing the current chief, Jacob F. Gerkins.

Contemporary sketch of a California hoodlum of the 1870s. *Author's Collection.*

Votes, then as now, were along political lines and resulted in five for Harris, two for Gerkins, and two blank ballots. On December 27, 1877, the thirty-eight-year-old Emil Harris was declared the new Los Angeles chief of police. More than that, he was the first Jewish police chief of Los Angeles. Also, for the first time, the police force had adopted uniforms for their guardians.

The appointment was well received, the *Daily Herald* reporting, "He is young, energetic and indefatigable. He will make for himself a striking record of efficiency, or we are much mistaken."

A party of warm, personal friends, who went to his residence that night to serenade him, found his home empty, as "both Mr. and Mrs. Harris were away from home...." The new chief took up his duties on the first day of 1878.

There had been problems and misuse of police badges for some time and one of the new chief's first proposals was that the city would provide badges for city officers. Heretofore, the officers bought their own stars and kept them when they left the force. The city council agreed that badges should not be in private hands and assented to the new chief's proposal.

The council knew they had made the right choice for chief when Emil made his first report to them at the end of January 1878. There had been 127 arrests for various offenses, and of a total of $758.50 that had been reported stolen, $618.00 had been recovered.

Emil Harris knew well that politics usually triumphed over talent, but he had made chief and Leda was quite proud. *Norton B. Stern Collection.*

On February 14, 1878, the chief was summoned to appear before the city council. Thinking the meeting concerned his proposal for suppressing the city's opium dens, Chief Harris hurried to city hall and was ushered into the council's quarters. He was startled when the mayor and councilmen asked him to sit among them, as reported in the press.

Los Angeles Daily Herald, **February 15, 1878:**

> ...*The climax of his surprise was reached when Mayor Frederick A. MacDougall, taking from his desk a handsome case, in a few well chosen words, presented to him a fine gold badge as the insignia of his office. The badge is in the form of a shield, consisting of solid gold elaborately wrought and enameled. The face bears the inscription "Los Angeles Chief of Police" and the reverse, "Presented to E. Harris by his friends—Los Angeles, Feb. 14, 1878." Mr. Harris was entirely taken by surprise, but he managed to utter a few words of grateful acknowledgement for the honor conferred*

*upon him. It was a very pleasant episode and one which the City Fathers
seemed to enjoy most heartily.*

When Pliney Fiske Temple married William Workman's fifteen-year-old daughter in 1845, they became the first couple with English names to be married in Los Angeles. Both Temple and Workman had arrived in the early 1840s and acquired large ranch properties as was the custom of the time. When he was baptized in the Catholic faith for his marriage, Temple also acquired a new surname, "Francisco." Both Temple and his father-in-law went on to acquire more property and both became prosperous cattle ranchers of the 1850s.

Wanting to invest in the growing city, in 1868, Temple became a partner in I. W. Hellman's bank, one of the first in Southern California. But he was no banker and when he began granting loans to every ragged immigrant who applied, Hellman bought him out while he still had a bank. But Temple saw his future in banking and in November 1871, he and his father-in-law, William Workman, opened the Temple & Workman bank. (It was Francisco Temple who dealt with Repetto's nephew during the Vasquez Repetto raid of 1874.)

Temple was not cut out for banking, however, and he was still careless in making loans. Also, both partners spent much of their time at their ranches and cared little for the mechanics of banking. But to the north, in the City by the Bay, a day of reckoning was at hand.

Virginia City, Nevada, was the mining center of the West at this time. The great mines of the Comstock Lode were shipping a constant stream of silver bullion to San Francisco, fueling unprecedented speculation and spending. William C. Ralston, a San Francisco banker of the same mindset as Temple, spent and lent his money with no regard for common sense, much less banking principles. When Ralston's Bank of California failed in San Francisco, the shockwaves of the resulting panic destroyed many banks, businesses, and lives throughout a wide area.

Los Angeles suffered with the rest of the state. Despite several bailouts from local rancher and silver baron Elias J. "Lucky" Baldwin, the Temple & Workman Bank was closed in January 1876, to allow for an accounting of the assets and liabilities. It was worse than they thought. They had mortgaged everything to secure Baldwin's loans and now lost their large ranchos and other possessions. William Workman solved his problem by committing suicide a few months after his bank closure. Francis Temple, stripped of his possessions, was crippled by a stroke and died impoverished in a sheepherder's hut in April 1879.

In February 1878, G. E. Long, a United States bankruptcy official for the now defunct banking firm, was still trying to collect debts and sell the properties of the estate. His bookkeeper, C. M. Phelps, opened the building on the morning of February 25 and entered the vault where the important papers were kept. The outer door was locked as usual, but secured with only one tumbler, instead of the usual three. Inside the vault there was a smaller, padlocked safe that had been broken into and the lock pried off with some tool. Nine thousand dollars in gold and $1,000 in silver was missing. Fifteen thousand dollars in silver coin and some personal funds of Mr. Long had not been taken.

Los Angeles Republican, **February 26, 1878:**

> *The robbery was undoubtedly carried out by a gang of experienced burglars, who had come into possession of a knowledge of the combination in use on the vault. This combination had unfortunately remained unchanged since the failure of the bank in 1876, and a large number of persons knew what it was, and some one of these parties must have given the information to the gang of burglars that committed this daring deed. As yet no clue has been obtained to the perpetrators....*

When Chief Harris arrived at the bank, he informed Long that he would require assistance since he was involved in another criminal investigation and could be called away at any time. Long agreed to hiring a second detective and Harris immediately telegraphed Captain Isaiah W. Lees, head of the San Francisco police detectives. In that era, San Francisco police officers routinely performed private detective work. Lees recommended officer Appleton Stone, who arrived on March 6 and was fully briefed on the case by Harris. When Phelps, the bookkeeper, noticed he was being shadowed by Stone, he complained to his employer.

The Temple & Workman Bank building, a few years after Harris' investigation. *Author's Collection.*

"Of course he is watching you," replied Mr. Long. "He is watching both of us, I suspect."

Los Angeles Herald, **March 17, 1878:**

> *All the avenues through which the thief could get away were scrupulously guarded. A careful examination of the lock led Harris to the conclusion that it had really been unlocked by someone possessing a key, and then taken away, hammered with some heavy iron instrument and replaced, to create the impression that burglars had been at work. The lock bore no signs of abrasion in places in which marks would inevitably have been left if it had been forced.*

After an immense amount of detective work had been done, much of it to eliminate faulty theories, Harris became convinced someone thoroughly familiar with the building was responsible. In other words, it was an inside job! Finally, Emil narrowed the suspects down to three, although Stone was not convinced that Harris was correct. When several men who had been seen in the area on the night of the robbery had been interviewed and eliminated, Detective Stone finally had to agree with Harris that it was an inside job. The culprit was either Phelps or Long. Emil was convinced "from his respectability, sterling character and actions that Mr. Long was as innocent as the babe unborn." The officers had their man, but now they must get a confession and recover the loot.

Detective Appleton Stone of the San Francisco police. *Author's Collection.*

On March 15, Harris summoned both Long and Phelps to the bank for a demonstration. He had obtained a padlock similar to the one used on the safe. He fastened this in place, then with a pick tried to pry it open. He pointed out to his audience the nature of the marks which he had made on the lock, then called attention to the missing marks on the original lock.

"The crime could only have been committed by one of us," said the startled Long as he turned to his bookkeeper. "As God is my witness, I am innocent. I have no motive since I would have to replace anything missing out of my own pocket." Phelps was looking increasingly uneasy.

That evening Harris and Stone called on Long and after thoroughly searching his house, found nothing. They next searched the Phelps's home, but again there were no results.

The next morning, Harris was chatting with several friends in the bank room, while Detective Stone was conversing with Phelps in the background. Suddenly, Stone called Harris over. Phelps had admitted to the robbery! The group then proceeded to some property near the Phelps home where the suspect supervised the excavation of the missing funds. "Every cent of the purloined deposits," stated the *Herald*, "was recovered."

The *Herald*, which had complained because the burglars had not been ferreted out sooner, now swiftly changed course.

Los Angeles Herald, March 17, 1878:

> *Thus closes a very singular and notable episode in crime. The suddenness and inexorableness of the retributions which overtook the robber should serve to discourage others who meditate similar offenses. The detectives have covered themselves with glory by the sagacity and celerity with which they ran down the criminal.*

Promptly arraigned, Phelps was held in lieu of $10,000 bail, to await the action of the grand jury which was to meet the following Monday. He was sentenced to two years in San Quentin. As a first offender with a wife and two children, Phelps won a pardon in November of the following year.

North of Los Angeles, events were taking shape that would involve Emil Harris in one of the most famous murder cases in California history. And, given the times, the fact that the incident involved a land grant squabble should surprise no one.

The 1848 Treaty of Guadalupe Hidalgo guaranteed the rights and property of the Mexican citizens in the territories conquered during the Mexican War. The Homestead Act of 1862, however, promised settlers 160 acres of land as their birthright. The resulting conflict over the Rancho Sespe Land Grant in Ventura County was a microcosm of what was happening all over the state. These huge Mexican land grants covered large chunks of California. Squatter troubles at Sacramento had resulted in some dozen men being killed or wounded over the Sutter Land Grant. In Santa Clara County during the Shore-Seale feud over another grant, three men were killed and several wounded. Sadly, a good-sized cemetery could be devoted solely to the victims of land violence in frontier California.

What the Ventura County Sespe Grant troubles lacked in body count, however, was more than made up for in drama and complexities.

Aside from all the legal maneuvering, this conflict was simply a clash of rights to a Mexican land grant with the American tradition of pioneers' homestead claims.

When Thomas W. More and his three brothers purchased the large Sespe Land Grant from the estate of Carlos Antonio Carrillo in 1854, it was done in good faith. The grant was located in Ventura County's fertile Santa Clara Valley and watered by the Sespe and Santa Clara rivers, and Tom More soon bought out his brothers and in time flourished. After the Homestead Act of 1862, however, squatters began appearing along the waterways of the More property. More tried to deal with the usurpers, but they always validated their presence by insisting the grant was flawed in some way; they claimed it was a forgery, had not been surveyed, or was in the public domain. Over time, both sides were becoming frustrated and increasingly desperate.

Thomas W. More, the murdered owner of the Sespe Land Grant. History of Santa Barbara County, *Thompson & West, 1883.*

Newspapers, both local and statewide, added their views and contributed to the troubles. Most argued against large landowners around the state who were popularly portrayed as greedy ranchers who wanted all the land for themselves. The fact that most of the squatters were poor people made them all the more sympathetic.

When More made application to add to his property and proceeded to form his own water district to control the rivers for his own irrigation, he unleashed the forces of his doom. To make matters worse, the area was heading into a drought.

The leader of the squatters was a man named Frederick Augustus Sprague, usually called "Frank." One day as Sprague was returning from a duck hunt carrying a shotgun, he was accosted by Tom More. In the resulting shouting match, each demanded the other vacate "his" land.

Ventura Free Press, **February 24, 1877:**

> *…They came together, More getting hold of the gun and with the assistance of another man getting it away from Sprague, both barrels being discharged in the struggle.*

142

> *More now struck Sprague with the shotgun, breaking it in the process. When the squatter now pulled a pistol, the two men separated and More headed for town to secure a warrant.*

The local squatters were all members of the local Grange and a plot was now hatched to get rid of More in the only way that now seemed possible. He had to be killed! On the night of March 24, 1877, a group of squatters led by Sprague met near the More ranch headquarters at one o'clock in the morning. The men were all masked and quickly moved over to the More barn and set it on fire. As the flames grew and leaped in the darkness, a Chinese cook in the nearby house was awakened by the glare. Yelling to foreman George Ferguson, the cook rushed out of the house, while Ferguson shook More awake. Juan Olivas also woke up and all now rushed outside in their long underwear.

In the barn More quickly ran to the horses and began untying them in their stalls. All was smoke, yelling, and confusion. Suddenly, there was a shot and More burst from the back door of the barn. Other shots exploded in the fire's glow and More fell, clutching his side. Four of the masked men ran up to him through the billowing smoke and Ferguson heard More say: "Don't kill me, I'm already shot!" Someone now reportedly said, "Now die, damn you, die!" Sprague, his rifle barrel at the fallen man's temple, pulled the trigger.

With their deadly mission accomplished, the masked figures now disappeared into the darkness and smoke, heading toward the Santa Clara River. Considering the parties involved, the murder was not unexpected and now a prolonged legal drama would begin.

Since the Gold Rush days, these squatter troubles had been erupting all over California. Just the previous January, there had been another shooting twelve miles east of the city. It was a typical situation. The Ranchita, a 1,000-acre land grant owned by Don Pio Pico, had recently been flooded by squatters under the same circumstances that had led to the More murder. A man named Anguisola was Pico's agent and he had lately been surveying fifty-acre tracts to

> **Murder of T. Wallace Moore.**
>
> SANTA PAULA, March 15.
>
> T. Wallace Moore was brutally murdered last night at about half-past three o'clock at his ranch, eight miles east of here. The parties first set fire to the barn, which stood some fifty yards from the house. The light from the burning barn awoke the inmates of the house, who ran out in their night clothes for the purpose of letting loose the horses. Moore and his foreman, Geo. Ferguson, entered the barn and cut loose all the horses, when they were fired upon by a party of of five men, who rushed from behind the house. Moore and Ferguson returned through the shed, part of the barn, and ran about one hundred yards, where the assassins overhauled Moore and shot him down. One shot from a Spencer hit him in the forehead. He was so near the muzzle that his face is ~~~ly powder burnt. Sever~~l ~~~ spots ~~ ~~ ~ ... the head

Notice of the More murder in the
Los Angeles Star, March 25, 1877.

143

offer to renters. At the same time, the squatters were surveying their own parcels on the grant and on January 9, 1878, the two surveying parties met.

There were angry words, but Anguisola remained calm and told the squatter party they were on Pico's land and they must not cross the Pico surveying line. After making sure the squatters knew where the line was, the two groups separated, apparently on good terms.

That evening, Anguisola loaned his horse to an employee named Hyme who proceeded on an errand. As he was riding quietly along the road, Hyme was fired on from ambush in the brush along the road. Hyme received four shots in his body and limbs, his horse also being killed. Mr. Anguisola, who was nearby and heard the shots, rushed to the scene. Putting his friend in the care of several others, Anguisola rode for town to bring back medical aid. Hyme was critically wounded and it was not thought he could recover. The shooting would be added to the bloody record of land troubles in California.

Pio Pico, the last Mexican governor of California. *Author's Collection.*

It was not too difficult to isolate suspects in the More murder. Frank Sprague, who had confronted More with a shotgun, was known as the leader of the local squatters. Just how to round up the other suspects was the problem! The More brothers, Alexander, Henry, John, and Lawrence,

The beautiful seaside village of Ventura. The county sheriff tacitly refused to participate in the More investigation because of the powerful interests involved. One of the several trials was held in nearby Santa Barbara. *California State Library..*

were large property owners, stock raisers, and farmers in Santa Barbara County who were determined to find and punish their brother's killer. When a large reward was offered for the killers, Emil had responded to the More brothers' call for detectives to work on the case. As it turned out, collecting the reward was as much trouble as collecting the evidence.

Harris spent the next year, off and on, investigating the murder and gathering evidence against the main suspect, F. A. Sprague, and his cohorts. Much of his time was spent in disguise as he prowled Ventura County seeking suspects and evidence. His work and the testimony of other witnesses clearly suggested Sprague as the principal instigator of the plot. In late March, Frederick A. Sprague, John S. Churchill, John T. Curlee, Jesse M. Jones, Ivory D. Lord, Henry Cook, and Julius Swanson were arrested and arraigned for the murder of Thomas Wallace More.

John, another of the pioneer More brothers. *Author's Collection.*

The case was called in the Ventura court of Judge Eugene Fawcett on April 5, 1878. The defendants were to receive separate trials, Frank Sprague to be tried first. The first and most damning witness, Nimrod H. Nickerson, testified that Sprague had called him to his house one night after the murder. He was afraid that a lynch mob was coming to get him from town and while they were waiting that night, Sprague told him all the details of the murder. Others would corroborate his testimony, despite threats of death from friends of the killers. Emil was present during much of the trial, but when the prosecution closed on April 9, it was reported: "Mr. Harris, the detective who made the arrest, leaves tomorrow, as it is expected the evidence for the prosecution will close tonight." The following day Sprague was convicted.

The Ventura County Courthouse where the More murder trials were held. *Author's Collection.*

On August 5, 1878, Judge Fawcett first turned down the Sprague attorneys' motion for a new trial, then proceeded to blister

145

Governor's letter authorizing a reward for the More murderers. *California State Archives.*

the prisoner's ears with a severe denunciation.

San Francisco *Daily Evening Bulletin,* August 5, 1878:

> F. A. Sprague, you have been convicted of the highest offense known to the law. You were skillfully defended at the trial. Every device was exhausted to save you, but the jury of your fellow citizens has pronounced you guilty of the great crime with which you were charged. In the dead of night, you, the leader of a band of masked assassins, applied the torch to the premises of your victim, and as he rushed, startled and half naked into the light of the flames, you closed upon him and shot him near to death. He attempted flight. You pursued. He fell before you with a pleading voice that should have wrung pity from a heart of iron, but you remorselessly riddled him with bullets....

Sprague was then sentenced to hang on September 27, but of course an appeal was immediately filed by Creed Haymond, the defendant's lead counsel. John Curlee was also convicted and sentenced to life in prison, but the other five defendants were all awarded verdicts of "not guilty."

It was a sad ending to a terrible crime, made all the worse by the hatred toward the murdered victim, who was only guilty of acquiring a large grant of land in a perfectly legal manner. Although most California newspapers condemned the vicious murder, at the same time they decried More and other large landowners on the theory that, somehow, they should share their property with the squatters who swarmed over their land.

Harris was inevitably caught up in all this as he now discovered the true character of Alexander More, one of the murdered man's brothers. More had a very bad reputation, and after his money had chiefly bought the convictions of his brother's killers, he now commenced to beat the detectives he had employed out of their rightful compensation.

Los Angeles Express, **December 6, 1880:**

> *Detective Emil Harris received notice today that a warrant for $500 awaits him as reward for the apprehension of the More murderers. Harris worked long and faithfully to bring the culprits to justice, and he richly deserves the bonus. A special reward of $2000 from Mr. More, brother of the murdered man, which ought to have been paid to Harris long ago, is not forthcoming without a suit. The detective, however, knows his rights, and knowing is going to try and sustain them.*

The $500 was a state reward that had been posted, while the $2,000 was Harris's bill for travel and expenses while spending a year sleuthing in Ventura County. When the detective filed suit in Santa Barbara in March 1884, presiding Superior Court Judge Hatch, a pal of Alex More, ruled that, in order to collect his money, Harris must prove that Sprague had killed More—this despite the fact that Sprague had been convicted of the murder and was now in prison. The parsimonious More, who claimed he had already paid Harris, must have been furious when the case was appealed. In December 1884, the California State Supreme Court ruled that Judge Hatch was in error in not allowing into evidence Sprague's conviction. In the new trial held in September 1885, Chief Harris finally won his $2,000. Again, smaller counties frequently asked larger police departments for aid in complex cases where rewards were involved as an enticement.

Meanwhile Sprague's lawyers had secured a new trial and his hanging was reduced to a life sentence, then later was commuted to twelve years by Governor George Stoneman. With time off for good behavior, Sprague was released from San Quentin on October 1, 1887. He had paid a small price for an extremely brutal crime.

On October 11, 1878, Chief Harris was prowling around the new Southern Pacific Railroad depot on Alameda Street. It was customary for lawmen in those days to watch passengers stepping down from trains in hopes of spotting a fugitive...hopefully, one with a reward on his head. On this particular day, Harris thought he recognized a passenger and followed him across the street to the Kansas City Hotel bar. He was soon convinced the man fit the description of one of three men who had killed a boy while escaping from a robbery of O'Shea's pawn shop in Portland, Oregon, the previous August.

Los Angeles Herald, October 12, 1878:

> *...The man when first approached by Harris gave the name of Harry Howard, and when arrested exhibited some reluctance to accompany him. Harris at once handcuffed him and brought him down town. Harris telegraphed the arrest to the Chief of Police of Portland, who last night answered the dispatch, telling Harris that if the prisoner was the right man he would find the letters "F.T." on his left leg. On examination the letters were found as described.*

Portland, Oregon, one of the boom towns of the Northwest.
Author's Collection.

The man's name was Johnson and it was an important capture. The three thieves had entered O'Shea's place about nine o'clock in the morning and immediately knocked down the proprietor with a slingshot. They then locked the door, packed up the jewelry and valuables and escaped by the rear entrance, passing through a dry goods store to the street. The crime was quickly discovered, however, and a pursuing party chased them down the street. When shots were exchanged, a small boy was killed, but the robbers were finally captured on the outskirts of town. One of the robbers, Johnson, managed to escape, however. "No clew could be discovered as to his whereabouts," continued the *Herald,* "until his capture by our Chief of Police yesterday. Johnson states that he walked nearly all the way from Portland to this city, avoiding all large towns on the way. His return will be accomplished at the cost of much less personal fatigue."

At the city election on December 2, 1878, Chief Harris distributed his men to cover the various precincts as best they could. Among other orders, the officers were instructed not to leave their posts unless relieved by another officer.

The chief was nervous. There were indications that the city council would be replaced and, politics being what they were, he was concerned about his re-appointment for a second term. After stationing his men at their various election posts, Harris began making the rounds of the precincts.

He was in the downtown area around noon when he noticed officer Godfrey Tribolet, who had just finished lunch in the Commercial Restaurant. Harris asked him why he had left his post in the 4th Ward at the Santa Monica Railroad depot. The officer at first said he was sick, but admitted no one had replaced him when he left for lunch. The chief had had a recent disagreement with Tribolet and he was in no mood for such disregard of a direct order.

Tribolet then claimed he had received word that some vote-buying was taking place and he was going to make an arrest. Harris was furious and demanded he return to his beat. Tribolet left, but a few minutes later Harris found the officer around the corner talking to several men. The chief again accosted him. Tribolet said he had a warrant to arrest Aaron Smith and a Frenchman named Levique for vote-buying.

Chief Harris now insisted the officer return to his beat, that he had no business arresting a vote-buyer when he was on duty elsewhere. When Tribolet again insisted on serving his warrant, Harris demanded his badge, but the officer refused to give it up. "I won't go," he growled, "I must do my duty." Harris then ordered officer Andy Fonck, who was nearby, to arrest Tribolet, and the trio returned to police headquarters.

Inside, Harris again asked Tribolet for his badge, but again was refused. After some shouting, the chief made a move to grab the officer's star, and Tribolet attempted to draw his pistol. As Harris raised a chair to defend himself, Tom Rowan jumped in front of Tribolet, while officer Jesus Bilderrain grabbed his arms. Harris then ripped the badge from the recalcitrant officer's uniform and suspended him from duty pending an investigation.

Tribolet preferred charges against Chief Harris and a hearing before the city council was scheduled for December 9. City Attorney Godfrey, who was representing officer Tribolet, was preparing to read the grounds on which a chief of police could be removed, when he was interrupted by the chief's counsel, Frank Ganahl. "All his client desired," reported the *Los Angeles Herald*, "was a full investigation of the whole matter."

Officer Tribolet was sworn first and related how he had left his post at the Santa Monica depot around noon to go up town for dinner. Leaving the restaurant, he met Jean Levigue, who told him he thought they were selling votes at the polls. Tribolet asked the Frenchman to go in and see if he could sell his vote. Inside Levigue met Aaron Smith, who bought his vote and offered to buy any others the Frenchman could bring to him. Tribolet was shown the money that was exchanged. It was at this point that Chief Harris appeared.

Other officers involved in the incident were interviewed and the chief gave his version of events. All the testimony was similar, Tribolet concentrating on his quest to arrest those who had been involved in buying votes. Aaron Smith testified that the Frenchman's charges of his buying votes was "false in every particular."

Despite Tribolet's efforts to suppress voter fraud, the officer's insubordination must be addressed, however, and the council found that the "Chief of Police is fully justified in depriving Officer Tripolet of his star for being absent from his beat without permission and for not returning to his beat when ordered by the chief to do so."

Another motion was adapted stating that the chief did not do his duty in following up on the vote-buying that officer Tripolet was so concerned about. Whether Harris neglected the fraudulent voting (which was quite common at that time), or whether he was so exasperated by the Tripolet incident that it slipped his mind, is not known. He must have realized, however, that it was not a shining moment for the police department.

Despite the incident, some Angelenos appreciated the dedicated service of Emil Harris, one of whom expressed his opinion in the local press.

Los Angeles Herald, **December 18, 1878:**

> *Editor Herald: In the midst of all this clamor and wire-pulling for the offices in the gift of the Council, you will allow me to draw your attention to the following figures from Chief Harris's report to the retired Council. I find that from January 1 to December 1, 1878, there were 970 arrests made and $1,708 paid in fines into the city Treasury. I also find that, out of $16,821 stolen by thieves, $14,534 was recovered through the official ability of the above named gentleman. On Thursday next the present Council will proceed to appoint a new Chief, and I hope, as a citizen*

and tax-payer, that they will put the right man in the right place, regardless of his politics....

But, politics was politics and a blacksmith named Henry King was named the next chief of police. Emil Harris left the force, but not his profession. He made himself available to local law enforcement for special assignments such as escorting prisoners to San Quentin and Folsom prisons. In March of 1879, he began advertising his private detective agency, located in the Downey Block. In the early 1880s, he secured a deputy constable's commission and served papers, rounded up witnesses, and kept order in the justice court of Judge R. A. Ling. He also operated a merchant's patrol for a time. In 1887, he traveled east to visit relatives, returning in the fall. When former sheriff James F. Burns became chief of police in 1888, Harris accepted the position of captain of detectives and served throughout the new chief's term.

In 1894, Harris became involved in a divorce case and was arrested on blackmail charges. The detective claimed that a check paid him was for routine work, but he was indicted and stood trial. While he was testifying in his own defense, the *Los Angeles Times* reported Harris "sat as cooly as if every eye in the courtroom was turned in the opposite direction instead of resting upon himself." Whatever the circumstances, the jury could not agree, and the detective was released.

The date of Leda Harris's death is not known, but in 1899 Emil married a Virginia girl named Mary who was ten years his junior. Late the same year, he was deputized to take a prisoner to San Quentin. Convicted of an assualt with a deadly weapon in September, one J. J. Clayton had attacked Earl Rogers, one of the most prominent criminal lawyers in the country. Emil and his prisoner took the train to Oakland, then boarded the ferry for San Francisco. Over Harris's objections, Los Angeles sheriff William Hammell had insisted Clayton not be handcuffed.

While crossing San Francisco Bay, Harris suddenly realized that Clayton was not beside him. "When the boat was out about five minutes," reported the *Los Angeles Times,* Clayton "suddenly disappeared." The ferry was promptly searched but no trace of the prisoner could be found. None of the passengers or crew had seen anyone jump from the boat and everyone disembarking was carefully scrutinized, but Clayton had vanished and was assumed to have drowned in the bay.

J. J. Clayton, the man who disappeared...for awhile. *California State Archives.*

It must have been very traumatic for the detective. Although the sheriff had dictated no handcuffs, that should have stimulated even more caution on the officer's part. Later, Clayton was picked up in a hotel room by Emil and several San Francisco police officers who delivered him to San Quentin.

After his second wife's death, Emil was invited to live with his younger brother Max during his twilight years. Max had a wife and two children, and Emil had the time to enjoy a family once again. He reportedly always delighted in telling the story of the Vasquez capture.

During his last years, Emil was retired and suffering from a heart condition. He was eighty-two years old when he died on April 28, 1921. He was buried at Home of Peace Cemetery in Los Angeles.

Today, Emil Harris is a long-forgotten pioneer who participated in stirring scenes of early Los Angeles history. Although only five-foot seven inches in height, Harris always kept in good shape, much to the dismay of various thugs he had encountered and arrested in early times.

But, it was with his sleuthing skills that he made his mark. Many future "private eyes" in radio, television, and film owe their heritage to the long, rugged shadow cast by Emil Harris, perhaps the first private detective operating in Los Angeles.

The old lawman had richly earned the few, final years of retirement. *Author's Collection.*

The End

Chapter Four

John J. Bogard

"He would follow a criminal to Hell!"

The lawman yawned as he climbed into his bunk. Trains were not the most comfortable place to sleep, but he was tired and looked forward to a night's rest. Sheriff John Bogard was returning from a business trip to Sacramento. The Oregon Express had left the Oakland pier at 7:30 that evening, Bogard boarding at Sacramento in the early evening. He had read a newspaper and talked to Redding attorney Charles Braynard for some time on the way north. Now, as the lawman listened to the clacking rythym of the wheels he relaxed and perhaps marveled at the wonders of nineteenth-century technology.

He was only ten years old when he had come west with his family in a covered-wagon train. It was a long and miserable trip, but now railroads spanned the whole country. People could travel much faster and more comfortably than was dreamed of in those past faraway times. Before he drifted off to sleep he may have mused about what travel would be like in another fifty years. Unknown to Bogard, Braynard

Young John Bogard in the 1870s, scratching a living out of sheep raising and the soil.
Henry Family Collection

had followed him to the sleeper a short time later. Soon both men were resting peacefully. The sheriff had no way of knowing that he was heading toward a desperate showdown.

Born in Chillicothe, Missouri, on June 22, 1851, John Jasper Bogard had been preceded by two brothers and a sister, who had all been born in

Indiana. Sister Sarah Elisabeth arrived three years later. George Bogard, the father, had moved several times before settling in Missouri. He had seen various neighbors and friends leave for California during the Gold Rush, and perhaps had received, or seen, letters from them. Although few were getting rich, most wrote about the luxuriant farmland and opportunity in the new territory. It was a time of movement and decision; a time for seizing an opportunity to get in on perhaps one of the last, great adventures. For good or ill, many heeded the siren call.

George Bogard preferred to stay behind and work his farm. It was too big a risk. He had his wife, Elisabeth, to think of, and the children. In the end he opted to stay put, rather than gamble on a long and dangerous trek that may, or may not, be rewarded by any kind of success.

By the end of the decade Bogard could still remember the exhilaration of that great Gold Rush. But, by 1860, excitement of a different sort was permeating the psyche of the country. Missouri had been admitted as a slave-holding state by the compromise of 1820, while other Western territories prohibited slavery. The neighboring territory of Kansas was populated largely with anti-slavery settlers and there was constant trouble along the border. With fanatics like John Brown stirring the pot, violence, kidnappings and murder followed. Throughout the South, this refusal to give up long-standing states' rights, culture, and traditions was manifest in the inevitable collision at Fort Sumter in the spring of 1861.

The fabric of George Bogard's Missouri was particularly ripped and torn by this conflict. While Confederate companies were being organized within the state, Federal units were also assembling for the coming conflict. Bogard's sympathies in all this are not known, but he undoubtedly did not want his family caught up in the dreadful Civil War that was already upon them. By late spring of 1861 the family had packed all they could carry and sold what remained. A sturdy wagon and two yokes of oxen were prepared and soon the family was headed west toward the Missouri River. The family also herded some 150 head of stock, but whether they started with them or purchased them along the way is not known.

The Bogards had joined a wagon train headed by a Captain Hunt. Besides Hunt and his family, others with the train were the Underhill, Boland. and Foster families. It is not known if the train was assembled at

Chillacothe or at Saint Joseph or at one of the other jumping off points. California, far from the local neighborhood feuding and battlefields, now seemed particularly inviting.

Although there is no record of the tragedy, family tradition states that eighteen-year-old Napoleon, the oldest Bogard boy, drowned during the crossing of the Missouri River. The ox teams were slow-moving and the party had to keep moving. "One of the most abiding memories of my existence," recalled Andrew Jackson Bogard many years later, "was that of journeying in wagons, drawn by several yoke of oxen, across plains where Indians more than once imperiled our lives and possessions." By late fall, travelers heading east had warned them it was too late in the year to cross the mountains of California. It was decided to stop for the winter rather than challenge the snow that lay ahead. The train probably wintered at Salt Lake City, then moved on at the first sign the trails were open ahead.

By 1861, the trails to California were well worn and rutted by thousands of wagons and years of travel. The California Trail followed the Humboldt River, finally branching off into a series of other paths into the state. The Hunt train wagons likely entered the state via the Lassen trail, in lieu of the flooded and snowy condition in the Sacramento Valley, making their way north into Shasta County. They had left Salt Lake City too early, however, and found themselves in a snow- and water-covered wilderness rather than the paradise they had expected. Fanny Reading, a pioneer of the Sacramento Valley area, described that harsh and bitter winter in a letter home written on February 3, 1862:

Street scene in 1860s Salt Lake City, a supply center for wagon trains and others heading west throughout the nineteenth century. *Author's Collection.*

> *"Yesterday we had another snow storm…the sixth we have had this year…you can form but the slightest idea of property loss and suffering in the state this winter. We generally have good grass all winter for the cattle and made no provision of other food for them. It is estimated that 80,000 head perished in the Sacramento Valley…."*

All the Bogard livestock were lost during that bitter winter. Although there were devastating floods and much resulting unemployment, George Bogard obtained shelter for his family, then managed to find work in the mining camp of Buckeye, founded in 1856 by Ohio settlers. In the midst of all this, seventeen-year-old Lydia Bogard had found a suitor during the trip west and was married to John Boland in early May 1862.

Located some three miles north of Poverty Flat, later renamed Redding, the Buckeye mines were proclaimed to be one of the richest diggings in California. The promise did not hold up, however, and by 1865 the Bogard family had taken up land to the south, in Tehama County. It is possible the death of Mrs. Bogard the previous year had something to do with the move.

The family had been whittled down considerably now with the loss of Napoleon, the marriage of Lydia, and the death of Elisabeth Bogard. This final blow must have been a bitter pill for the family after all the hardships they had undergone. Still, the children now rallied to pick up the slack left by their mother. Sarah Elisabeth was ten or eleven and could hold up her own end of the chores. John was in his mid-teens and worked with brother Andrew, called "Jack" by the family, in looking after stock and in any of the heavier chores.

By the time a final tragedy struck, the Bogard children were accustomed to looking after themselves. When George Bogard died on March 23, 1867, the survivors had to evaluate their situation. Sixteen-year-old John and his nineteen-year-old brother Jack were probably anxious to get on with lives of their own, but the welfare of thirteen-year-old Sarah was a serious concern. The boys may have worked the family farm for a time while they decided their best course of action. We know little of all this, but it must have been a difficult time in all three lives.

In the end it was decided to talk to their married sister, Lydia, to see if Sarah could stay with her family for awhile. Lydia and her husband,

John Boland, already had three young children and having a fourth thrust upon them by her brothers probably did not sit well. Still, Boland was a farmer and Sarah could help out with the chores to pay her way. The Bogard boys were free to begin their new lives.

There are indications that Sarah was not happy in her new home, however, apparently feeling she was overloaded with chores. Sarah's responsibility was perhaps to care for her niece and two nephews, among other tasks. If she was unhappy with her new home, she must have longed for a way out of the situation. Not long after Sarah met a young sheep herder named William Ashurst, the couple were married in Red Bluff on September 13, 1871.

The 1870 census listed John Bogard as living in the village of Paynes Creek, a short distance northeast of Red Bluff. Perhaps the brothers were able to attend their sister's wedding. Ashurst took his sheep flock to the mountains that summer of 1871, then

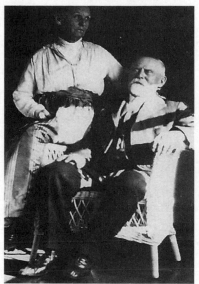

Sarah and Jack share a quiet moment many years after their pioneer days were over. *Henry Family Collection*

moved to Nevada. Jack Bogard had established a sheep camp at Geary Springs by now, and John was thought to have been involved in sheep raising at an early date, although in the 1870 census he is listed merely as a "laborer."

There was a great deal of sheep raising going on in Tehama County at this time. The Spanish sheep, first brought to California as stock for the missions, were coarse-woolled churros. Kit Carson reportedly brought the first flock overland to California in 1849, while many of the Gold Rushers also brought their own wooly herds with them. Mutton and lamb became a welcome relief from beef and bear meat in the early days and on the coast sheep prices increased from 75 cents and $1 per head to $12 and $14 in 1849. The rolling plains of Tehama County were ideal for grazing sheep and it was estimated that between 75,000 and 100,000 sheep were trailed from Ohio, Michigan, Illinois, and Missouri between 1851 and 1861.

The green and blooming prairies of Tehama were spectacular in the spring and fall. "For months now," wrote a Tehama farmhand in the early days, "the plains have all been in flowers here, with every kind of flower; one kind resembles tulips and other marguerites. The plains give a superb view."

In 1857, two brothers named Rawson brought in the first recorded fine-woolled French Merino sheep to Tehama County. They had started from Missouri with 7,000 head, but upon reaching California only 4,000 had made it through.

And, if sheep could be herded west to California, they could be driven anywhere. In 1865, Tehama sheep rancher John Burgess successfully drove some 3,500 head of sheep to Idaho. It was a profitable move and by the 1870s others were doing the same. In the summer of 1877, Henry W. Brown hired sheepman Eugene Reardon to drive ten thousand woolies to Colorado, where a ready and profitable market was found.

Joseph S. Cone, whose brand was registered in 1859, acquired the Rancho de los Berrendos in 1869. Consisting of some fourteen thousand acres across the river from Red Bluff, the ranch spread from the broad plains to the hills in the north. Cone stocked his ranch with thousands of sheep, hogs, and cattle, planting his fields in wheat, barley, orchards, and gardens. His flocks, consisting of some 20,000 sheep, were pastured in the hills in the summer and on his wheat stubble in the winter. He was one of the most successful ranchers in the county, besides having mercantile and property interests in Red Bluff.

Through their mutual interest in sheep, Jack Bogard was acquainted with Cone and reportedly became foreman of the Cone sheep operation. It

Sheep raising in old Tehama County was hard and dirty work, but good sheep dogs made it much easier. *United States Forest Service.*

was probably in the late 1870s when Jack successfully drove a flock of 5,000 sheep to Montana for Cone and a rancher named Ward. Later he made three trips to Denver, Colorado, spending six months on each trip. One of these drives involved 18,000 sheep in three bands. The dates of these journeys are not known, but John Bogard was probably on the trips, also.

Along in the late 1870s, John's life was influenced by his meeting a girl. Annie Gibbs had been born in California, but her family was from John's home town—Chillicothe, Missouri. Her father, Talton Gibbs, was a Mexican War veteran who had joined the rush to California in 1849. He had tried mining, but finally used his government bounty land warrant to acquire land in Tehama County.

The mutual attraction between John Bogard and Annie Gibbs ripened into love and they were married on June 15, 1879, in Mill Creek, some miles northeast of the Gibbs family home in Tehama. John was probably running sheep in the area and found it difficult to get away from his sheep herds. A year later, John and his new wife were living with her family in town during Annie's pregnancy. Since another family was living in the same dwelling, Talton Gibbs was either running a boarding house or renting rooms in his home. The census, taken on June 1, 1880, listed John and Annie living there with their newborn daughter, Della, who had just been born on May 31.

Five days later, on June 5, 1880, Bogard and his wife and baby are again listed in the census, but this time living with Jack Bogard some miles away in the town of Red Bluff. Both men are listed as "sheep raisers." Seven other young men are listed as living at this boarding house, most being sheep men, carpenters, and laborers.

Like most new fathers, John suddenly became aware of the family responsibilities that he had acquired.

Mr. and Mrs. John Bogard pose for a tintype on their wedding day. *Henry Family Collection.*

He filed on some property and registered his brand in June 1883. An 1885 Lassen County directory lists John Bogard as a "sheep raiser" with 160 acres in property. There had been additions to the family by this time, also; Della was five years old, Eleanor was four, and baby George was just one year old.

Both brothers were firmly ensconced in sheep raising and farming and were popular and active in Republican party politics. When John was nominated to run for the office of sheriff, he accepted and began campaigning in the fall of 1892. All of John's photographs show a stern expression, but his many friends all commented on his cheerful and jovial disposition.

J. J. BOGARD,

REPUBLICAN NOMINEE FOR

SHERIFF OF TEHAMA COUNTY.

Your support is desired

SENTINEL PRT. RED BLUFF.

Bogard's calling card, used during his campaign. *Henry Family Collection.*

"I knew John well," recalled J. D. Sweeney, of Red bluff. "He lived within fifty feet of our home for years. Many times we went hunting doves, quail, or rabbits after school hours in his dashing buckboard. Two weeks were spent together in the vicinity of Tyler's [now Child's Meadows] while he solicited votes. He was whole-souled, feared no man, was a dead shot and fond of joking."

And, he was a good campaigner. He comfortably won the general election and took up his duties as the new sheriff. One of his first actions was to appoint his brother, Jack, to the post of office deputy—now known as undersheriff. Putting family members on the public payroll was common enough then, as now, but Jack Bogard also had an excellent reputation and was expected to make a good officer.

During the nineteenth century, the sheriff's duties were in constant flux, but generally he was an officer of the courts in criminal and civil matters and in charge of the county jail. He summoned jurors and looked after them during trials, executed warrants, foreclosed property, and held public sales resulting from civil actions. The odious duty of hanging convicted criminals had been taken out of the hands of sheriffs in 1891, and executions now took place at the two state prisons. The new sheriff had a lot to learn, but he took to his lawman's calling like a duck to water.

Sheriff Bogard was well aware that Red Bluff was no Dodge City, but opportunities for crime persisted in a county that contained many thousands of acres and only three major towns, plus a scattering of villages. Petty crimes, sheep thefts, and cattle rustlers kept lawmen on their toes, even if bank and train robberies were practically unheard of.

The early 1890s was a period of depression and uncertain futures. Besides hordes of tramps that plagued California and the country, there was almost an equal number of the unemployed just trying to find jobs. In Shasta County, the times were so hard that county salaries were reduced and the local sheriff, and his opponent in the local election, both vowed not to do any advertising. Neighboring Tehama County wasn't much better off, but perhaps it was more interesting as indicated by one of sheriff Bogard's early cases.

Red Bluff was the main supply center for Tehama County. It was a fast-growing village on the banks of the Sacramento River. *Red Bluff Public Library.*

By late February of 1893, there had been several months of complaints from isolated farms and ranches in the hills behind the city of Red Bluff. Various witnesses had reported seeing or being confronted by a wild man. The reports were sporadic and vague enough so that other locals claimed the witnesses were just seeing things. "Those that saw the man," reported the Red Bluff Beacon, "averred that they could not be mistaken, but everybody else poo-poohed the story and declared the wild man a myth and fancy of the brain."

During the last week of the month, a report was received by the sheriff that there had been another sighting. Two ranchers, named G. W. Balis and Adin Bullard, claimed they had been "frequently frightened almost out of their wits" by the sudden appearance of a human being who looked more like an orangutan than a man. The creature would suddenly appear for an instant, then dash into the brush and disappear. When these incidents were repeated several times, the sheriff decided an investigation was in order.

Yreka Journal, **March 1, 1893:**

> *...Accordingly, Sheriff Bogard, accompanied by Constable Birmingham, went out to Mr. Bullard's in a double vehicle Sunday morning at 4 o'clock, and learned that the wild man was asleep in a shed near a farm house half a mile from Mr. Bullard's.*
>
> *The officers went to the place and found the fellow asleep. Having taken precautions against an assault either with a knife, gun or pistol, Sheriff Bogard got hold of the man's cane, near where he slept and called to him to get up. He raised up, parted his long, dirty, shaggy hair that hung down over his face and shoulders, and gazed wildly at the officers. The sheriff says he looked more like a grizzly or hyena as he sat there than a human being. When asked where he came from the only answer was "The mountains." The officers got him into the buggy and brought him to town and put him in the jail.*

The wild man's hair was some eighteen inches long, with a ragged beard to match. Both were black and dirty and his clothing was a "stinking mass of dirty, filthy rags." Stripping off his garments, it was found that he had on "four coats, three vests, three pairs of pants, three pairs of undershirts and

A home in old Tehama County. Although the occupants are unidentified, they are probably Bogard relatives or friends. *Henry Family Collection.*

drawers, half a dozen sock legs, the feet worn off," and an old pair of shoes and no hat.

The man's clothes were burned and he was thoroughly hosed down in the jail bathing facility. Bogard had procured clean garments for his prisoner, but after he had been dressed he still refused to talk or eat. He relaxed on the bunk in his cell, however, until about 4:30 that afternoon, then suddenly began to greedily gulp down the food offered him.

In going through the man's meager belongings, Sheriff Bogard found little of value, although indications were that he had traveled widely between Chicago, Texas, and the coast. Various written material was in the German language, and the following day Bogard secured a local resident named Lang who could speak German. The "wild man" was a German immigrant from Hanover who had been in the United States about nine years ago. He had held several jobs, but claimed that after breaking his arm he could not do any hard work and had turned to begging. The sheriff decided to hold him for several days to see if he developed any signs of insanity.

"He looked," said Sheriff Bogard, "more like a wild beast than a man, and his wild stubborn look and stolid indifference to all the surroundings added to the cognomen 'The wild man of the mountains.'"

Later that year the sheriff would have bigger and more dangerous fish to fry. In October 1892, a seventeen-year-old young man left his home and parents in Oakland, across the Bay from San Francisco. Robert Moody was tired of clerking in his father's grocery store and wanted to get out on his own and do some traveling. Moody and a friend made their way east, winding up in Placer County, where they worked at various odd jobs for eating money. Before long, the two split up, Moody going to Marysville for a few days, then traveling north, working his way to Portland, Oregon, before again returning to California.

At Ashland, Oregon, he met a young man named John Moore and the two traveled south for a time, then split up. Moody was thrown off a train at Vina in Tehama County, and then continued walking south along the Sacramento River. At the village of Jacinto, near the Glenn Ranch, Moody again met his friend Moore, who was working on the river levee. When Moody asked if Moore could get him something to eat, he was told; "I have a scheme that will beat begging all hollow."

Moore explained that he had previously made and passed counterfeit dollars at Puget Sound. He claimed that the bogus coin was so good that officers never caught on to it. Moody at first declined to get involved, but the older man soon talked him into it. Moore knew a blacksmith in Jacinto named Charley Ackers through whom he obtained plaster of paris and the metal needed. Stealing a boat at Tehama, the two men found an abandoned cabin on an island in the river. After obtaining a new dollar coin as a master, the two men retired to their island and soon had cast a quantity of counterfeit coin.

The two men now crossed the river and began passing the coin at farmhouses and in Butte City. Their method of operation was simple; they would buy an inexpensive item with a counterfeit dollar and their change would then all be in good coin. Returning to the river, they paid off the blacksmith, Ackers, then decided to move downriver as they thought they were being sought by officers. Packing up their meager belongings and taking along one hundred phony dollars, Moody and Moore again headed out into the river. Sheriff Bogard, however, was already tracking the boat stolen at Tehama.

The jail is just to the left of the Tehama County Courthouse in Red Bluff, shown here as they appeared in Sheriff Bogard's time. *Tehama County, California Illustrations.* San Francisco, Elliott & Moore, 1880.

The two men drifted with the current downriver during the night, then rested out of sight during the day. They had been seen, however, and Ed Todhunter, a constable at the village of Washington, received a telegram alerting him to the presence of the suspected counterfeiters on the river. Todhunter was busy, but asked his father to take his younger brother, Louis, along and intercept the two suspects. Armed with a shotgun and pistol, the elder and younger Todhunter secured a boat and began rowing upriver from Washington. In the twilight a boat was soon seen coming toward them, an incident reported later by young Moody.

Woodland Daily Democrat, April 12, 1893:

> *About 7 o'clock in the evening just as the dark was coming on we met a boat coming up the river in which were two men. They came near us and I saw that the man in the stern was a much older man than the other. I learned later they were the Todhunters—father and son. One of them shouted to me to throw them our painter [a rope]. I stopped rowing and one of them seized the gunwale of our boat. The man in the stern had a gun and Moore wrenched it from his hands. In the meantime the current turned their boat around and the young man [Todhunter] began to shoot.*
>
> *He fired twice and the first bullet struck me in the hip. Moore then shot the older man and their boat drifted away into the night and was soon lost in the gloom....*

Louis Todhunter had been killed in the exchange and the two counterfeiters jumped into the water and swam to the nearby levee.

Meanwhile, Yolo County Undersheriff Sehorn and Sheriff Bogard had learned that the Glenn Ranch blacksmith, Charley Ackers, had purchased the metal and plaster of paris used in the counterfeiting. By watching his mail, the two lawmen discovered Ackers had received a letter from Moore and one from a man named Martin. The blacksmith wrote back to "Martin," who turned out to be Moody, who had fled north to Siskiyou County. In the letter were numerous newspaper clippings giving accounts of the death of young Todhunter. Moore's letter was written from Nevada.

Sheriff Bogard now arrested Ackers and placed him in jail at Willows. The two lawmen caught the first train north and soon had young Moody in custody at Mott, Siskiyou County. He was returned and placed in jail at Sacramento, where he made a full confession. Yolo County Sheriff David Wyckoff, acting on a statement made by young Moody, took the train for Reno, but returned empty-handed when the fugitive could not be located.

Woodland Daily Democrat, May 23, 1893:

> *Charles G. Ackers was found guilty by a jury in the United States district court in San Francisco Monday, on two counts of the indictment*

charging him with aiding and abetting John Mohr and Robert E. Moody in counterfeiting coins. Moody gave State's evidence in the proceedings yesterday against Ackers. This is the crowd of counterfeiters who are responsible for the death of Louis Todhunter.

Two days later, Robert Moody had his hearing before a Washington Justice Court and was promptly discharged when no evidence was presented against him for the Todhunter murder. Moore was finally located under his real name of Whitfield and arrested in San Jose. He came from a bad family, and "Doc" Whitfield, his notorious brother, had been sentenced to ten years by a federal court in October 1893, for counterfeiting.

It was all valuable experience for the new sheriff and he was learning what all public servants discovered sooner or later: You don't have to be rich to serve the public, but it sure helps. Although there were perks to the sheriff's office, he quickly learned that many unforeseen expenses would have to be put before the county supervisors for reimbursement. Often, poor counties would deny compensation to their lawmen and they would have to swallow such items as travel charges while chasing criminals.

Leaving his Missouri home in 1866, Milton A. Sharp headed west, where he worked at mining in both California and Nevada. For twelve years he was an honest miner, but his continual investments in poor mining stocks kept him broke. He was working on a California farm when he made the acquaintance of a new employee, one William C. Jones. Having recently made another one of his bad investments, Sharp was open to Jones's suggestion that they hold up a stagecoach and make some real

money. Jones had recently been released from San Quentin, and the quiet, mild-mannered Sharp was now in very bad company.

Quitting their farm jobs, Sharp and Jones stopped the Auburn to Forest Hill stage on May 15, 1880. The passengers were lined up and robbed, and the two bandits then headed east into Nevada. They robbed the Carson City stage on June 8, as reported locally.

Milton Sharp was a crafty and dangerous stage robber who once shot a Wells Fargo guard.
Author's Collection.

Carson Valley News, June 11, 1880:

...The robbers leveled shotguns at the head of Cambridge, the driver, and ordered him to throw down the box. The box containing nearly $4,000 was pitched down. The pas-

sengers...were ordered out, placed in the road and made to stand in a line while they held up their hands....Six watches were taken and small amounts of cash...

Their spirits buoyed by their first two robberies, Sharp and Jones stopped the Bodie coach a week later and relieved the treasure box of $300.

With a $600 reward now on their heads, the two highwaymen crossed back into California and laid low for awhile. They were back on the road in August when they again stopped the Forest Hill stage and obtained $1,500 from the strongbox. They robbed the passengers also before waving the stage on and disappearing into the wild brush and tree-covered country.

Luck had been with the bandits in these initial robberies. On September 4, Sharp and Jones returned to Nevada and stopped the Bodie to Carson stage. The robbery had been interrupted and they had fled with nothing to show for their effort. The next morning they planned to stop the return stage, but when the guard, Mike Tovey, saw footprints in the road he got down to investigate. Suddenly there was a shout and two shots were fired. One of the stage horses was killed as Tovey stepped back behind one of the lanterns on the coach. When Jones abruptly appeared in the lantern light, Tovey shot and killed him, but received a shot in the arm from the other bandit. As Sharp disappeared in some brush, Tovey, who was bleeding badly, was taken to a nearby farmhouse for first aid. Sharp then returned to the coach and told the driver to throw down the box. After securing $700 from the treasure box, the highwayman fled before Tovey and the others returned.

A posed stage robbery in the mountains. Holdups usually took place on a grade where the driver would be kept busy controlling his horses. *Author's Collection.*

167

A San Francisco bankbook in the dead highwayman's pocket was seized by Wells Fargo officers and sent to Detective Captain Isaiah Lees of the San Francisco police. Lees, a twenty-seven-year veteran of the force, put a surveillance on the bank and a Minna Street boarding house, and Sharp was soon in custody. Various items taken in the robberies were found in the highwayman's room and he was whisked back to Aurora, Nevada. The bandit was convicted on October 30, 1880, and placed in jail while waiting for transportation to the state prison at Carson City.

A local election caused enough excitement and celebrating in town for Sharp to engineer his escape from the Aurora jail a few days later. After some ten days of freedom in the desert, the fugitive was recaptured and on November 12 entered the state prison at Carson City to begin serving his twenty-year term.

Over the years Sharp made many attempts to escape, but his efforts were always frustrated. He was thrown into dark dungeons, heavily ironed, and made to carry around a large iron ball, but still he kept up his escape attempts. Finally, he realized other means must be utilized. He wrote home and asked his family to intercede for him and he began regularly applying for parole. He had earned eighteen months' credit to be subtracted from his sentence when he saw an opportunity he could not ignore.

His prison record was considered "exemplary" by the summer of 1889 and his sudden disappearance caught prison officials by surprise, as noted in the local press.

Carson Morning Appeal, **August 17, 1889:**

> *Sharp was a trusty, doing garden work and was seen in the garden about 5:30 o'clock. It is customary to shut everything up at 6 o'clock, and it was at this hour that he was first missed. As soon as possible means were taken to recapture him, and Warden McCullough came to the city and requested the Governor to offer a reward, which was done. Early this morning Indians were put on his trail, and it was discovered that he had headed...towards Clear Creek. It is thought that he will be retaken before he gets far.*

Despite a massive manhunt and notices sent out to both California and Nevada authorities, Sharp vanished and was not heard from for the next few years. Utilizing a variety of aliases, the fugitive worked throughout northern California and apparently led an honest life. His freedom came to an abrupt end in the fall of 1893, however. He had been working as a cook in Trinity County for some time and had saved enough money to invest in a farm when his world fell apart once again. He was on his way to Redding when he stopped to buy a pair of shoes in Red Bluff. Sheriff Bogard's story of Sharp's capture appeared in the Carson City press.

Carson City Appeal, **October 5, 1893:**

> *Not long ago I was hunting a horse thief and met Sharp on the road. He was riding in a wagon and heavily armed. He answered to the pictures and descriptions I had of him, and I concluded he was Sharp, but still I was not certain.*
>
> *Next day I found a man named Randall, an ex-con, who knew Sharp, and said he could identify him. We found him next day in a shoe-maker's shop. He came to town with an old hunter named 'Turkey Tom,' to whom he paid $5 for a ride. They got off the wagon, and Sharp had unstrapped a brace of six-shooters in his belt and left them in the wagon, throwing a gunny sack over them. When I arrested him in the shoemaker shop as Sharp the stage robber, he merely turned to the shoemaker to whom he had given the order, and said: "You needn't mind about those shoes, I won't need 'em."*
>
> *He hired some lawyers to make a habeus corpus fight but it was no use. We found $880 in a sack in the wagon. Of course there were plenty of lawyers ready to stand in when they heard of this. He said to me after the arrest: 'If I had been with my guns you would have had to kill me to have got me.' I guess it was a good thing that he had no gun, for I hear that he will fight at the drop.*

The usually cynical *Redding Press* was delighted with the capture.

Redding Republican Free Press, **October 7, 1893:**

> *Sheriff Bogard of Red Bluff made a very important arrest last week in the person of Milton Sharp, a famous Nevada criminal, who broke out of jail at Carson City about four years ago, after serving about four years of a twenty-two year term....Detective Hume has identified Sharp as the right man, and he has been taken back to Carson to serve out his term.*

When Sharp was fully identified, Sheriff Bogard escorted him aboard the train to Sacramento where they were met by Warden Frank Bell of the Nevada State Prison. The two officers then escorted Sharp to the prison located outside Carson City.

When Sharp's various employments and honest lifestyle had been verified, he was able to apply for a pardon and in July 1894 he was a free man again. It was the last ever heard from one of the most notorious stage robbers of record.

Although Sharp's capture had been a prosaic affair, Bogard's detective work in recognizing the fugitive after all those years was acknowledged as fine police work. The sheriff had no sooner returned from Nevada when Southern Pacific railroad detective Will Smith called on him.

The past summer of 1893, Smith had been involved in the Evans and Sontag train robbing case in Tulare and Fresno counties. He had smelled gunsmoke on several occasions and was no doubt disappointed that he had not been in on the final shootout and capture of the bandits at Stone Corral. Smith was later interviewed by a Red Bluff reporter and discoursed on various subjects of the meeting in the local press.

Red Bluff Sentinel, October 15, 1893:

Southern Pacific detective Will Smith presented Sheriff Bogard with an engraved, double-action revolver.
John Boessenecker Collection.

I know of no sheriff in the entire state that possesses greater abilities as a detective than your own sheriff, Mr. Bogard. He has been remarkably successful and the people will hear more of him in years to come. He works quietly and independently, is tireless and conscientious. When he makes an arrest you may count on him having the proper evidence to convict.

I was in Red Bluff last Fair time after some safe crackers [continued Smith]. The subject of the highway robberies committed near here came up and Sheriff Bogard named Jim and Dan Ford as the guilty men. The arrests of Sunday and the confession of one of the Fords is an example of Mr. Bogard's good judgment.

Detective Smith's praise of Bogard was so effusive that the following day the reporter questioned a courthouse official on the same subject:

"He is the best sheriff in the state today, and his detective work marks him as a man of unusual shrewdness," said the official. "He is close mouthed and a dozen men couldn't keep track of him. It is no unusual thing for him to go home and remain there until two or three o'clock in the morning and then make some sneak into the country on some mission and return home in time for breakfast. And if you wait for him to say where he

was, or what he was working on, you will die in suspense. Captain Lees of San Francisco regards Bogard as an exceptionally bright officer, and this I have straight."

Smith's real purpose in visiting Sheriff Bogard may have been other than just a social visit with a brother lawman. Peace officers and detectives of the time often kept mementoes of their contact with criminals. Just as Scotland Yard had its Black Museum of confiscated criminal guns, knives, bludgeons, and brass knuckles, some California sheriffs had their own collections of outlaw memorabilia. Probably the most extensive collection was that of Sheriff Thomas Cunningham, of San Joaquin County. Other lawmen, notably railroad detective Len Harris, had their own private collections of acquired weapons of captured criminals. Detective Smith may have had aspirations of this nature in his own mind when he called on the Tehama sheriff. Smith's setbacks and lapses of judgment during his pursuit of Evans and Sontag were seriously questioned in the press of Tulare and Fresno counties and perhaps he was initiating his own private collection of weapons as an ego-boosting device.

The two lawmen probably began discussing guns when Bogard noticed the pistol Smith was carrying. It was a unique weapon, distinctly different from the Colt and Remington handguns that were so popular. The pistol was a Merwin, Hulbert & Company Double Action, 44-73 Pocket Army with folding hammer revolver. It fired 1873 Winchester rifle ammunition, and to reload, when the cylinder was pushed forward, the empty rounds were ejected. The Red Bluff reporter described the weapon further as follows:

Red Bluff Sentinel, October 15, 1893:

> *Smith carries one of the finest revolvers ever made. The barrel and cylinder are finely plated and chased and the handles are of the finest pearl. One side is a buck's head magnificently carved. It is suspended from a belt by a patent contrivance which does not necessitate the use of a scab-*

Detective Smith's gift to Sheriff Bogard in exchange for one of Milt Sharp's pistols. The beautifully engraved Merwyn and Hulbert revolver is still cherished by the family.
Henry Family Collection.

171

bard. It cannot be lost from the belt in a scuffle, yet one movement is all that is necessary to remove and bring it to bear on a man. It may be thrown into any position without removal from the belt and can be fired from the coat pocket also. The weapon cost $55 and is perfect in mechanism. It is the most rapid loading revolver yet devised. Detective Smith is to make Sheriff Bogard a present of a similar weapon as soon as he can procure one in the city. Smith carried away with him one of the revolvers found upon Milton Sharp, the Nevada stage robber, when arrested by Sheriff Bogard in Red Bluff two months ago.

This sounds for all the world like a trade had taken place; when Smith admired the Sharp pistol, perhaps the sheriff responded that since he had two, Smith could have one if he wanted it. Of course Smith wanted it, but he graciously said he would later present Bogard with an engraved Merwin and Hulbert in return. Such trades would be frowned upon today, but in the distant past it was considered a perk of the office. Soon, Sheriff Bogard had a new pistol, and it was a beauty.

A new handgun takes some getting used to, especially since no holster was needed to house his new weapon. Called a Bridgeport Rig, the system consisted of a stud welded to the pistol, just above the handle, that fit into a slotted device attached to a cartridge belt. To fire, the handle was grabbed and the pistol swiveled into position. This took practice, but soon the sheriff was accustomed to, and proficient with, his new weapon. The pistol could also be swiftly detached from the belt if more latitude was desired.

A massive manhunt had involved Sheriff Bogard and many other lawmen during the summer of 1893. The fugitive's name was William Fredericks and he more than proved he was a desperate man. Fredericks was not his real name and the evolution of his knavery is only imperfectly known, but he was born in the Alsace region of Germany around 1867. He claimed to have gone to sea at an early age and probably jumped ship in the United States about 1878. He showed up in California in 1889, drifting north to Shasta County where

Mug shot of William Fredericks. He lost an eye while attempting to rob a San Francisco bank. *Author's Collection*

he is thought to have worked as a barber. By early 1890, he had traveled south to Mariposa County where he found himself indigent and hungry. He resolved his problem in a manner he was probably already familiar with from his stay in the north.

On the night of May 10, 1890, Fredericks robbed Dorsey Ramsden's cabin on the outskirts of the town of Mariposa, then four days later stopped the Merced to Mariposa stage. Holding a shotgun on driver Fernando Davila, the highwayman directed him to break open the treasure box. When the noise of pounding on the lock irritated Fredericks and he yelled for Davila to stop, the bandit then called for the lone passenger to throw out any money she had. Millie Farnsworth tossed out some thirty or forty cents in loose change to the disappointed robber, who then waved for the coach to move on. A few days later Fredericks was captured and jailed.

On May 23, 1890, the outlaw had his hearing in the superior court of Judge J. M. Corcoran, who sentenced Fredericks to four years in the state prison at Folsom.

In Folsom, Fredericks soon gravitated to those of his own ilk. A stage robber named Frank Williams had been admitted shortly before Fredericks and in time the two became friends. When train robber George Sontag, who had adopted a stepfather's name of Contant, began serving his life term, Williams made his acquaintance, also. Both men were lifers. Along with his brother, John Sontag, and a Tulare County farmer named

Crouched alongside the American River, Folsom Prison was a foreboding sight to those who saw those granite walls and Gatling gun posts scattered around the perimeter. A few did manage to escape, but very few. *Author's Collection.*

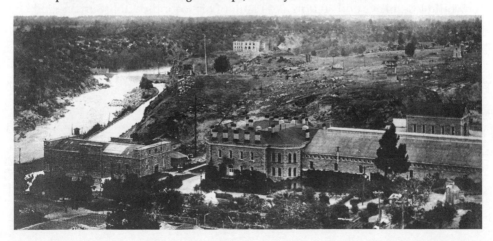

Chris Evans, George Sontag had robbed trains in California, Wisconsin, and Minnesota. As such, Sontag was held in awe by the burglars and petty thieves who filled the cells of Folsom.

Life termers spent much of their time plotting to escape. Few, however, acted on their schemes, as it was extremely dangerous. Although Folsom had no outside walls, as such, it was situated on the American River, with buildings as a barrier and open space securely covered by Gatling gun towers. Some convicts drowned in the river and others were shot down. Few, however, escaped from Folsom.

Despite this fact, when Fredericks came up for parole, he was involved in an escape plan with Williams, Sontag, and several others.

When Warden Charles Aull learned from the guards about the association of Sontag, Williams, and the others, he knew it meant trouble. Calling Fredericks into his office, he told the convict he would be better served not to get mixed up in any escape plots with someone like Sontag. Fredericks said he did not know what the warden was talking about, and on May 26, 1893, he walked through the gates as a free man.

The plan was a simple one. Fredericks was to contact the Evans family in Visalia and, through them, obtain guns to be secreted in a pre-arranged hideout in the Folsom quarry. Eva Evans, Chris Evans's teenaged daughter, helped Fredericks obtain the needed guns. As the ex-con headed back to Folsom, he probably heard the news of the gun battle at Stone Corral, a few miles east of Visalia. Chris Evans and John Sontag had been ambushed and captured, both men being desperately wounded. Evans would lose an eye and an arm as a result of his wounds, while Sontag died of his injuries a short time later. Not knowing how this might affect the escape plans, Fredericks kept moving and soon had the weapons safely concealed in the prison quarry.

Fredericks now hid out at an abandoned stamp mill and waited for the convicts to join him after the break. The escape attempt took place on the afternoon of June 27, 1893. Sontag and his fellow plotters obtained the weapons and seized a guard to use as a shield. When guard Frank Briare leaped over a precipice, taking one of the escaping convicts with him, Sontag and his pals found themselves exposed and in the open. As they scurried for cover on the rocky ground, the Gatling guns and Winchesters of the guards began cutting them down. Ricocheting bullets and bits of rock careened everywhere as the horrified convicts scrambled to protect themselves. It was over in less than an hour. Frank Williams was killed, along with convicts Anthony Dalton and Ben Wilson. George Sontag and Charles Abbott, wounded and covered with blood, surrendered and were hustled to the prison infirmary.

Fredericks read about the debacle in a newspaper and hastened to flee the state. With a hobo pal, he was riding on top of a train near Colfax when they were spotted by brakeman James F. Bruce. "Bruce ordered him off," reported the *Grass Valley Union*, June 29, 1893, "and as he approached within a few feet of him the murderous tramp drew a revolver and fired at the brakeman. Immediately after having fired the shot the tramp exclaimed: 'Run, God damn you, or I'll give you another.' "

As the mortally wounded Bruce climbed down and staggered toward the engineer, Fredericks leaped from the train and headed for the town of Grass Valley. Word of the Bruce shooting quickly spread, and Nevada County Sheriff William H. Pascoe thought he spotted Fredericks outside the Pacific Saloon in Grass Valley. When the man moved down the street, Pascoe followed him toward a local foundry. Realizing he was being followed, Fredericks suddenly whirled and fired one shot. The startled Pascoe managed to fire three shots before dropping with a bullet through the heart. Fredericks quickly ran off into the night.

Fredericks reward poster.
California State Archives.

Sheriff Bogard and officers from Yreka to Sacramento joined the manhunt, but the fugitive had disappeared.

Hopping a train at the first opportunity, Fredericks kept moving through the states of Nevada, Arizona, New Mexico, and Colorado. Eventually he turned up in Butte, Montana, where he kept a notebook record of various crimes he committed. He was constantly looking over his shoulder, afraid he would be recognized. In January 1894, he was in Salt Lake City. By the following March, he was back in California where he committed several robberies in San Francisco.

On the morning of March 21, Fredericks walked into the San Francisco Savings Union Bank on the corner of Market and Fell streets. He knew that only two cashiers were on duty and thought the bank would be easy to rob and that then he could make a fast getaway in the streets outside. Walking up to one of the windows, Fredericks confronted cashier William A. Herrick. The desperado later recalled the events that followed:

> "I handed a note to the cashier and told him that unless he did as I ordered I would blow up the bank, at the same time showing him the bottle to which a fuse was attached. I told him the bottle contained nitroglycerine, but there was nothing in it except alcohol.

> "He read the letter and went over to a drawer. Instead of giving me the $5000 that I told him in the note I wanted, he commenced shooting at me. One shot hit me in the right eye and another in the side. I fired at him then in order to save my own life."

Actually, Herrick's first shot had shattered a glass partition, sending a sliver of glass into Fredericks's right eye. The bandit's first shot had misfired, but Fredericks had fired again and Herrick staggered backwards with a mortal wound. The other man, bookkeeper Charles Melvin, also had his pistol out by now and was firing. Fredericks had taken a spent bullet in his side and wanted nothing more at this point than to get out alive. Rushing out the door through a gathering crowd of pedestrians, the outlaw fled up Market Street and vanished into an alley.

Policeman W. J. Shields was quickly at the scene and was told the direction in which Fredericks had fled. Tracking him to West Mission Street, the officer was told the desperado had last been seen running into a cellar. Shields and another officer cautiously descended into the cellar and soon made out Fredericks sitting in a corner. The bandit's wounds were not serious and after a visit to the receiving hospital, Fredericks was jailed

Contemporary illustration of the site of Fredericks's bungled bank holdup. *Author's Collection.*

and Detective Captain Isaiah W. Lees arrived to interview him in his cell. At this point, the identity of the suspect was not known.

It did not take Lees long to figure out that he was getting nowhere grilling the erstwhile bank robber. Asking for the prisoner's personal effects, Lees retired to his office and began going over a notebook found on the man. It was written in a code and soon the detective began recognizing some of the people mentioned. The names of "Evans" and "Sontag" now jumped out at him, as did the name of "Eva Evans," Chris's daughter. Shouting for his secretary, Lees now asked for a wanted poster from his voluminous files. When the poster was in his hands, the old detective scanned it quickly and looked up smiling. From the description of Fredericks on the poster, including many body tattoos, the detective knew that the most wanted man in California had been caught at last.

When Lees summoned the desperado to his office, Fredericks readily admitted his identity and the smuggling of weapons into Folsom. Neither did he deny the bank robbery charges, although he insisted he had shot Herrick in self defense. He denied the killing of Sheriff Pascoe and various other crimes, however.

There was a surprise visitor at the city jail on the morning of April 2, 1894. Eva Evans, accompanied by Fredericks's lawyer, appeared and asked to see the prisoner. Eva stood outside the bars and talked of her experiences since they had last met in Visalia. Eva and her mother were appearing in a local melodrama enacting a highly fictionalized account of the train-robbing careers of Chris Evans and John Sontag. The family was destitute due to Evans's criminal career, and they needed the money now to finance his impending trial. Eva must have enjoyed the opportunity to tell him of her new career, and the outlaw was no doubt flattered that she took the time to visit him. They had exchanged a few letters, but both probably knew this was their last meeting.

A snapshot of Sheriff Bogard who always seemed to be on the alert.
Henry Family Collection.

When Eva left, Captain Appleton Stone, in charge of the jail, asked who she was. When told, he promptly recalled Eva's involvement in the Folsom gun smuggling operation and instantly ordered a search of Fredericks's cell. Nothing was found, but a small hole was discovered in the wall. Fredericks just laughed and said it was the work of rats, but it was promptly decided that he would not be permitted any more visitors.

Fredericks's arraignment for the killing of William Herrick took place later that afternoon. His lawyer tried to obtain a change of venue, but when that failed he sought a delay that would allow him to contact the defendant's parents in Germany to learn if there was any insanity in the family. This, of course, was to be the plea for the trial that Judge Levy had scheduled for the following Thursday morning.

During the course of his trial, Fredericks was behaving oddly, but it did him no good. After his conviction his appeals began and in early May 1894, he actually managed to pick the lock of his cell and nearly succeeded in escaping. From then on a guard was stationed outside his cell around the clock. He kept up his insanity act, but a panel of physicians finally threw cold water on that routine.

Like many officers in northern California, Sheriff Bogard was disappointed that Sheriff Pascoe's killer was not apprehended that summer of 1893. The fugitive was never far from his mind after that. Although hanged for his crimes on July 26, 1895, the ubiquitous William Fredericks was to invade Bogard's life one more time.

After a brief campaign, Sheriff Bogard was re-elected to a second term by an increased majority in November 1894. In mid-March 1895, he was called to Sacramento on business. What little we know of the trip was reported later.

Sacramento Bee, **March 30, 1895:**

> *Sheriff Bogard had been in Sacramento for two or three days on business connected with a reported plot to assist murderer Fredericks in making his escape from the State Penitentiary.*
>
> ### *The Plot in a Letter.*
>
> *Sheriff Bogard, in some manner, which has been kept concealed by the authorities, intercepted a letter addressed to Fredericks....The letter advised Fredericks to make his escape by all means and no matter at what*

hazards. It contained also a map showing the locality in which Fredericks could find a lot of stolen money buried. This money is believed to be the proceeds of a train robbery, probably some of the money taken at the Yolo train robbery several months ago.

Bogard remained in this city for three or four days, hunting up clues connected with the authorship of the letter. He consulted with railroad and express detectives....

Various other newspapers alluded to Sheriff Bogard's mission to verify this letter, but so little was known of the matter that nothing was said or speculated as to just how such a letter could be obtained. At the time of Fredericks's trial, however, an article in the San Francisco press tried to explain what had transpired.

San Francisco Examiner, **April 6, 1894.**

Long ago, at the time of the Pascoe killing, Marshal [George E.] Gard detailed Deputy Harry Johnson on the case, and that officer, with requisition papers in his pocket, traced his man from time to time – first to Ogden, then to Pocatello, then to American Falls, then to Buffalo, Idaho and then to Butte, Montana, where the clew was lost. The chase was an arduous one and cost Marshal Gard a lot of money, but neither he nor Johnson gave up and a few days before the killing of Herrick a tip was received that Fredericks was again in San Francisco.

While investigating this affair a letter from Fredericks to Eva Evans fell into Marshal Gard's hands, in which a confession is made of his participation in the attempt to rescue his friends in Folsom...

The letter was published also, but is not pertinent other than to indicate that Eva captivated every man she encountered. What is important is that Gard, as a federal officer, apparently asked the post office to keep him appraised of any correspondence directed to known associates of Fredericks. Marshal Gard, then, probably acquired the letter Bogard was investigating from the post office. Just why Bogard was selected for the job is not known, but it is another indication of his reputation as a detective.

Gard was a noted lawman of the time. He had cut his teeth as a police officer, detective, and sheriff in Los Angeles County during the 1870s and 1880s before being appointed United States marshal of Southern California in 1890. It was George Gard who led the posse that shot it out with, and captured, train robbers Chris Evans and John Sontag at Stone Corral.

As Sheriff Bogard dozed in the sleeper car, the train clickety-clacked through the night, stopping at the Wheatland depot, just south of Marysville. It was about 1:15 on the morning of March 30, 1895, when the train began moving forward again. No one noticed the two dark figures that crawled on top of one of the cars. Engineer Amos L. Bowser was in the cab of the train with his fireman when the two masked men suddenly appeared. The engineer later recalled what happened next.

San Francisco Examiner, **March 31, 1895:**

> *It was when we were about a half mile this side of Wheatland that someone punched me quite forcibly in the ribs and I turned around to see that it was a masked man, a tall fellow armed with two pistols, which he held uncomfortably close to me. Behind my fireman I noticed another man, a shorter one, also masked and armed similarly. I said to the tall man; "Hello, what do you want?" He replied; "We want you to stop at the next crossing." I asked which crossing he meant and he said, "the next main highway."*

When the train had stopped, the bandits led the two trainmen back to the express car where Engineer Bowser was instructed to call for the express messenger to open up. Sliding open the door, the messenger jumped to the ground when told to do so. The shorter bandit then climbed into the car. There was no combination for the safe's lock, so he returned with the messenger's shotgun and tossed a package to his partner.

"Here's a bouquet for you, Bill!" he grinned, then suggested they pay a visit to the passenger cars.

The captive fireman, Barney Nethercott, the messenger, and Engineer Bowser were motioned on as the two bandits headed for the nearest passenger car. Nethercott was given a sack consisting of the leg of a pair of overalls with one end stitched together. The five men then entered the car

It was on a passenger train such as this that Sheriff Bogard was forced to confront a very dangerous situation. *California State Library.*

and startled the inhabitants by shouting, "Hands up!" The passengers were told to stay in their seats and throw their valuables into the sack held by Nethercott. Things went well enough until a passenger from Redding named Sampson refused to give up his money. The taller bandit lurched forward and brought his pistol down on the man's head, opening a four-inch gash. His cash was promptly forthcoming, along with a rush of blood from his head wound. When everyone in the car had been robbed, the procession of bandits and train personnel moved on to the next car, the smoker. Passenger A. S. Berger later recalled that startling moment.

Engineer A. L. Bowser was the first to be made aware of the bandits. *Author's Collection.*

San Francisco Examiner, **March 31, 1895:**

> Some one of the passengers had jokingly said, as cause for the wait, "Guess it's a hold-up," when the door opened and the fireman entered holding a sack and guarded by a masked man—robber No, 1. Back of them was robber No. 2. "Throw up your hands!" was the order. I was the first man, and mine went up very quickly. The robber said, "Give us your money."
>
> "How can I, when my hands are up?" I said. "Hand over and hurry up," he rejoined.
>
> I handed him the contents of my pockets, a knife, keys and about $5 in money. They had just passed on a few seats when I heard the door in the other end of the car open and the firing began. All was noise and smoke and the ten other passengers and myself were only too glad to duck our heads out of range of stray shots. It was all over in a few minutes, though it seemed hours…

Sheriff Bogard was startled as he sat up in his sleeper car bunk. A porter was shaking him while whispering something about the train being robbed. "Robbed—Where?" asked the now wide-awake lawman as he was buckling on his belt and pistol. "In the smoker car up ahead," responded the porter. Slipping into his overcoat, the lawman now detached his pistol from his belt and swiftly headed for the forward cars, followed by the porter and a brakeman. With all the excitement in the smoker car, Bogard was able to slip into the car unnoticed, while the porter and brakeman stayed outside. He crouched between two seats without being seen.

The robbers' procession was led by Engineer Bowser, who must have moved some distance ahead of the group and suddenly saw the lawman and later commented:

"As we entered the smoking car I noticed a man crouched between two seats on his knees, and immediately recognized…an old acquaintance, Sheriff Bogard of Tehama County. He whispered to me these words: 'How many?' I replied: 'Two.' "

The sheriff then fired at the tall robber, who was keeping an eye on the passengers being robbed. The bandit dropped to the floor, shot through the heart. "Don't leave me, Bill!" was all he could gasp, and then he was gone. The shorter bandit in the rear now fired at Bogard, who had stood up to get a clearer shot at the other bandit. The sheriff had Nethercott and the engineer in the aisle to be concerned with, as well as the passengers, and he hesitated for a clear shot. The bandit had no such concerns. When he shot, the sheriff's right side was facing him and the robber's bullet struck a cartridge in Bogard's pistol belt, then glanced off driving into the lawman's back severing a main artery below the kidneys. The sheriff staggered backwards, and then collapsed in the aisle.

In a panic now, the bandit fired several more shots, striking fireman Nethercott in the neck and shoulder, as well as the thigh. A third shot tore off the heel of an exposed shoe of a salesman named Fish, who was crouched on the floor between seats. As the bandit jumped from the car and fled into the night, the wounded Nethercott staggered into the next car and announced he was "shot to pieces." He was still holding the makeshift sack full of loot.

The conductor checked Sheriff Bogard and saw that he was still breathing. Awakened by the shots, attorney Braynard rushed from the sleeper and burst into the car and saw Bogard on the floor. He was quickly told what happened as he kneeled to hold up his friend's head. Bogard had left Braynard in the smoker and had perhaps hoped he would have an ally when he confronted the train robbers. But the attorney had retired to the sleeper shortly after the sheriff had left. Braynard had his pistol with him and was regarded as a splendid marksman. The lawyer now sat down and wept as he thought of how he might have aided his friend if they could have coordinated their attack on the robbers. But it was too late now.

The bandit was dead and the train was quickly put under steam for Marysville, where a physician could be obtained for the wounded sheriff and Nethercott. Yuba County sheriff Sam Inlow was notified of the events, and as telephone and telegraph lines flashed the news around the state, a massive manhunt was instituted for the escaped train robber.

A team of Marysville physicians quickly took charge of Bogard and Nethercott, and after an examination and some bandaging, the fireman was returned to the train and sent on to the railroad hospital in Sacramento. Nothing could be done for the lawman, however, and he died on the examination table. He was forty-three years old.

A call was made to the Bogard home in Red Bluff and the sad news related to the family. Jack Bogard, the undersheriff, planned to leave immediately for Marysville to help coordinate the manhunt and bring his brother's body home. Word quickly spread around town, and groups were soon discussing the news on streetcorners. It was a terrible tragedy, but those who knew Sheriff Bogard were not surprised. That was the kind of man he was.

Shortly after hearing the news, a prominent Sacramento detective remarked that "Bogard was a man who would follow a criminal to hell!"

"Wells, Fargo & Company," reported the *San Francisco Examiner,* March 31, 1895, "today purchased a handsome casket in this city and have given undertaker Bevan instructions to forward the remains of Sheriff Bogard to the bereft family at Red Bluff."

Jack Bogard arrived that same day and after viewing his brother's body, consulted with the local officers concerning the manhunt for the fugitive killer. Wells Fargo detective John Thacker, his son Eugene, along with another officer, were already in the field scouring the area around the robbery site. The dead bandit had been wearing clothes indicating he was a bicycle rider and he had been recognized as being in Marysville just prior to the robbery.

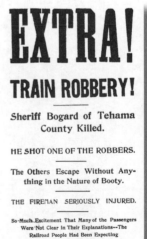

EXTRA!

TRAIN ROBBERY!

Sheriff Bogard of Tehama County Killed.

HE SHOT ONE OF THE ROBBERS.

The Others Escape Without Anything in the Nature of Booty.

THE FIREMAN SERIOUSLY INJURED.

So Much Excitement That Many of the Passengers Were Not Clear In Their Explanations---The Railroad People Had Been Expecting a Hold-Up.

Marysville Daily Appeal, **March 30, 1895. The robbery was headlined all over the country and the brave sheriff mourned throughout the state.** *Author's Collection.*

When a bicycle was found nearby, it was brought to town and the name of the rental company telephoned to Captain Lees in San Francisco. Lees found the firm of Baker & Perkins on Van Ness Avenue and a check of their records showed that two men had rented the bicycles a few days previous to the attempted robbery. A member of the firm caught the next train for Marysville where he identified the dead bandit as one of the men. The second cyclist was described as short and stoop-shouldered. With lawmen from four or five counties as well as the detectives of Wells Fargo, the Southern Pacific, San Francisco, Stockton, and Sacramento officers working on the case, information was coming together by the hour.

Oscar Brown, or Browning, the dead bandit killed by Sheriff Bogard. *John Boessenecker Collection.*

The dead bandit had used various aliases. He had rented the bicycle under the name of Sam Maguire, his companion using the name Jack Brady. Both men had used various aliases throughout central California, but the dead bandit's name was apparently Brown, or Browning. His fugitive partner, Brady, was finally determined to be Henry Williams, or Ury.

In a matter of days the tall and short bandits had been linked to a series of holdups in Sacramento, Stockton, and San Francisco. George Gard, head of the Southern Pacific Detective unit, was investigating an unsuccessful train robbery on March 3, at Ben Ali, near Sacramento. Afterwards the tall and short bandits had robbed a Sacramento saloon. On March 8, the same duo attempted to hold up the same train, but only managed to steal the shotgun and pistol belonging to the express messenger. A series of robberies in San Francisco also were noted as being perpetrated by tall and short bandits.

Marysville photographer P. W. Griffiths took this photograph of a man dressed in the dead bandit Browning's clothes and holding his two pistols. *Author's Collection.*

By now both men had been identified as ex-convicts who had done time in San Quentin for horse theft a few years previously. Their prison identification clearly indicated Samuel Oscar Browning as the tall bandit and Henry Williams, alias Jack Brady, as the shorter one. When both Marshal Gard and a Wells Fargo official contacted San Francisco police detective Captain Isaiah Lees and gave him an address on Grove Street thought to have been the address of the tall cyclcist, it was a major breakthrough. After interviewing the suspect's landlady, Captain Lees and several detectives were let into the room. Later, Lees gave an interview.

Jack Bogard was appointed to his dead brother's office and was active in the pursuit of Brady. *Henry Family Collection.*

San Francisco Chronicle, **April 2, 1895:**

> *I found a trunk belonging to Williams, alias Brady, who had been rooming there since November 1. I opened the trunk and found two tintypes of Williams and Browning together on their bicycles....*

> *My investigations led me to a room on Van Ness Avenue which had been rented by the tall man, S. O. Browning, on November 1, but which he left about two months ago and went to room in a house on Golden Gate Avenue....I found a large trunk in Browning's room in the house on Golden Gate Avenue. I picked the lock and got several pictures taken in St. Louis...There were also tintypes taken here since November of him and Williams together on their bicycles. That was about half past 1 this morning.*

Newspaper sketch from one of the tintypes found by Captain Lees in the San Francisco rooms of the train bandits. *Author's Collection.*

Lees was quite ill at the time with a flu-like malady, but he knew now he was working on a series of San Francisco crimes, as well as the Bogard murder and this latest train robbery. Alonzo Stagg, proprietor of the Ingleside Resort, a few miles inland from the Cliff House, had been shot and killed during a robbery there on March 16, 1895. Little money was obtained, but once again a tall and shorter man had been involved. Other robberies in Sacramento and San Francisco all had this similar M.O. of the taller bandit being the more aggressive and the smaller one nervous and shaky. The same two bandits were now suspected in two train robberies near Stockton and the theft of over $50,000 from a train stopped west of Sacramento at a place called Sheep Camp.

Jack Brady, the second train robber. Like his partner. he was an ex-convict. *California State Archives.*

On April 2, 1895, Sheriff Bogard was laid to rest in Red Bluff's Oak Hill Cemetery. Crowds of people gathered on the streets that morning, many from distant villages and towns, as well as farmhands from the country and the great many friends and family of the deceased. A $10,000 reward had been raised by the people of the county and Jack Bogard was about to be appointed to take over his dead brother's post. The previous day, the late sheriff's good friend Judge J. F. Ellison paid eloquent tribute to the fallen lawman.

San Francisco Chronicle, April 4, 1895:

In adjourning at this time the Court deems it proper to say a few words concerning the untimely death of its executive officer John J. Bogard, who had been a resident of Tehama County from early boyhood. In 1892, the voters manifested their appreciation of his work by electing him Sheriff of this county. In 1894 so well had he performed his duties that he was re-elected by an increased majority. Last Wednesday night he left for Sacramento on an important piece of detective work, the nature of which he had confided to only a few of his intimate friends, including the Judge of this court.

...It has been said by one of earth's wise men that it is just as natural to die as to be born. This may be true when death comes from old age, from a gradual extinction of vital powers, but in this case there was nothing natural about it. In the prime of life, of great physical power, in full possession of all his faculties, his eye undimmed, his natural forces unabated, and suddenly without warning he went over the river to join the great majority. We who knew him well will miss his familiar form and presence from the circle of official duty.

Another photo, found in one of the bandit's San Francisco rooms, shows the dead outlaw Browning with a lady friend. *Author's Collection*

186

As sheriff of this county he performed every duty faithfully, diligently and fearlessly. In his sudden death we can reflect that he died at his post of duty with his armor all on, displaying a courage never excelled and rarely equaled...."

The board of supervisors also adjourned for the day as did all the county offices, many businesses, and even the saloons. Flags were at half-mast all over town. A troop of the members of the late sheriff's Masonic brethren marched to the Bogard home, where leading citizens and county officers served as pallbearers and carried the casket to the hearse, then followed it to a local church for services. The hall was filled with a great many large floral arrangements to complement the sermon and choir.

"It was without doubt the largest funeral ever held in Red Bluff," concluded the *San Francisco Examiner*, "and showed the feeling in which Sheriff Bogard was held by his neighbors."

Most of the major newspapers showered praise on the fearless sheriff who had rushed to duty no matter what the odds. In neighboring Shasta County, however, one newspaper saw fit to criticize the sheriff's actions.

Redding Republican Free Press, **April 6, 1895:**

Bogard was a man of undaunted courage, a good detective, but not endowed with the necessary caution. His determination and courage prompted him to take too many chances. He had been following the track of these men, and expected a hold-up in the near future, but not at that time. He was buried in Red Bluff Wednesday under the auspices of the Masonic lodge, quite a number attending from this city. He leaves a large family to mourn

The crowds at the Bogard funeral must have looked much like this street scene in old Red Bluff. It was a sad day for the family and Tehama County. *Red Bluff Public Library.*

his sudden death. They will receive $2,000 from the Workmen lodge of which he was a member. A good man and brave officer has perished.

It was a long and difficult day for Annie Bogard and the three children. Della was now fifteen, Eleanor was fourteen, and George would be eleven in May. They would have to do the balance of their growing up without a father.

Annie Bogard, shown here with son George, had three children to comfort her at this terrible time, but her husband was gone.
Henry Family Collection.

Sketches made from the photographs of the bandits appeared in all the large city newspapers and were instrumental in the manhunt for Brady. Since this was the first train robbery where the bandits used bicycles, pedestrians were looking at all cyclists with a jaundiced eye. Berkeley constable John Teague saw a man wearing a bicycle jacket trying to catch a ride out of town and immediately arrested him as a suspect. He was released when no corroborating evidence could be produced.

A San Francisco cyclist traveling to Virginia City over the Sierra reported being stopped thirteen times by officers. He finally gave up and returned home. Another bicyclist near Woodland crossed the river on a ferry, the ferryman later deciding his passenger must have been Brady. The man was tracked down by a dozen pursuers, but this cyclist also proved he was not the fugitive killer.

Prominent Oroville attorney Colonel A. F. Jones arose early one morning, dressed, then jumped on his bicycle and made a dash for the local depot to catch the Sacramento train. As he neared his destination, he heard a voice shout; "Hey there, you fellow! Halt!"

Thinking a footpad was after his wallet, Colonel Jones began pedaling even faster when the voice again shouted; "Halt, I say, or I will shoot!" It was a local lawman looking for Brady.

As the colonel skidded to a stop, the voice came closer and said in a disappointed manner, "Oh, it's only you, is it," as he recognized Jones' magnificent whiskers.

Brady himself would later talk of his flight to avoid capture. Between April and late July, he claimed to have roamed from Marysville to Fresno, then up to Red Bluff and down to Stockton and Sacramento. While in the north he was recognized by two manhunters who nicked him with some buckshot, then fled while Brady rushed in the opposite direction.

On July 26, 1895, there was a telephone report of Brady being seen in Freeport, a river village south of Sacramento. A man answering Brady's description was seen reading a newspaper in Riehl's store while eating lunch. Suddenly, the man appeared startled, and abruptly jumped up and rushed out to the street. The owner, after witnessing this, looked at the newspaper and it clearly appeared that the man had been reading an article about the Brady search. He immediately called the Sacramento sheriff .

John Bogard's tombstone in the Red Bluff Cemetery. *Henry Family Collection.*

Sheriff Johnson recruited Deputy Alexander McDonald and several other lawmen and immediately began tracing the fugitive's trail. After he alerted various towns in the area, Sheriff Johnson left Deputy McDonald on a road, telling him to stay on the lookout, while he returned to Sacramento on some business. Another manhunter named William Johnson met McDonald on the road and told him he had seen a man under a bridge a short distance away. The two men carefully made their way to the bridge where they caught the suspect by surprise.

"What are you doing down there?" queried McDonald.

"Oh, just resting," responded the man.

Drawing his pistol, Deputy McDonald growled; "Come out of there."

After looking carefully at their captive, the two lawmen were sure they had the right man, and the three men traveled in a buggy back to Sacramento. The manhunt was over!

During the next few days, Brady admitted his identity, even confessing to some of the robberies he and his partner were accused of committing, except of course, the Ingleside resort robbery and the Wheatland robbery, both of which involved killing. The Sheep Camp train robbery, where the loot totaled over $50,000, was also their work. They had buried this haul across the river from Sacramento, taking only a portion of it at the time and stashing the balance. Later, when they returned, they were unsuccessful in locating their treasure. A hobo had stumbled across it and most of it had been spent by the time detectives had tracked down the lucky bum.

In the Sacramento jail the prisoner had a visitor he would have preferred to avoid.

Sacramento Bee, July 27, 1895:

> *A Bee reporter, accompanied by Sheriff Johnson, Sheriff [Jack] Bogard and A. L. Brown, of Red Bluff, had an interview with Brady shortly before noon today.*
>
> *Brady's sunburned face flushed as he took his seat between Sheriff Bogard and the reporter, and he tapped first one foot and then the other foot nervously upon the floor....*

It was a long interview, the officers looking for holes in Brady's stories. The outlaw insisted he was not involved in the killing of Sheriff Bogard since he had split up with Browning the previous night. Earlier, Brady had told a visitor that he thought Browning had killed the sheriff because "there were so many persons behind him (Bogard). Brady then quickly qualified his comment:

Marysville courtroom scene as pictured in the San Francisco *Examiner*, November 7, 1895. Brady is seated in foreground.

"But, that was not admitting that I was in the holdup."

"But you spoke about Brady," persisted Sheriff Bogard.

"Yes," replied Brady with a big smile, "because Brady was supposed to be in the holdup, and I was supposed to be Brady."

It became very clear to the officers they would have to make their case in court, with no help from Jack Brady:

"You fellows would have made quick work of me if I was taken in Tehama County," grinned the outlaw. Both Bogard and Brady had flushed faces as the interview concluded.

In August 1895, Brady was tried in Marysville for the murder of Sheriff Bogard. There was concern that the prosecution's case was weak because of a lack of hard evidence. Captain Lees was in court to arrest the defendant for a San Francisco murder and several robberies in case of an acquittal. The jury convicted Brady of murder, but could not agree on the penalty. Finally, on November 18, 1895, he was sentenced to life in Folsom State Prison. He was saved from the death penalty by one vote. Nevertheless, an aged Jack Brady was paroled in 1913. He died in 1940, while still on parole. Prison records establish Jack Brady, alias Henry Williams, was in reality one Henry Ury, a native of Illinois.

Jack Brady in his well-deserved prison stripes.
California State Archives.

When Annie Bogard contacted the Fidelity and Casualty Insurance Company concerning her $3,000 policy, she was told her claim was invalid in that the premium had not been paid and the dead sheriff had "unnecessarily placed his life in jeopardy by opposing the attacks of robbers." Mrs. Bogard was then forced to sue the company, with results that were triumphantly published in the California press.

Oakland Tribune, January 13, 1896:

> *Red Bluff, Jan. 13. – The jury in the case of Mrs. Anna Bogard, the widow of Sheriff Bogard who was killed while resisting train robbers, against the Fidelity and Casualty Insurance Company has given a verdict for defendant.*

Bogard's life was insured in the company named. His widow's claim for the amount of his policy was refused by the corporation on the ground that in fighting the robbers, Bogard had unduly exposed his life to danger."

Listen carefully! With a little concentration, you can almost hear the courtroom cheering on that one!

The End

Chapter Five

Hiram L. Rapelje

A gunfighting lawman with a dark side

"**H**e is five feet eleven and three-quarters inches in height, has dark brown hair and mustache, a grayish-blue eye, full round face and fair complexion. He will weigh about 220 pounds. He is of happy temperament, always seeing the sunny side of every situation.

"In conversation he has an easy, pleasant manner, and is a very ready conversationalist and is very communicative about everything except his official business. He does not at all strike one as the pictured gun fighter with the fierce eye and fiercer mustache, loaded down with a various assortment of small ordinance. In short, like Byron's Lambro, he is 'the mildest mannered man that ever cut a throat or scuttled a ship.'"

Hi Rapelje's description, at the height of his Stone Corral celebrity, was written by a newspaper reporter just after the desperate gunfight that saw the reign of terror of two train-robbing desperadoes brought to a close. The description was of Rapelje

Hi Rapelje, the morning after the battle at Stone Corral. *Author's Collection.*

in his prime, at that moment a famous man in California. He would find his newly acquired stature an illusory and fickle appellation.

Some gain fame in politics or war. Premier inventors, sports figures, and entertainers also acquire recognition for their talents and skill. Hi Rapelje's renown was garnered mainly from a photograph. Oh, he was given much notice for being one of the principal officers who shot it out with two train robbers in Tulare County in 1893. A photograph taken at the time shows the wounded bandit John Sontag lying in the foreground with a group of gun-toting men posing behind him. Holding his Winchester rifle, Hi Rapelje stands in the group in what has become one of the most published and famous photographs of the Old West. Although most historians would concur (as did an autopsy report) that it was Hi's rifle that did most of the shooting at Stone Corral, it was the photograph, and not Hi, that gained the lasting fame.

Still, in the great San Joaquin Valley, in his day, Rapelje was a widely known stage driver, city marshal and hard-riding deputy sheriff. Despite his pursuit and capture of stage robbers, train robbers, horse thieves, and cattle rustlers, his long career as a lawman is little-known today.

A scrappy, hard-drinking brawler on occasion whose judgement was sometimes in question, Hi usually landed back on his feet. It is high time his colorful story, spanning the riotous California frontier days and well into the twentieth century, was told.

The original Rapeljes in America were descended from Joris (George) Janssen Rapalje, a Dutch Huguenot exile from France. Fleeing his native country, he took up residence in the Hudson Valley in New Amsterdam (New York) in 1623. The family later moved to Long Island, to an area called Breucklyn, later Brooklyn. George's daughter Sarah, born in 1625, was unquestionably the first white child of Dutch parents on the island. Later, in the early nineteenth century, the Rapeljes moved north, settling in Ontario, Canada, where Daniel Rapelje was a founder of the village of Saint Thomas, in Elgin County. Daniel's son Daniel Barkley Rapelje, and his wife Anne had six children; Almira (Myra), George Henry, Susannah, Daniel Lambert, Hiram Lee, and Malcolm.

Hiram Lee Rapelje had been born in Saint Thomas on March 20, 1851. When both parents died in 1860, the children were taken in by relatives Barclay Lambert Rapelje and his wife, Nancy. When Hiram's older sister Myra married and moved to Port Huron, Michigan, young Hi soon joined her there, moving on to California when he was still a teenager. Indications are that other Rapeljes accompanied or followed him to the state. His brothers George and Daniel both served the Union during the Civil War.

Coast Line stagecoach ad.
Los Angeles Daily News,
February 23, 1869.

Hi later reminisced about driving stage-coaches in San Luis Obispo County where he became a skilled reinsman while still a teenager. Although coaches running along the coast route seldom carried the potential of a rich treasure box, as did the inland mining camp stages, young Hiram was held up at least once. He recalled not paying much attention to the robbers as it was all he could do to control his horses at the time. It was a rough route in other ways also, climbing through craggy mountain passes and dropping down along the surf-washed beaches where the coach running gear often acquired trailing links of dripping seaweed.

Flint, Bixby & Company's Coast Line featured both the gorgeous red and yellow Concord coaches, as well as the hardy and practical mud wagons. Driving both types of coaches, helping with the stock, and learning to "read" the idiosyncrasies of his horses was wonderful training for young Hi, and he learned his craft well. Many years later, coast stage driver Thomas Green recalled those halcyon days of mountain and seacoast stagecoaching:

"We drove matched teams of six. Nothing but six, and always matched. To the last buckle everything shone. San Luis Obispo must still remember Bill Blackmore's team of six bully blacks, with red leather on the bridles and sixty ivory rings. Over Cuesta Pass, through the Coast Range, there were grades and turns that called for the best of driving by the very best of linesmen…"

A coastal stagecoach crossing the Santa Ynez River. Such crossings could be quite treacherous in bad weather. *Len Gralleri Collection.*

And Hi Rapelje learned to be as good as the best of the drivers.

After learning every bump and curve in the road of his stage route, there came a time when Rapelje realized just how huge California was…. and he had seen very little of it. He was particularly curious about the wondrous valley of Yosemite. By the late 1860s, stagecoaches out of Mariposa covered the twenty-six-mile route to a hotel and station at Wawona where horses carried visitors the twenty-seven remaining miles on into the valley. The dusty roads and jarring horseback rides could not discourage the mounting flood of tourists that by 1870 were arriving from all over the country and the world. In a letter to Mariposa acquaintances from Stockton, the renowned P. T. Barnum gushed excitedly about the trip.

Mariposa Gazette, **June 17, 1870:**

> *"Our party has just arrived from the Yosemite and Big Trees — tired, but delighted. It is a fatiguing trip, but the wonders and delights it affords pays one ten times over for making it. The first view from 'Inspiration Point,' is worth crossing the Atlantic and the Continent to see…."*

Exactly when Hiram traveled across the valley and made his way to the village of Mariposa is not known. In the early 1870s, the Southern Pacific Railroad was building south down the San Joaquin Valley. Where depots were designated, towns began springing up and Lathrop, Modesto, Merced, Madera, and other villages assumed their places on the map. California was growing out of its Gold Rush days, although horses as a means of travel would last for forty more years.

In the early 1870s, Mariposa was still a mining town, but it was also the hub of the Yosemite tourist trade and its spectacular giant Sequoia

The village of Mariposa was hospitable and Hi had no trouble making friends in Joe Miller's saloon. *Author's Collection.*

trees. The Washburn brothers had come out from Vermont in the early days. They bought Galen Clark's hotel and developed the property as a packing station for tourists to the big trees and Yosemite Valley. Henry Washburn also owned the local stage line, as well as a livery business in Mariposa.

In Mariposa, young Rapelje looked around and liked what he saw. A trip to Yosemite Valley left no doubt that he was indeed in God's country. Returning to Mariposa, Hi stepped into the Capital Saloon, which was housed in a new brick building. He was struck by the friendliness of the owner-bartender, the very popular Joseph H. Miller. Bartenders were a combination public relations firm and chamber of commerce in those days, and when Hi mentioned that he might be settling down, the friendly barkeep told him of the local work opportunities. Perhaps Miller invited Hi home for supper, where he met the saloon man's wife, Ann, and their three young children. It was not long before the two men became good friends.

Henry Washburn and his brothers had many interests in Mariposa County. *California State Library.*

It was probably Miller who introduced Rapelje to Henry Washburn who, with two partners, owned the local livery stable and stage line. When there was an opening, Hi demonstrated his coaching abilities and soon found himself holding the ribbons and making the stage run from the new town of Merced up to Mariposa and Wawona.

Over time Rapelje met most of the stage drivers on the route. George Monroe, a black man, was regarded as one of the best drivers, while George Powell, Jack Ashworth, Rice Markley, Al Sleeper, and Al

"Buffalo Jim" Cody were all experienced reinsmen. Another driver, Johnny White, was about Hi's age and the two became good friends while exchanging news about their respective routes.

Concord stages were used in good weather, and the hardy mud wagons put in service the rest of the year, but passengers did not like being enclosed in a coach when such splendid scenery was to be seen. At an early date, the Washburn operation ordered specially designed coaches for their operation.

Yosemite stage driver George Powell. *Author's Collection.*

Mariposa Gazette, May 26, 1871:

New Stage—Washburn & McCready, who are running a daily line of stages between Mariposa and Clark & Moore's, [Wawona] where they connect with their saddle train for Yo Semite, received on Saturday last a splendid eleven passenger stage, which they immediately placed upon the road. It runs smooth and is just the thing for the mountains. It was made in Stockton.

Yosemite stage driver Al Sleeper. *Author's Collection.*

Hi enjoyed his mountain route and his passengers, who came from across the country and around the world. Stage drivers often selected the two passengers who were allowed the privilege of sitting on the seat with them, and Hi would regale his seat mates with tales of his experiences. When he tired of that, there were always the adventures of the other drivers. Buffalo Jim's coach once approached a grizzly bear dining on a mule alongside the road. "The bear gave a snort and ran," reported Jim, "and the team was equally frightened. For about three-quarters of a mile the time is reported the best recorded for that track."

In late June 1875, the *Mariposa Gazette* heralded the completion of the wagon road from Wawona down into the Yosemite Valley. Now stages and freight wagons could go all the way from either Merced, Coulterville, or Mariposa to Yosemite Valley, eliminating those last miles on horseback. It was a great and difficult achievement.

Loading passengers at Wawona. Hi must have found driving the Yosemite route much more colorful than the bleak coastal trails. *Mariposa Historical Society.*

It is not recorded who introduced Hi to Zella Henry, but the two were soon keeping steady company. She was a Missouri girl four years younger than the rollicking stage driver. Joe Miller was a widower now and his oldest daughter, Josephine, was in charge of the house. Hi was a frequent visitor and it may have been Josephine who introduced the couple. After a courting period of country dances, community picnics, and rides through the countryside, the two were soon talking of marriage. The date was set for November 8, 1876, with the Miller family hosting the affair at their home. The local press gave the happy event a proper send-off.

Mariposa Gazette, November 11, 1876:

> *...Accompanying the above were the compliments of the newly married couple, together with a superabundance of excellent cake and a bottle of Heidsick wine. We wish the happy couple, so long as they both may live, a full share of earthly blessings. May Hi—never be required to use more than six lines to hold his beloved one in check, but with skill "rein" her into a path that will lead them both safely to joy and happiness.*

Zella probably knew she had a bear by the tail and it was indeed destined to be a long and hectic union. Their son, Harrison, called "Harry," was born the following year.

The steady stream of visitors to Yosemite ceased during the snows of winter, but began again in early spring. Washburn had ordered a new coach capable of carrying twenty or more passengers into the valley. There was still snow on the hills, and a drizzling rain when the first coaches left Mariposa in mid-April. "Hi Rapelje, the skilled reinsman," commented the *Gazette*, "smiled complacently, the responsibility of holding six lines, and with a magnificent coach loaded with passengers, and a team of six fine horses, making an attractive picture to many people here."

William J. Howard was one of the colorful characters of old Mariposa. He was a forty-niner

Many of the Yosemite stages were convertible, allowing the top to be removed for maximum enjoyment of the magnificent scenery. In this early view, several of the passengers have climbed atop one of the fallen, giant redwoods of the area.
Author's Collection.

and early ranch and store owner who had served in Harry Love's California Rangers. He had sold supplies to Grizzly Adams, bred fine, blooded horses for racing, and engaged in several disputes resulting in desperate pistol duels. In 1878, he was living at his summer home in Yosemite while serving as district attorney of the county.

Howard was driving a wagon down to Mariposa in late May when one of his horses began fighting with its mate and became tangled in the harness. Frightened and trying to free themselves from the entangling traces, the two animals ran away down the mountain road. When the wagon struck a rock, Howard was thrown violently in front of the wagon, which rolled over his body, bruising him considerably. In great pain, Howard tracked his animals down the grade; he found one dead and the other standing quietly by its mate. He was assembling his harness when help arrived.

Mariposa Gazette, June 1, 1878:

>*...After working for nearly an hour to get things to rights, the stage came along, and Hi Rapelje and passengers gave him such assistance as to enable him to continue his journey to his home, a distance of twenty-five miles, where he arrived in a badly bruised and damaged condition.*

In the late summer of 1878, Collis P. Huntington and an entourage of some fourteen people took a vacation trip to Yosemite to hopefully cool off in the high Sierra during the hot summer months. Huntington was a member of the "Big Four," the group of Sacramento business men who financed the great transcontinental railroad. Their Southern Pacific railroad was spreading throughout California, bringing in settlers and developing the state while charging exorbitant rates for its services. Huntington, Leland Stanford, Mark Hopkins, and Charles Crocker all made vast fortunes through their endeavors and they lived like the kings they were proclaimed to be. Editor Angevine Reynolds of the *Gazette* could not help but notice the group.

Mariposa Gazette, August 17, 1878:

>*...It was the 14th day of August, with the thermometer ranging at 106 deg. At the time o' day the August bodies passed this office on board of one of Washburn & Bruce's largest clipper handcrafts, with Hi Rapelje as Cap-*

Collis P. Huntington, the railroad mogul and merchant.
California State Library.

tain. We couldn't help but admire Rapelje on this occasion, for with reins in hand of six, he appeared quite as majestic as any one of the representatives of millions of dollars, whose lives were to a great extent in his hands and dependent upon his good reinsmanship and careful driving.

Whether he had space to fill, or was really serious, Reynolds went on to rave about Rapelje's skill and Huntington's deep pockets, suggesting that the driver should be given a gratuity of one thousand dollars for his skillful driving. "It would not have been as much to him as 10 cents... for Rapelje did actually save the lives of the whole party by his great care, good judgment and skill as a first class driver." Editor Reynolds, however, should have known that Huntington was as parsimonious with money as he was skillful at making it.

In October, after a disagreement with another coach driver, there was a scrap, and Hi was charged with battery. The hearing was held a few miles north of Mariposa in Bear Valley. Rapelje's attorney, Newman Jones, apparently had little to work with, and Hi was found guilty and paid a five-dollar fine.

It was just a year later when the Central Valley was alerted that former president Ulysses S. Grant was making a tour of the West. Mrs. Grant, the former Julia Dent, was from Knight's Ferry in nearby Stanislaus County. On a September day in 1879, the large Grant party passed through Stockton and arrived in Madera at midnight, traveling in two "splendid silver-palace cars" of the Central Pacific Railroad. Madera was one of the

The Yosemite Hotel, where Rapelje and the other stage drivers picked up tourists and dignitaries for the trip to Yosemite. *Madera Historical Society.*

stagecoach centers leading to Yosemite. Despite the late hour, the train depot and Russell Mace's hotel were thronged with crowds from both Madera and nearby Fresno.

Grant and his entourage remained in their cars until sunrise, when Henry Washburn and Mace boarded and invited them to the hotel. Inside, Grant, Mrs. Grant, and various notables with the party signed the register and shook hands with anyone who wanted to meet them. Soon it was time to go. The Grants and their family and guests stepped outside, where a line of stagecoaches were lined up, ready for boarding. As was customary, Grant was helped up to the driver's seat of a sparkling Yosemite coach, as noted in a dispatch to the Fresno press.

Daily Evening Expositor, October 1, 1879:

> *Gen. Miller ascended the driver's box, with a handful of cigars, and took his seat on the left. The ex-president and ex-commander-in-Chief of all the armies and navies of the United States, in slouch hat and duster, sat in the middle, with a fresh cigar in his mouth, and the driver, Hiram Rapelje, six-in-hand, sat on the right.*

Hi had driven many celebrities and foreign notables over the mountains to Yosemite, but this was his shining moment. We can assume he told Zella every detail of what must have been a most memorable trip. The coach arrived at Wawona just after dusk and was greeted by huge bonfires and the Mariposa brass band playing "Hail to the Chief." The hotel was decorated with pine boughs twisted into a huge "Welcome" greeting with candles glowing on the balcony. Soon it was time to go, and Grant climbed aboard George Monroe's coach for the final lap into the great valley.

George Monroe was one of the more skilled of the Yosemite drivers.
Author's Collection.

"As Mrs. Grant mounted the seat of the coach," reported the *Gazette*, "she showed some anxiety by asking George Monroe, the genial coachman, 'Are you a good driver?' to which he modestly replied, 'No, m'am.' Actually, the popular black man was selected to drive the Grant party because he was one of the best drivers on the route.

Hi had been driving stage for more than ten years by now and he was keeping his eyes open for work that would keep him closer to home and his family. When he saw an opportunity, the young reinsman seized it. In a let-

Fresno Flats was a stage stop and supply center on the road to Yosemite when Hi went into the saloon business. *Author's Collection.*

ter written at Fresno Flats (now Oakhurst), one of the stops on the Yosemite road, a traveler recorded the local business enterprises.

Mariposa Gazette, October 22, 1881:

> *...If you are in the habit of irrigating, you may be dry by this time, and if you are, a short way up the street you will find Hi Rapplegee [sic], who keeps a first class assortment of liquors and cigars, and who can mix you a cocktail as gracefully as he can handle the strings over six bronco horses. Hi has built up a good trade by his courteous treatment to all, and bids fair to be very popular in his new home.*

Indications are that Hi enjoyed bartending and the companionship of his saloon patrons. Although he had been on the committee for the New Year's Ball in Fresno, in late October he made a court appearance for selling liquor on Sunday. When a stage driver was needed in nearby Crane Valley, Hi hired a bartender and took the job, but he was back working at his saloon in late October 1883, when tragedy struck.

Mariposa Gazette, November 3, 1883:

> *Hi Rapelje of Fresno Flats is unfortunate. His house and furniture was entirely destroyed by fire on Thursday of last week. Loss estimated at $1,000, no insurance.*

The jovial Rapelje was a natural-born bartender. *Author's Collection.*

It was a terrible blow to the little family, but Hi knew exactly what he must do. Henry Washburn promptly hired his ex-driver and when Zella and Harry were situated in a boarding house, Hi was ready for work. The Yosemite stages had been hauled off for the winter, but Washburn had a

Snelling was the first county seat and a growing supply center for the surrounding area. *Merced County Historical Society Archives.*

four-horse stage running between Madera and Fresno Flats and this was turned over to Rapelje, "the pleasant and urbane driver."

It was good to be handling the reins again, but it also made Hi realize that he missed his saloon business. He enjoyed people, but now he was freezing or baking again on the seat of a rocking and noisy stagecoach. It did not take many trips before Hi was again looking for another business opportunity. In early May 1884, the *Merced Star* announced that "Hiram Rapelje, a stage driver for many years on the Yosemite line, has opened a saloon in Snelling…"

Summers in the San Joaquin Valley are quite warm, but Hi enjoyed being back in business. Saloons were the social clubs of their day, but also the source of many problems and trouble. Liquor was the curse of nineteenth-century America. Aside from saloons being on almost every street corner, nearly all hotels, theaters, grocery stores, and boarding houses also offered a bar. Drinking was a way of forgetting your problems and long workdays, and Hi enjoyed the companionship of the sheepherders, cattlemen, and farmers who frequented his place. He came to know county officials, also, whom he regaled with stories of his staging days in the pine-studded Sierra.

Hi had met various Merced County deputy sheriffs while staging and they now dropped by his saloon while out chasing horse thieves or serving papers. For some years

There were problems with a saloon and long hours, but at least Hi was closer to home again. *Author's Collection.*

204

he had been active in local Republican politics and was quite friendly with J. L. Crittenden, who was elected sheriff in the fall of 1884. Perhaps it was friendship, or the way Hi could quietly calm a troublesome drunk in his saloon, but when Crittenden was elected sheriff in the November elections, Hi was appointed a deputy sheriff of Merced County.

The new deputy already knew most of the routines of his position. Deputies would hunt up jurors, deliver warrants and other official papers, and serve as a peace officer in the city of Merced when not otherwise occupied. Drunks were a big problem in the growing city, particularly when the gangs of cowboys, sheep herders, and farm hands came into town on weekends. On the night of January 17, West Hereford, the town watchman, was terribly beaten by a crowd after he shot a troublemaker in Egan's Saloon. It was a good lesson to the other officers to work in pairs whenever possible.

When three horses and two saddles were found missing from a local stable on January 23, Sheriff Crittenden discovered two young men who had been employed locally were missing also. Further inquiries substantiated the officer's suspicions and deputies Rapelje and Al Dowst were sent east and south as far as Madera, but with no results. Crittenden now sent the two lawmen to the Coast Range. Working their way north and obtaining fresh horses as they went, the deputies came to the village of Tres Pinos, where the two fugitives were discovered. The recovered property and the thieves were shipped by railroad back to Merced where they were held on three charges, with bail set at $2,000. The new sheriff got rave reviews in the press and Hi had received a crash course in a successful hunt for horse thieves.

Several of the Yosemite stages had been held up and robbed in the early 1880s, and on the evening of May 22, 1885, there was a repeat performance. Two men held up two Yosemite coaches at a spot between Fish Camp and Wawona, near Fresno Flats in Fresno County. The first report of the holdups reached Mariposa some hours after the occurrence, and the posses began gathering.

Fresno Weekly Expositor, **May 27, 1885:**

> *E. H. Cox, agent of the C.P. Railroad at Madera, telegraphed to Sheriff Meade late Friday night last that two of the Yosemite stages had*

been robbed at about 5 o'clock on the road near Benford's place by two men; one a short man, the other a man of lighter build, but taller. The short one was armed with a rifle and pistol, and the other with a shotgun and pistol. There were a number of passengers aboard the stages, and the robbers divested them of their money, watches, sleeve buttons, charms and jewelry of all kinds…The robbers were evidently well acquainted with the drivers as they told the first driver, Phillip Toby, to "Drive on, Phil," when they had got through stripping his passengers, and to the other driver, Geo. Foster, they said, "Drive on, Foster." The men were dressed in black, but had their clothes on wrongside out. Sheriff Meade at once set out in quest of the robbers

Hi's experience as a mountain stage driver was known to Fresno Sheriff O. J. Meade, and he took the train to Madera where he joined forces with Deputy Rapelje and headed for the hills. The two lawmen were in Mariposa on the 25th and, with William Howard and several others, aided materially in tracking the two robbers to the home of a local rancher named Charley Meyers. William Prescott, Meyers's brother-in-law, was found asleep in the house. Prescott told the officers that Meyers had gone to see his wife who was visiting in Coarsegold. Prescott had a weak story of hunting for hogs in the hills at the time of the robbery. The officers were sure they had their robbers, however.

Fresno County sheriff O. J. Meade helped capture the robbers, but lost the case when he tried to influence the jury. *Author's Collection.*

William Howard stayed to question and guard Prescott while Hi and Sheriff Meade rode over to Coarsegold to arrest Meyers. After the house and barn had been thoroughly searched for evidence, the two suspects were taken to the justice court at Fresno Flats. When the suspects could not make their bail, they were escorted to Fresno by Sheriff Meade and locked up.

There had been considerable riding entailed in the pursuit of the robbers and all of the possemen hoped for a share of the reward as reimbursement. By now some $1,200 in rewards was being offered by Wells Fargo, the state, and the Washburn stage line. Much evidence had been gathered and it looked like a good case and a quick trial until word was received

Wm. Prescott,
Robbed Yosemite Stage
May 22" 1885

Prescott's mug shot. He and his partner luckily obtained Pat Reddy for their defense. *Author's Collection.*

that Patrick Reddy had been hired for the defense. Reddy specialized in criminal cases and had become rich trading legal fees for mining claims. The local press announced the arrivals of witnesses.

Fresno Weekly Expositor, June 17, 1885:

> *Deputy Sheriff Howard, of Mariposa County, Constable Moore, of Fresno Flats, and Deputy Sheriff Rapelje, of Merced County, are in town. They were the assistants of Sheriff Meade in the capture of the parties accused of robbing the Yosemite stage.*

After numerous delays the trial was commenced on September 2, and it continued for sixteen days. District Attorney James Daly and George Goucher prosecuted the case. The circumstantial evidence was very strong and when the jury pronounced the defendants guilty, Pat Reddy's co-counsel, Walter D. Grady, merely smiled and asked for time to file an appeal. This was granted and on October 22, Judge J. B. Campbell asked Attorney Reddy if there was any reason he should not pronounce sentence on the defendants. Reddy responded:

Although one-armed, Reddy was still a formidable opponent in either a courtroom or a fist fight. *Eastern California Museum.*

"The reason a new trial should be granted, your honor, is that I have affidavits showing that the jury did not obey the admonitions of the court by communicating with outside parties!"

It seems the sheriff, in his zeal for a conviction (and the rewards), had taken the jury to a local saloon to drink and mingle with the crowd, a clear infraction of the law. Surprisingly, on November 2, Judge Campbell denied the new trial and sentenced the defendants to twenty years at San Quentin. This was successfully appealed, however, by the capable Reddy.

During much of September, Hi was on call as a witness for the

Subpoena for Rapelje's appearance as a witness in the stage robbery trial. *Fresno Superior Court Archives.*

View of the Fresno County Courthouse in 1881, where the trials of Prescott and Meyers took place.
Author's Collection.

prosecution. When not in court, he would spend time at the Fresno sheriff's office with Deputy Sheriff Johnny White, his friend from stage-driving days in Mariposa. On September 1, 1885, Sheriff Meade received a dispatch from a Bakersfield constable asking that a fugitive be arrested. He was a horse thief named Gervasio Romero who worked as a sheep shearer. Deputy White was detailed to look for the man. When he asked Hi if he wanted to come along, the big Merced deputy promptly agreed since the stage robbery trial was not scheduled to begin until the following day.

While searching the sheep camps west of town, the two lawmen found Romero working at Frank Serradell's shearing pens. It was reported that Romero had previously said he would never be taken alive. After studying him carefully to make sure he fit the description, the officers waited until he finished shearing his sheep, then approached the fugitive, as White called out his name. Both officers knew they were facing a showdown.

Fresno Weekly Expositor, **September 9, 1885:**

> *Romero picked up his vest, in which he had a revolver concealed, and throwing it across his arm so that he could grasp the hilt, he approached Officer White, who read to him the dispatch, and told Romero that he wanted him. Romero commenced to back away from the officer, and when about eight feet distant he threw his revolver in view and discharged it at Mr. White, the ball passing near his left side. Almost immediately the Mexican turned and shot at Deputy Rapelje, the ball whizzing in close proximity to the officer's left ear. The officers then drew their revolvers and fired two shots at the Mexican's legs, but failed to bring him to bay. Romero again raised his pistol and shot at Mr. White, when both officers fired at his breast, and the Mexican fell dead....*

The coroner stated that there were scars all over Romero's body, his right thigh looking as if a charge of buckshot had been fired into it. The coroner's jury pronounced the lawmen fully justified in the shooting.

Meanwhile, after having been back and forth several times as a witness in the stage robbery case, Hi had now returned to duty in Merced. Apparently he was doing too good a job.

*San Joaquin Valley Argus,*October 23, 1886:

> *Snelling, Oct. 22—Last night, between eleven and twelve o'clock, Hi Rapelje, while walking down one of the streets of this village, was knocked down by a club in the hand of some unknown person. He was found senseless some time after and cared for by friends.*

In Fresno, Pat Reddy had appealed to the California Supreme Court for a new trial and was able to show that some of the evidence was inconclusive and the jury had been taken to a saloon against the judge's wishes. Reddy made no bones about the sheriff's motives for the action; clearly, he needed the rewards to compensate for his own out-of-pocket expenses. The high court concurred and a second trial was set to begin on January 3, 1887.

This time the prosecutors were District Attorney Aurelius "Reel" Terry and S. J. Hinds. There was little new evidence, but the trial dragged on for some two weeks, finally resulting in a hung jury in late January. Pat Reddy was doing what he did best, and nobody liked what was happening. The jurors and witnesses were often called from distant points in the county and there was no remuneration for their trouble. County officials were upset at the continuing costs of the two trials.

The third trial began on November 30, 1887. It was more of the same, only in more detail. On December 25, 1887, the jury returned saying they could not agree on a verdict and Reel Terry moved that the prisoners be discharged. More than $25,000 had been spent on the trials. There was no point in continuing and Judge Campbell declared the case closed.

Sheriff Meade, Deputy Rapelje, Howard, and the others all kissed the rewards goodbye. If it was any consolation, Pat Reddy probably received little for his trouble either. In 1880, when Wells Fargo had offered to pay only half of his bill for prosecuting noted stage robber Milt Sharp, Reddy refused to take anything. Instead, he vowed to defend anyone being prosecuted by the company and over the years he cost Wells Fargo very much more than they had refused to pay him. Unless he took stolen loot from stage robbers as payment, Pat Reddy received precious little for these three trials.

Hi had been subpoenaed for all the trials and he was undoubtedly relieved to get back to work in Merced. He spent much time assisting local officers in keeping order in town. Hoboes were a constant source of trouble in the fall, with Hi arresting half a dozen one night in late October 1886. It was no doubt one of these worthies who had clubbed him that night in Snelling.

When Sheriff Crittenden lost the sheriff's election, Rapelje went back to work for the Washburn stage line. Besides designing their own stagecoaches, in 1876, the Washburns had put into operation a snow plow of their own invention that could clear the road from Wawona down into the Yosemite Valley. This had allowed an extension of the tourist season, which was a boon to merchants and tourists alike.

Fresno Daily Evening Expositor, **April 16, 1887:**

> *Hi Rapelje, who is driving on the Yosemite line from Wawona into the valley, reports that there is an average of two wagon loads of tourists a day going into the valley.*

Occasionally, Hi was called on for other duties. At the 1887 Fourth of July celebration at Bernard's Hotel in Yosemite, a man named Johnson Ridley took on a little too much high octane headache tonic and pulled his pistol, firing into the crowd. Hi and others promptly seized and disarmed him and no one was harmed. When Hi left on his down trip at three the next morning, a handcuffed Ridley was taken along and deposited at the Mariposa jail.

Rapelje was re-hired as a Merced deputy in January 1888. In December, he was invited on a hunting trip with former Merced sheriff A. J. Meany, George Goucher, John Stevens, and one "Mustang Ed." They were looking for ducks, but only bagged two, plus several jack rabbits. The most fun of the trip was when Senator Goucher and Stevens fell into the water while trying to sneak up on some game. "This bursted the party," reported the *Expositor*, "all being afraid to speak to Goucher for the balance of the day...."

In January, Rapelje was back in Merced rousting hoboes out of railroad freight cars and breaking up Chinese fan tan games. It was a dull period in Merced, but by the end of the year the first electric lights were installed along Front Street. The town was growing up and needed the benefits associated with incorporation as a city. As a former stage driver and prominent peace officer, Hi was well known and had many friends. When approached to run for the post of city marshal at the March 1889 election, he seized the opportunity. When the votes were counted, Hi Rapelje, running as a Republican, had been elected the first city marshal of the newly-incorporated city of Merced.

Senator George Goucher was a prominent attorney and drinking pal of Rapelje. *Author's Collection.*

The new city clerk, J. O. Blackburn, visited Sacramento and secured all the laws and information on establishing the new municipality. A set of rules required for the working of an orderly city were soon established. Hi's job was maintaining peace and order by arresting vagrants and those accused of any crimes and misdemeanors. This included irresponsible riders or those who allowed their horse, bicycle, or cart to block the sidewalks. It was a misdemeanor to allow a stable or pen within the city to become smelly or otherwise offensive. The secondhand shops in town were required to keep records and be carefully monitored for stolen merchandise. A chain gang worked on city projects and a guard was provided.

Fire was the great tragedy of these largely wooden frontier towns and obtaining firefighting equipment was high on the priority list of the

In the 1880s Merced was no longer a scraggly railroad town, but a bustling city that was now the county seat. *Merced County Historical Society Archives.*

officials. Meanwhile, the new marshal enforced fire ordinances by warning the merchants of Front Street to clean up weeds and debris close to their buildings. In late June, Hi noticed a man selling spectacles on the street and advised him to obtain a license. An hour later, he caught the man selling his wares in Stoddard's stable. Hi took the peddler to the city recorder, who fined him $20 and kept his sample case as security.

Other crimes made his stomach churn:

San Joaquin Valley Argus, **July 27, 1889:**

> *Brutal Treatment—Mrs. R. K. Vestle, a Spanish woman living near Landram's mill, "on the other side of the track," was arrested yesterday by officer Rapelje for brutal treatment to a little girl aged fourteen named Marie Consiano. The child was left in her charge by its mother, and Mrs. Vestle, it is said, treated it most brutally by burning it to make it mind. The woman was taken before City Recorder Robertson this morning and on the woman's promise to give the child up she was turned loose. The child was put in charge of Mrs. Harrison who will see that it has kind treatment hereafter.*

When two self-styled "bad men" blew into town in October, they proceeded to get liquored up in the nearest saloon. After spending what money they had, the two thugs staggered down Front Street demanding handouts. If refused, they began abusing the pedestrian before moving up the street. Hi saw what was going on and hunted up Deputy Fred Griffith. The two lawmen promptly escorted the "bad men" to the sheriff's "hotel."

In early November 1889, Hi paid $9,913.59 into the city treasury as collector of the business license fee and taxes. Later in the month, Marshal Rapelje appeared before the city recorder for examination on an assault charge after a prior fistic encounter with one Milt Reeves. Recorder Robertson bound Hi over to await the action of the superior court. The following April, Hi was convicted and paid a fine of $250 rather than serve 125 days in jail. It was not what the electorate expected from their marshal, and Hi was defeated that month in his bid for re-election.

In May, Hi joined a group of friends on a trip to Fresno for a baseball game. He also probably looked up Johnny White to see if he knew of any job prospects in the sheriff's office. Hi enjoyed Fresno. Like Merced and Modesto, it was a railroad town, born when the Central Pacific Railroad established a depot there. Hi remembered the town when it was just a cluster of false-fronted frame buildings lining the main avenue. Now, Barton's large opera house was going up on the corner of J and Fresno streets. Looking down Mariposa Street's cluster of banks and commercial buildings, with their turrets and spires, reminded Hi of pictures of eastern European cities. And the saloons...Hi especially enjoyed Jay Scott's White Fawn or the colorful emporiums in Fresno's Chinatown, where the crowds were sometimes rowdy, but always friendly.

When Charles Warfield was elected sheriff of Merced County, he had to leave his job as foreman for Henry Miller's Santa Rita Ranch. This was the center of Miller's vast land holdings in California and neighboring states. In late October 1890, Hi took over the job until the sheriff could return early the following year.

After finishing his stint at the Santa Rita, Hi obtained work at Toll House, a small village some thirty-five miles east of Fresno. There was a blacksmith shop, corrals, a hotel, a box factory, and about thirty houses. Hi managed the Toll House Hotel and tended the bar for nearly two years before another opportunity turned up. This jumping around from one job to another must have been a tough period for Hi, but in October 1892, he accepted a position in Fresno as deputy for Constable George Matheson. Finally, he was back in law enforcement, where he wanted to be.

Constables were officers of a particular justice court and had pretty much the same duties as a sheriff, but within a township rather than a county. Sometimes, constables could make as much as a deputy sheriff's salary. For serving such process papers as a summons or citation, there was

Tollhouse as it appeared when Rapelje worked there. Yancy's Saloon is center right, while the toll road can barely be seen at the foot of Sarver's Peak. *Fresno County Library California History Room Collection.*

a fee of $2. For serving other papers a flat fee of 5 percent of the amount involved was charged. Hi was still hoping for a deputy's commission from the newly elected Republican sheriff Jay Scott.

Born in Illinois in 1850, the infant Scott was brought to California during the Gold Rush days of 1852. As an adult, he farmed for many years, later engaging in the hotel business in Sonoma County. When he moved to Fresno County in the 1880s he operated the White Fawn Saloon, engaged in local politics, and made a wide circle of friends. His popularity can be gauged by the fact that during the campaign a contest was held in Madera at the Catholic Ladies Fair for the most popular candidate for sheriff. Despite the fact that the incumbent sheriff was a resident of Madera, Jay Scott won the contest 140 votes to 8 for Hensley. The prize was a beautiful silver-plated Merwin, Hulbert & Company .38 calibre revolver. The cylinder was gold-plated and it was described as "an elegant piece of workmanship."

Jay Scott, the popular Fresno saloon owner, had his hands full as sheriff. *Author's Collection.*

Scott easily won the general election and Hi looked forward to the announcement of his deputy appointment.

Fresno Morning Republican, **December 13, 1892:**

> *Sheriff Scott has already made his appointments as follows: Undersheriff, Frederick T. Berry; deputies, Frank Bedford, L. P. Timmins and P. F. Peck; jailor, C. C. Connolly, and chain gang deputy, J. Smythe, of Madera.*
>
> *Mr. Berry is a brother-in-law of Mr. Scott, and until recently was ticket-agent in the Palace Hotel office of the Atlantic & Pacific....*

Exactly one month later, on January 13, 1893, Sheriff Jay Scott signed the deputy sheriff appointment papers for Hi Rapelje. Since his job was as night watchman at the jail at only $65 per month, he might have held on to his day job as a deputy constable. There would be times in the next few years when the sheriff would bless and curse the name of his new deputy.

Rapelje was well aware, as were all Californians, that the San Joaquin Valley had been plagued by a series of train robberies. These robberies had evolved gradually as the railroads themselves spread out over the country. On August 30, 1881, a train was intentionally wrecked at Cape Horn Mills in the high Sierra, above the town of Colfax. Although unsuccessful, it was the first attempted train robbery in California.

When train No. 17 was stopped near Pixley by two masked men on February 22, 1889, it was a much more serious event. Two curious passengers were mortally wounded by shotgun blasts and some $400 was reportedly stolen from a dynamited express car. A year later, on January 22, 1890, a second train was stopped and robbed some thirty miles north, at Goshen, California. Here again, the trigger-happy bandits killed a curious tramp who crawled out from under a car. Amounts between $25,000 and $40,000 were taken, according to the press, although Wells Fargo did not confirm the reports.

Train fireman George Radcliffe was mortally wounded in yet another holdup near the village of Alila (now Earlimart) in early February 1891. Again, two masked men were involved and it seemed likely it was the same pair involved in the other train robberies. Grattan Dalton was arrested and convicted of the crime, while brothers Bob and Emmett fled to Indian Territory with Tulare County Sheriff Eugene Kay hot on their trail. Grat managed to escape from jail and joined his brothers. Bill Dalton, a well known rancher of Merced and San Luis Obispo counties, had aided his brothers in avoiding the law and was charged with complicity in the Alila holdup. He was tried and acquitted, but his life was changed forever.

It seemed clear now that the Dalton brothers were responsible for the series of train holdups in the valley. While searching in Indian Territory, Sheriff Kay was convinced that the Daltons were there, but he was unable to locate them he and returned to California.

Shortly after Sheriff Kay returned, there was a series of train holdups between May 1891 and July 1892 in Oklahoma and the Indian Territories. There

Grat Dalton as he appeared during his California

was no doubt that the bandits were Bob and Emmett Dalton, assisted by three or four others. Emmett later admitted these robberies in his various writings. With Grat Dalton in the Tulare County jail and Bill in trouble locally, also, it was a shock when another train was held up at Ceres, California on September 3, 1891. No Daltons had been available for this latest robbery, and the lawmen began looking in other directions. Meanwhile, two train robberies in the Midwest would have an ominous impact on the seemingly unrelated California holdups.

Train robbers flourished during the later half of the 19th century, the Daltons and Evans and Sontag being the most colorful. *Author's Collection.*

John Sontag, a former railroader, visited his family in Mankato, Minnesota, during the fall of 1891. He had left home as a teenager in 1878 and traveled about the West, settling in California. On the coast he found work with the Southern Pacific Railroad. After being injured and laid off by the railroad, Sontag had worked for, and roomed with, a poor Visalia farmer named Christopher Evans and his family. In time, the erstwhile trainman took an interest in Evans' teen-aged daughter, Eva, and soon it was generally understood that the two would be married. Meanwhile, Sontag complained bitterly to anyone who would listen about his poor treatment at the railroad hospital.

Indeed, the Southern Pacific was not popular in California. Its high freight rates, exorbitant land prices, and high-handed methods, coupled with a shootout and killing of six farmers who were being evicted from their land at Mussel Slough, resulted in animosity throughout the state. When the train robberies began, Californians felt compassion for the innocent people who were shot, but most had little concern for the railroad's losses.

In Minnesota, John Sontag startled his younger brother George by bragging about the train robberies in central California. John boasted that he and Chris Evans had committed all but the Alila robbery, and the way John told it, it was easy! At their most recent robbery, near Ceres, a railroad detective named Leonard

John Sontag, the ex-brakeman, had a grudge against the railroad. *Author's Collection.*

Harris was seriously wounded and no loot was obtained. And, when Evans and Sontag leased a livery stable in Modesto, it burned down, putting them in further debt.

George listened to his brother's tales. His own past was marred by terms in reform school and the state prison. It was not difficult for John to talk George into a robbery and on the night of November 12, 1891, they held up the Chicago train at Western Union Junction in Wisconsin. George later claimed they had taken over $9,000, but newspaper accounts stated much of the loot was in bank drafts that were cancelled immediately.

Christopher Evans, the simple farmer and family man turned train robber. *Author's Collection.*

The brothers returned to California where Chris Evans took them on a tour of the mountains in a search for convenient hiding places when they resumed their train robberies. However, before they could make any plans, George received word that his wife had delivered her baby and he returned home to Minnesota. Chris Evans, traveling under the name "Charles Naughton," followed George east where the two men planned another holdup. They stopped the westbound Chicago train on the night of July 2, 1892, near Kasota, Minnesota, but got no loot when the guard hid the money. The two bandits fled into the night, back to Mankato. They were quickly identified—George because he had a criminal record and was spending money when the officers knew he had been out of work for some time. Also, he had often been seen with Naughton, a stranger in town and now a suspect also.

The two bandits announced they were going fishing at a nearby lake, but instead headed separately for California, via Oregon. They were tracked by detectives and, despite using assumed names, in California they were quickly identified as Chris Evans and George Sontag.

Unaware that their real identity was now known, the two fugitives and John Son-

Newspaper illustration of damaged express car doors of robbed train. San Francisco Examiner, *August 5, 1892.*

217

tag planned a new robbery near Collis, west of Fresno. They struck on the night of August 3, 1892. After disabling the train, they blew out the express car doors, and reportedly escaped with some $15,000 in silver coins. They then disappeared into the night. Chris and John took their buggy and loot on to Visalia, while George Sontag caught the robbed train at Fresno the next day and joined his two associates at the Evans' home on the outskirts of Visalia.

The following day, George toured various Visalia saloons, boasting that he had been aboard the Collis train that was robbed. A bartender, who thought George was telling more than he could know about the holdup, notified Deputy Sheriff George Witty. After taking Sontag to headquarters for questioning, Witty was soon convinced that George could very well have been one of the Collis robbers.

Deputy Witty and railroad detective Will Smith were told to go to the Evans home and pick up Sontag's trunk, hoping it might contain evidence of the robbery. It was the afternoon of August 5, 1892. Evans' daughter, Eva, let the two officers into the house, where they were confronted by an armed Evans and John Sontag, who began shooting at the two lawmen. Both Smith and Witty were wounded as they fled the house, while the two fugitives drove off in the officers' buggy.

In this dramatic fashion the Valley train robbers were unmasked and a massive manhunt was promptly underway. That same night, Evans and John Sontag returned to the Evans farm for supplies and engaged in another shootout, mortally wounding Deputy Sheriff Oscar Beaver. Again, the two outlaws fled and disappeared into the foothills and mountains to the east.

Meanwhile, investigating officers had proved much of George Sontag's tales to be false, and the trio was considered prime suspects for the two Midwestern train robberies as well as the local valley train holdups. The clincher came on August 29 when detectives dug up two bags of stolen coins on the Evans property. Clearly, the officers were not dealing with a trio of minor characters, but deadly and desperate criminals willing to do anything to maintain their freedom.

Less than a week later, a posse arrived in Visalia from Arizona. The Southern Pacific had lost faith in bumbling local lawmen and had brought in a posse composed of grim and serious manhunters. Vernon C. "Vic" Wilson, a former Texas Ranger and now a Southern Pacific detective, was the leader. Yuma deputy sheriff Frank Burke was along, in charge of two Indian trackers, Pelon and Camino, and all were determined to get a piece of the $10,000 reward being offered for the outlaws. The group joined forces with Southern Pacific detective Will Smith's posse, which included Al Witty, Andrew McGinnes, John Broder, and Sanger constable Warren Hill. The combined posse wasted no time and was in the field by September 9.

Working through foothill country known to be frequented by the outlaws and their friends, the posse managed to find footprints that were tracked to a camp where the fugitives had spent the night. Encouraged, the lawmen began checking cabins in the area. At one point they found Mrs. Evans visiting a friend and were sure a meeting with her husband was her intention.

On the morning of September 13, the posse rode over to the cabin of Jim Young to leave a note for posse member John Broder. Dismounting at the gate, Vic Wilson and Andy McGinnis began walking down the path to the cabin, followed by Frank Burke and the two Indians. Burke later recalled what happened that deadly morning.

Vic Wilson, leader of the posse, met more than he bargained for at Young's cabin. *Robert G. McCubbin Collection.*

Visalia Weekly Delta, **September 15, 1892:**

Suddenly, when the men were about five steps from the house, we saw the two men run out and shoot. Wilson and McGinnes fell dead, but Wilson was reaching for his revolver and fell with it in his hand. Evans stepped over Wilson's body and started toward us, firing. He fired at Witty and one shot struck him in the neck. I fired at Evans and he then began firing at me with a Winchester. The first shots were fired from shotguns. I ran to a pine log about fifteen yards away and Evans fired at me three times. I fired at him, and as he was standing aiming at me I got a good shot at him and when I fired he dropped his gun and fell....

Evans managed to rise, and he and Sontag ran out of sight. The shot-up and disorganized posse assembled and assessed damages. Warren Hill was sent off to the nearest telephone to report the tragedy, while Al Witty sought medical help for a neck wound.

For the posse to have approached a cabin without first some reconnoitering was foolhardy to say the least. To make matters worse, the front door was the only way out of the place. In the minds of the two fugitives, they had no recourse but to shoot their way out. Three officers dead and as many others wounded was the terrible total to date. New posses were forming in Fresno and Tulare counties, as newspapers cried out for something to be done. Sheriff Hensley, of Fresno County, told a reporter that no more chances would be taken with the outlaws. They would be shot on sight!

Camino, one of the Indian trackers who shot it out with the outlaws. *Author's Collection.*

In Fresno, enough evidence had been produced to hold George Sontag for the Collis robbery, and on October 24, the trial began. Many witnesses testified against him and the coins dug up in the Evans yard were frosting on the cake. George took the stand on October 29 and denied any involvement, but he was convicted and on November 2 he was sentenced to Folsom State Prison for life.

George's brother and Chris Evans had successfully disappeared into the mountains again. Sontag had been shot in the arm during the fight, while Evans had suffered a gash over his eyebrow. They knew the posses would be coming again—more careful and more deadly. The two outlaws wintered in Dark Canyon, three or four miles northeast of Camp Badger. Surprisingly, they were interviewed by a San Francisco reporter who claimed he had chanced upon them at a mountain cabin. Others claimed to have seen them that winter, also.

In mid-April 1893, the two fugitives visited Evans's Visalia home for clothes and supplies. Sheriff Kay learned from some school children the outlaws were in town and he quickly had a posse

TWO OFFICERS SHOT.

The Collis Train Robbers Resist Arrest.

THEY WERE FOUND HIDDEN IN TULARE COUNTY.

Neither of the Officers Fatally Hurt. A Posse of One Hundred Men is in Active Pursuit — The Highwaymen Will Probably be Caught.

Visalia, August 5.—Detective Will Smith and Deputy Sheriff Witty were shot by the Collis train robbers one mile north of Visalia, about 2 o'clock today. Smith was hit in the back and Witty in the neck. Neither was dangerously wounded. Chris. Evans, an old resident here, shot Witty. A hundred men with rifles are in pursuit and will probably capture the robbers.

Fresno Weekly Expositor, August 10, 1892.

surround the property. However, the fugitives again escaped when shots were fired by Kay and his officers became rattled.

Kay and a posse were in the saddle early the following morning, as were Sheriff Jay Scott, Hi Rapelje, Wells Fargo's John Thacker, and others from Fresno. Once again, the posses were unsuccessful.

Fresno Morning Republican, **April 22, 1893.**

> *Sheriff Scott returned yesterday from Visalia, where he went in pursuit of Sontag and Evans. The Sheriff and Detective Thacker went as far as Monson, accompanied by Deputy Rapelje, Constable Irwin of Sanger and Deputy Smiley. At Monson the party separated, Scott and Thacker going to Exeter and thence to Visalia. The others made for the mountains on horseback. At Visalia Thacker sent another posse in pursuit.*

The deadly ambush was staged for a photographer at the scene a few days afterward. *Tulare County Historical Society.*

The $10,000 reward for the outlaws had lured the famous Harry Morse to send two operatives into Sontag and Evans country. A very prominent sheriff of Alameda County, Morse now operated a private detective agency. He hired Tom Burns and Samuel Black to find work at Camp Badger and see if they could pick up information on the outlaws. The outlaws quickly discovered the situation and on the night of May 26, 1893, they ambushed the two spies and badly wounded Black.

John Thacker, a thoroughly experienced detective and former Nevada sheriff, had for many years been chasing stage and train robbers while working under James B. Hume of Wells Fargo. Thacker had learned his business well and it now seemed clear that these two extraordinary outlaws would not be captured by ordinary means. Contacting George Gard, U.S. marshal for Southern California, Thacker asked that they meet

221

in Fresno to discuss the situation. The two men met secretly at a Fresno hotel shortly after Gard arrived from Los Angeles.

Thacker's plan was to put three or four men into the hills east of Visalia under cover of night. They would stay out of sight during the day and search the area at night, eating crackers and sardines so no cooking fires would be necessary. Gard liked the plan and at Thacker's suggestion, he agreed to deputize Hi Rapelje, Fred Jackson, and Tom Burns for the job. Gard insisted in leading the posse, saying, "It was a duty I owed to the people to try and assist in their capture." After swearing in the three men as deputy U.S. marshals, Gard caught the next train for Los Angeles to secure federal warrants for the outlaws. He would return and join the posse in the hills east of Visalia.

U.S. marshal George Gard— a lawman of wide experience. *Author's Collection.*

The men were a collection of first-class frontiersmen and good shots. Gard himself was a twenty-year veteran of the Los Angeles police and sheriff's offices, having served as a detective, police chief, and sheriff, beginning in 1870.

Rapelje's record as a lawman and crack shot was well known locally. Tom Burns, although he had been a Harry Morse operative with Sam Black, was an unlikely choice since he was an ex-convict. His main value seems to have been that he was familiar with the area and had worked with Evans and could identify him. Fred Jackson was perhaps put on the team because he was a friend of Thacker's son, Eugene. Jackson was in Fresno visiting a sister at this time and was in need of a job. His real merit, however, was his skill with a rifle. "Fred was a crack shot," recalled his niece, Mrs. Ada Schmitz of Fresno. "We used to live in the hills above Red Bluff. I was a little girl then and he was about seventeen....He was such a good shot they finally barred him from the (local) rifle matches."

On the night of June 3, 1893, the three officers were smuggled in a wagon out of Fresno and into the foothills. Gard joined the group in a few days. Hi Rapelje later gave an account of the expedition and its results.

Visalia Weekly Delta, June 15, 1893.

We spent all last week in the mountains looking for signs of the desperadoes or obtaining information regarding their whereabouts. We were assiduous in our search, and as a result became greatly fatigued with travel.

Sunday morning we camped at a vacant house about a half mile from Stone Corral, near the foothills, and about six miles west of Wilcox Canyon. Stone Corral is about eighteen miles from this city. We had spent the day in sleeping and making preparations for the campaign.

About twenty minutes of sundown, I went toward the rear door of the deserted cabin, and I saw the desperadoes coming down the hill and towards the house. I did not know who they were, but judging from their appearance and the arms they carried I suspected they were the outlaws. I turned around and said to Jackson, "Hello, here comes two men down the hill."

Jackson rushed to the door and said, "They are the men we have been looking for," so Gard and Burns, who were asleep, were woke up. They jumped up immediately and grabbed their guns and prepared for the fight.

Evans was in the lead, and he carried a Winchester rifle and a shotgun. Sontag was in the rear, armed with a rifle.

The officers went out of the front door of the house and as they went around the back corner, Evans, ever on the alert, espied the men. Elevating his Winchester to his shoulder he took deliberate aim and fired into the crowd of officers, but his shot did not take effect. Jackson stepped around behind me and fired at Evans. Then the fusillade became general, and it took place at a distance of seventy yards. During the firing Sontag was seen to throw up his hands, stagger and fall backwards to the ground, and we thought he was killed outright or mortally wounded.

Evans jumped behind an old straw pile, out of sight, but he did not cease to shoot at the officers. The gathering gloom handicapped the men, and they were unable to distinguish the forms of the desperadoes readily.

Jackson went around the far end of the house, hoping to get a better place from which to shoot. As he was going around the corner he was shot in the left leg. He limped back to where I was standing and told me that he (Jackson) was shot, and told the boys to keep up the fight and not give up.

After a short while firing ceased. Evans was seen to crawl from behind the straw pile on his stomach, and I at once commenced firing at him. Evans then rose to his feet and ran as hard as he could toward the hills, *myself pursuing and shooting at him. It was then so dark that the retreating form of Evans could not be distinguished, and he was soon out of sight. He did not turn and shoot at me, but ran as fast as he could.*

Fred Jackson, probably the best shot in the posse, was knocked out of the fight early and lost his lower leg from the wound. *Author's Collection.*

The abandoned cabin from which the posse fought was known as the Bacon place, but at this time was not in use.

Returning to the posse, Rapelje and the others saw that Jackson was badly injured and had lost a lot of blood. A wagon was obtained from a local rancher and while Hi drove the wounded officer to Visalia for a doctor, Gard and Burns stood guard over the outlaw in the field. At the time, the lawmen did not know that Sontag was wounded, and the two officers kept their distance throughout the long night.

In town, Rapelje summoned a physician, then placed Jackson in a room at the Palace Hotel. As soon as Jackson was in the doctor's hands, Hi gathered a posse of citizens and officers. E. M. Davidson, a local photographer, heard of the gathering expedition and secured permission to go along. It was after midnight when Hi and several others headed back to the Bacon place in the wagon. Several buggies followed with the balance of the impromptu posse.

It was just before dawn when the procession from town reached the Bacon cabin and the battle site. They had picked up Burns on the road. He and Gard had become separated during the night, but now the group cautiously approached the man in the field. They found the bloodied, whiskered outlaw covered with straw and barely conscious. "Where's John, Chris?" queried Rapelje. "I'm John," muttered the prostrate figure. He was seriously injured, a bullet having plowed through his shoulder and entered a lung. He was given some water, then propped up and when it was light enough, several photographs were taken by Davidson.

As the posse looked around the area for the missing Evans, Sontag was carried to a wagon and driven to the Visalia jail where he was tended by a physician. Evans's hat and rifle were found splattered with blood and it was obvious he was wounded, but he had vanished.

A large crowd of townspeople had met the posse and wounded outlaw outside of town and followed the procession to the jail. Jo P. Carroll, a correspondent of the *Fresno Morning Republican*, shaded Sontag with an umbrella and interviewed him during the trip. In Visalia, Carroll promptly contacted his editor with the most exciting report of his life. The local Visalia and San Francisco press soon had the story also.

Hi contacted Sheriff Jay Scott and informed him of the fight and capture of Sontag. Advising Scott to put together a posse, the sheriff soon joined Rapelje with deputies Lindsey P. Timmins, P. F. Peck, along with Bill Henry, Ed Miles, Jack Irvine, and Tom Burns. Shortly after their arrival, about ten o'clock at night, it was learned that Evans had been found. He had made a painful, six-mile trip to the widow Perkins ranch in Wilcox Canyon. It was dawn when he washed up at their pump, then went upstairs and lay down. He was discovered there by Elijah Perkins, who patched Chris up as best he could, then slipped off to Visalia. Perkins informed Undersheriff Bill Hall of the wounded outlaw's location at his mother's farm.

The news quickly spread all over town and since most of the sheriff's people were guarding the Evans home, it took Hall precious time to

One of the most famous photographs in Western history. The heavy-set figure second from the left is Hi Rapelje. Marshal Gard is hatless, third from the right with Tom Burns on his right. The rest are ranchers and officers from Visalia. The cabin is in the background. *Author's Collection.*

put together another posse. Scott's posse piled into their buggy and headed north. Hall learned of their departure and, in company with Deputy George Witty and Jo P. Carroll, soon had the Scott buggy spotted ahead of them. Whipping their horses into a run, Hall's buggy careened around Scott's vehicle into the lead in the frantic race.

Scott's men were unaware of the occupants of the buggy that passed them. It could have been friends of Evans, for all they knew. Both buggies raced into widow Perkins's yard about one o'clock in the morning, Hall's men jumping onto the porch as Scott's party bounded out of their buggy.

"Who goes there?" demanded Deputy Timmins.

"Yes, speak or I will blow your head off," shouted Rapelje.

Contemporary newspaper sketch of widow Perkins's house, where Evans sought refuge. *Author's Collection.*

The men on the porch shouted, "Wait a minute," then quickly disappeared through a door. Once inside, Hall's party rushed upstairs where they found the fugitive Evans lying, pale and weak, on a bed. Hall pushed up a window and yelled down to Sheriff Scott, "All right—come on. Evans is my prisoner!"

The Fresno officers could not believe their ears. Rushing up the stairs, Scott, Rapelje, and Timmins confronted reporter Carroll, who blurted out, "All right, boys, we've got him." A frowning Rapelje walked over to where Evans lay.

"Hello, Chris; you're pretty badly shot up."

"Yes," Evans responded weakly, "pretty badly shot."

As Carroll began taking down a statement from the outlaw, Rapelje, Scott, and Hall stepped out of the room.

Fresno Weekly Expositor, **June 14, 1893:**

> *Rapelje then claimed Evans as his posse's prisoner, but was willing to let Hall take him into custody as Hall represented the sheriff of Tulare County, provided Hall would give Rapelje a receipt for him.*

Hall replied: "No, I will give you no receipt; I claim the man my-self."

Rapelje said in a determined manner: "Then you will never take him; if that is the case I will take him to Fresno with me tonight."

"You will?" asked Hall.

"Yes, I will," replied Rapelje, "and that's all there is about it; you can't get him."

"That's all right," remarked Hall significantly.

"Yes, that's all right," continued Rapelje in a manner equally as significant.

Both men had their blood up, and there is no knowing what might have happened had not Sheriff Scott interfered as peacemaker, and suggested that it did not cut any figure in the case which one of them took Evans into custody.

"If Hall wants the man, let him take him," continued Sheriff Scott. "You have offered to turn him over and he won't give you a receipt; then let it go."

Hi was not happy, but everyone knew Scott was right. It could all be settled after Evans was safe in the Visalia jail. The Fresno sheriff and his men followed Hall's party back to Visalia and watched as Evans was placed in jail about 5:30 in the morning, June 13, 1893.

That morning, as Hall, Thacker, and George Witty were having their morning "eye-opener" in a local saloon, Rapelje and Tom Burns walked in. It did not take much to veer the conversation over to Evans's "capture" at the Perkins place. During the discussion Witty remarked that he did not want any reward money—Marshal Gard's men were entitled to that reward. That was all Rapelje needed to insult Hall and the manner in which he had taken Evans from the Perkins place. Burns stepped up at that point and all three men reached for their pistols. Thacker stepped between them and ordered Burns and Hi to go to bed, and they wisely left.

Evans was made comfortable at the jail, where his family was allowed to visit him. He had been shot in the right eye and his sight destroyed. He also was wounded in his back, where a bullet had ripped a furrow. Another bullet had struck his right wrist, passing up through his forearm before exiting. Another had smashed both bones in his left wrist resulting in a very painful wound. Later that day the lower part of his left arm was amputated.

Sontag's injuries were mostly superficial, except for the wound caused by a bullet that entered his shoulder and side, then lodged in the lung. Dr. Mathewson said that it was possible he could recover, but that he seemed to have lost the will to live.

"Several officers arrived from Fresno this evening," reported the *Visalia Delta*, "and the town is alive with officers, detectives, and newspaper correspondents representing journals far and near, all confident that they are to be in at the death."

Chris Evans was patched up in the Visalia jail, but he had lost an eye and his left arm. *California State Library.*

News of the gun battle at Stone Corral and the capture of two of the most notorious outlaws in the West was headlined throughout the state and country. All the major dailies in San Francisco carried the story in much detail. The *Examiner* chartered a special engine, hauling one passenger car filled with reporters and artists. Ordinarily the trip from Oakland to Goshen took ten hours by train, but this day they did it in half the time.

The Visalia jail cell in which Chris Evans was placed before being moved to Fresno. *Author's Collection.*

The Redding *Republican Free Press,* a few miles north of Jackson's home in Red Bluff, reported: "Fred Jackson, the Nevada officer wounded in the Evans-Sontag fight, lived in Red Bluff for several years up to ten years ago, with his father, mother, and a sister named Mattie....Jackson is a large, good-looking young fellow, and said to be a dead shot with a rifle. He is a man of sober habits and fearless."

The *Mariposa Gazette*, June 17, 1893, also had a long article on the fight. "Rapelje," reported the *Gazette*, "one of the arresting officers, was a former resident of Mariposa, and is well known as a man of unimpeachable bravery...."

On June 15, it was decided to prosecute Evans and Sontag in Fresno County for the Collis train robbery and the Wilson and McGinnes killings. Mrs. Sontag, mother of the brothers, had arrived in town and was staying with the Evans family. The two prisoners were taken to Goshen by Sheriff Kay, where they were met by Undersheriff Berry, Hi Rapelje, Lindsay Timmins, and other Fresno officers. The train trip to Fresno was uneventful, although one flare-up indicated Rapelje and other officers were still very touchy about the Evans capture. Jo Carroll, the reporter, was on the train and insisted on interviewing Sontag during the journey. When they had crossed the county line, Timmins told Carroll to "let Sontag alone, as the poor man had a hard enough time without being obliged to expend his little strength in talking."

Fresno County Deputy Sheriff L. P. Timmins. *Author's Collection.*

In Fresno, the two prisoners were locked in their cells and the officers went out to do a little celebrating. Hi, Timmins, and several others were talking in the Grand Central Hotel bar when they overheard Jo Carroll discussing his presence at the capture of both Evans and Sontag. "I was with George Witty when he arrested Sontag," he boasted at one point. …"I was also with Billy Hall when he arrested Evans."

Witty had been one of the first to reach the wounded Sontag the morning after the fight near Stone Corral. He made a point of arresting the comatose outlaw as a basis for a later reward claim. Hall had done the same thing in the Evans capture at the Perkins house. Rapelje was furious when he overheard Carroll's boasting and his hot temper quickly boiled-over.

CAPTURED.

John Sontag Wounded and in Jail

AFTER A HARD FIGHT

Deputy Sheriff Jackson Loses His Leg.

RAPID FIRING IN THE DUSK

Sontag Shot Himself in the Head After Being Disabled by the Posse—Brave Conduct of Rapelje. Jackson, Burns and Gard—One Hundred and Thirty Shots Exchanged Between the Outlaws and the Officers—Evans was Located Late Last Night in Wilcox Canyon and the Posse have gone Thither — Sontag Cannot Live More Than a Day or Two.

Evans and Sontag have neared the end of their rope at last.

Sontag has been mortally wounded and Evans at last accounts had taken refuge in flight with a posse of determined men at his heels.

Nothing was talked of on the streets yesterday but the story of the desperate

Newspaper headlines around the country hailed the great battle at Stone Corral. *Author's Collection.*

Visalia Weekly Delta, **June 29, 1893:**

Rapelje heard the statement, and shaking his fist at Carroll said; "You are a liar, and if you say that again I will smash you!" Carroll repeated the words, and Rapelje hit him a blow on the right hand side of the face. The blow knocked Carroll's head back, but he did not fall. Deputy Sheriff Timmins also made a pointed remark, and Rapelje said, referring to the obnoxious statement: "If you ever repeat that, I will hit you again." Carroll merely answered, "I said it, didn't I?" and the affair ended.

Hi would later comment in disgust, "I only hit him with my open hand."

George Sontag and various other convicts attempted to break out of Folsom on June 28, 1893, but it was a disastrous failure, three of the prisoners being killed while Sontag was badly wounded. Poor Mrs. Sontag, the boys' mother, had hardly returned from visiting the shot-up George when her son John died.

Jo P. Carroll came close to a thrashing when he sided with the Visalia officers. *Author's Collection.*

Hi had been guarding Sontag at the time and would glance in at mother and son from time to time. The worn out woman had slept little since arriving in California, one observer noting that her eyes were like "two burning coals." As he looked at the sad pair, Hi must have wondered if she knew that the guard was the man who had shot her son. The autopsy would establish that it was a bullet from Rapelje's .44 calibre Winchester that had ripped into the outlaw's upper arm, then passed into the body, causing his most serious wound.

Hi testified at the coroner's inquest as to the circumstances surrounding Sontag's wounds and ultimate death. He also attended the outlaw's burial in the Fresno cemetery on July 4, 1893. But the saga of Evans and Sontag was far from over.

A Fresno saloon of the period. *Fresno County Historical Society Archives.*

George, still on crutches when he testified against Chris Evans at his December trial, had already confessed to Wells Fargo detectives. Evans was tried for the murder of Vic Wilson in the ambush at Young's cabin. George's testimony locked up the prosecution's case. Evans was convicted and a date for sentencing was announced.

The Evans and Sontag story was unique to Western history in many ways, not the least of which was its reincarnation as a stage play at the time of Chris Evans's trial. The playwright, R. C. White, sought and obtained permission from Chris Evans for his wife Molly and daughter Eva to play themselves in the production. The destitute Evans family needed the money to pay Chris's lawyers. The drama opened in San Francisco to good crowds, but mixed reviews, and it soon petered out when it went on the road.

This should have been the end of the story. On the evening of December 28, 1893, however, Evans escaped from the Fresno jail with the aid of daughter Eva and an ex-convict known as Ed Morrell. The two fugitives were at large until February 19, when they visited the Evans home in Visalia. Discovered there, Evans and Morrell surrendered to Marshal Gard, who had just arrived from Los Angeles. Worn out from weeks in the snowy mountains avoiding pursuing posses, the one-armed fugitive and his new partner gave in to the inevitable. The following day, escorted into court by Sheriff Scott, Hi Rapelje and Lindsay Timmins, Evans was sentenced to life in Folsom prison. Sheriff Scott delivered his prisoner to Folsom the next day. In April, Morrell was tried and received the same sentence.

With the Tulare officers trying to get in on the rewards for the captured outlaws, Hi was sent to San Francisco to file their claims with Wells Fargo. In mid-June, a *San Francisco Examiner* reporter was scanning the register of the Grand Hotel when he recognized the name of one of the heroes of the Stone Corral fight. He sought an interview with Rapelje in his room and obtained a long story of the fight for his trouble. When the matter of rewards was brought up, Hi bristled.

San Francisco Examiner, June 18, 1893:

> *Rapelje frankly admits that he did not go man-hunting for his health or glory, and adds that he proposes to profit by the risk he took if*

231

there is any justice in the division of the bloodmoney....I think there will be no question about the reward, however. There is not a mark on the two men but what the doctors and caliber of the guns will prove I put there, save for the cut across Evans' eye, which was inflicted by the first shot Jackson fired. I am not proud of being a man-hunter, but when I take the chances I did, I want all there is coming to me for it.

...There was no intention of attempting to capture Sontag and Evans alive. We would have been foolish to try any such game as covering them and asking them to surrender. It was our calculation to kill them without giving them any show whatever. This may sound a little cold-blooded, but they had made the pace, would undoubtedly fight instead of surrendering, so we planned to treat them just as they treated McGinnis and Vic Wilson.

In late July 1893, the *Fresno Morning Republican* announced that five thousand dollars of the reward offered by the Southern Pacific and Wells Fargo had been paid to U. S. Marshal Gard for the capture of John Sontag. The marshal stated that he wanted none of the money himself, but that "the largest share should be given to Hi Rapelje and Jackson, the latter of whom was wounded at the stone corral."

This was good news for Hi and he immediately planned a trip to Merced to take care of some neglected business. The visit would also be an opportunity to see some old friends and perhaps bask in his current celebrity.

Mariposa Gazette, **August 12, 1893:**

Hi Rapelje, who used to be City Marshal of Merced and who was one of the posse who captured Sontag and Evans, spent one day last week in Merced. He received part of the $5000 paid for the capture of Sontag and remembering that before he went to Fresno he had left a number of debts in Merced, contracted while undergoing a long spell of sickness, he thought he would stop over and pay as many of those debts as he could. As a consequence several people are happier than they were before Rapelje came.

George Witty and the other Visalia officers who had rushed out to grab Evans at the Perkins place, now applied for a share of the reward for Evans. Although this was expected, Gard and his posse were furious, but had to go to federal court in Los Angeles to argue against the Visalia lawmen's claim. In April 1894, the judge ruled that Gard and Jackson each receive $1,000, with Burns and Rapelje getting $500 apiece. Undersheriff

Hall, Witty, and Elijah Perkins were to divide the remaining $2,000.

Gard's posse was understandably upset about the decision, but they were hopping mad when George Witty suddenly announced that it was he who had "arrested" the wounded John Sontag at Stone Corral. Worse yet, Witty insisted he was entitled to all of the already-paid $5,000 reward!

After hearing the case in Los Angeles on October 6 and 7, 1895, U.S. district judge Olin Wellborn announced he would give a decision at a later date. The litigants then left and while waiting for the next train to leave for the valley, they congregated at the nearest saloon to wet their respective whistles. It was not a good idea.

THE CHRIS EVANS REWARD

Hi Rapelje's Snap Shot at the Tulare Claimants.

Several weeks ago our readers will remember that the Southern Pacific Company commenced a suit in the United States Court at Los Angeles against Marshal Gard, Hi Rapelje, Tom Burns, Fred Jackson, W. F. Hall, O. P. Byrd, E. H. Perkins, Henry the Fourth, Charles' the Sixth and others, to set forth their claims for the reward money offered by the railroad company for the capture of Chris Evans, the bandit. Hi Rapelji, who is a deputy United States marshal, served the summons on the Visalia defendants to the action. As Mr. Rapelje is a defendant in the action himself his service of the summons is invalid. The defendants will all have to be reserved with summons by some officer who is not interested in the result of the suit.—Visalia Delta.

Fresno Morning Republican,
September 8, 1893.

Several shouting matches at the bar were calmed down, but when the lawmen took their seats in the train's passenger car at the depot, there were more flare-ups. Witty was drunk enough to be combative and he and Tom Burns again began arguing. Rapelje, for once, left the group to sit at the end of the car. When Witty went out the back door to the rear platform, Burns followed. As the train clacked along, Burns pulled his pistol and fired as the two men clinched. Shot in the hand, Witty wrestled desperately with the gunman and both men fell from the moving train. Neither was seriously injured, but it was a close call.

Judge Wellborn's final ruling was that Witty had no right to the $5000 reward for Sontag, and there was a collective sigh of relief that no one had been killed in the reward wrangling.

While Hi went about his deputy duties, far to the north, in Siskiyou County, a miner named Donati Probasco and an acquaintance named Charles Hammil decided to visit the town of Etna. They set out from Yreka in June 1892, and unfortunately they had included a bottle of whiskey in their provisions. They camped out that night and during a drunken quarrel, Probasco killed his companion. By the time the Siskiyou County sheriff had discovered the crime, Probasco had fled the area. Sending descriptive telegrams throughout the northern part of the state, Sheriff Walker soon heard that his man had been captured on the coast by a Humboldt County deputy sheriff. Before he could be taken into custody, however, Probasco escaped and again disappeared. With some $700 in rewards being offered for the fugitive, Sheriff Walker vowed to catch him at any cost.

Probasco obtained funds from his wife, then boarded a ship in San Francisco for British Columbia where he prospected for a time. He kept on the move to Idaho, then Oregon, where he mined at Pendleton and Spokane Falls. Everywhere he traveled, the fugitive saw the reward posters sent out by the assiduous Sheriff Walker. Finally, the fugitive was located in the mountains above Madera, working under an assumed name. Learning that Probasco's wife was leaving for Redding, Walker thought there was a good chance she would be visiting her husband. He knew he could not travel on the same train as Mrs. Probasco for fear of her becoming suspicious, so Walker deputized a local blacksmith named John E. Harmon to shadow her. He was just the man for the job.

Harmon followed Mrs. Probasco to Redding, then to Pendleton, Oregon, where her husband's brother lived. The fugitive never showed at either place. By this time, Sheriff Walker had learned that Probasco was likely still in Madera County, working under the name Webster with a partner named George Bagby. Wanting some backup, Harmon proceeded to Fresno, where he was told to "hunt up Rapelje, one of the four men who captured Evans and Sontag."

Donati Probasco, the fugitive murderer. *California State Archives.*

After securing a team and buggy, Rapelje and Harmon started off early in the morning and by late afternoon they had located the cabin of the fugitive in the hills near Coarse Gold Gulch. As they approached the cabin by a circuitous route, they saw Probasco coming from another direction with a shotgun over his shoulder. Still unseen, the two officers entered the cabin and explained to Bagby what was up and to keep quiet.

They waited until Probasco entered and put down his shotgun, and then Harmon stepped into the room and called on him to surrender. The startled outlaw was taken completely by surprise and desperately attempted to seize his weapon, but Harmon snatched it from him.

Fresno Morning Expositor, **September 22, 1893.**

He [Probasco] then bolted out of the door and Harmon fired over his head, which disconcerted the murderer and he fell on an embankment and the officers pounced onto him.

He made a desperate hand to hand fight of it. In the tussel he got a clasp knife out and tried to open it with his teeth. Rapelje, who did not wish to shoot him, managed to get a chance to clip him on the side of the head with his revolver and laid him out. He was then handcuffed and brought to Madera and yesterday morning Harmon returned to Siskiyou County with his prisoner in irons.

Tried in Yreka in late November 1893, Probasco was convicted of second degree murder and received a long stretch in Folsom state prison.

Hi had resigned his position as jailer in August, but according to county records he was kept on the payroll as one of Scott's assistants. Since he was continually referred to in the press as "Deputy U. S. Marshal," apparently Hi was also kept on staff by Gard for his stellar performance at Stone Corral.

Frontier days still lingered in a state where telephones now united many communities and businesses throughout California. William Farrow was a forty-two-year old Kentuckian who had a home in the West Park Colony. The previous year, he was the People's Party candidate for tax collector, but he primarily supported his wife and seven children by raising alfalfa and fishing. He was disabled and walked with the aid of crutches. On November 13, 1893, Farrow was puttering around his fishing camp on a West Side slough when two men, each driving a wagon, appeared. At gunpoint they stole a heater from Farrow and some fishing tackle from John Ballogh, then drove away in two separate wagons.

Driving to Fresno, Farrow and Ballogh located Deputy Constable Will Henry. The three men then set out in Farrow's wagon to find the two thieves. About a mile and a half from town, Farrow pointed out their quarry ahead of them. Whipping up their team, Henry passed the two fugitives' wagons, then blocked the road in front of them.

Jumping from the wagon, Constable Henry told the men in both wagons he had warrants for them and they would have to return with him to Fresno. Will Henry later reported what happened next to a *Republican* reporter:

"I was about to mount his wagon, intending to drive to Fresno, when he slid over to the right side of the seat and to my surprise drew a 44-caliber Smith & Wesson revolver and pointed it at me. He told me to 'git.'

"I stepped back, but supposing he was joking, smiled, I soon saw by his appearance that he was in earnest, upon which I advised him not to make a foolish break like that.

"I had no sooner taken another step backward than he fired, the bullet whizzing past my left ear. He continued shooting rapidly, missing me, however. I drew my six shooter, a 45 Colt's, and returned fire.

"At my third shot, I believe, he cried out that he had enough, but on my stopping a moment he recommenced firing, this time with his Winchester. I discharged the remaining chambers at him, and then, being out of ammunition, and having no other weapon, I went to Wharton's to get a rifle or something."

When the shooting began, Farrow's team jumped, overturning his wagon and spilling both Farrow and Ballogh onto the road. Losing his crutches, Farrow could not get up and he was shot and killed at some point during the melee. Riding to Fresno for assistance, Henry returned to the site with Hi Rapelje and Deputy Constable Henry Russell. They found one of the thieves missing, but sixty-seven-year-old Charles Robinson was discovered a mile down the road. The old man had two serious wounds; one of Henry's bullets had pierced the abdomen, while another had entered the thigh and ranged upward. The wounded Robinson and the body of Farrow were returned to Fresno.

Back in Fresno, Sheriff Scott immediately organized squads of officers to search for Joshua D. Hobson, the missing accomplice. Scott took Deputy Lindsay Timmins and several others to search to the north, deputies Bedford and Peck rode west toward Easton, while Constable Henry and Hi Rapelje headed south for Caruthers. Hi and Henry returned that evening and, after some refreshment at the White Fawn saloon, proceeded north after Sheriff Scott's party.

The fugitive Hobson's wagon had a wobbly wheel and left a distinctive track, and it was just a matter of time before the party's Indian tracker found him. As the posse rode up, Deputy Timmins pulled his pistol and yelled, "Throw up your hands, and no monkey business about it!"

Hobson immediately surrendered. During the return to Fresno, the captive denied over and over having anything to do with the shooting, saying it was all done by Robinson. "The old man did it all," he kept repeating, stating he had no weapons. From the men's stories, this seemed to be the case, although both men lied at various times. When Robinson died a week later, it had been determined by testimony at the coroner's inquest that Robinson had a violent temper and reportedly appeared to be mentally unstable. Deputy Constable Henry was absolved of any responsibility in the shooting. Two men had died over what was, at most, a petty and minor offense.

Hobson was later released for a lack of evidence, while a collection was being taken up for Farrow's wife and children.

While Hi, Deputy Constable Will Henry, and Deputy Constable Henry Russell were out hunting for Hobson, the hero of Stone Corral had an experience which, for a moment, shook his own self-confidence. The men had been riding along the San Joaquin River when they spied what appeared to be several geese in the water.

Daily Evening Expositor, **November 17, 1893.**

"Just wait, I want one of those geese," spoke Rapelje in a whisper, and throwing his trusty Winchester to his shoulder he fired quick as lightning.

The geese never moved a muscle. A look of wonder came over Rapelje's face; for he could not understand why he should miss a goose only a hundred yards away. But the best marksman will sometimes miss; and perhaps he thought he had fired too quick. So he raised his rifle again and took long and deliberate aim. Bang went the gun.

Scene along the San Joaquin River in Hi Rapelje's time. *Fresno County Libary, California History & Genealogy Room.*

"Listen at that," exclaimed Rapelje, "I heard the bullet hit the feathery whelp!"

But the "feathery whelp" and its two feathery companions did not budge. Rapelje began to suspect there was some trick in it; but he fired again for luck, and the bullet was heard to strike the broad side of the goose.

An examination was made and the three geese were decoys, made of wood, and had been set there to deceive.

Although Rapelje is usually good natured, yet it is decidedly unsafe to mention the subject to him; and those who were with him were afraid to tell it, but a boy who saw it came in this morning and gave the joke away.

When Rapelje escorted a prisoner to Folsom that same month, he took the opportunity to visit with George Sontag. The convict was still recovering from wounds incurred in his recent escape attempt but was hobbling around "quite lively."

Fresno Weekly Republican, **November 10, 1893:**

He told Rapelje that the confession attributed to him concerning the train robberies he and his brother John and Chris Evans committed was a genuine one, and that the circumstances related therein were true. He made the confession, he said, because the Evans family treated his mother badly.

When told that Chris Evans had said he, Sontag, had lied, he answered; "Well, Chris never could tell the truth."

When ex-convict Ed Morrell aided Chris Evans in his escape from the Fresno County Jail on December 28, 1893, it added a new episode to the sensational saga of Evans and Sontag. During Evans's first few weeks of freedom, Hi Rapelje was enjoying a trip to Inyo County and Nevada. He heard the news at Reno and quickly saw to it that the eastern slope of the Sierra was guarded in case Evans attempted to flee eastward.

Back in Fresno by mid-January, Hi quickly learned that much was expected from the hero of Stone Corral. "His name," noted the *Republican*, "has been frequently mentioned the past three weeks as one who would be a good man to send after the escaped desperado...."

The *Expositor*, also, put on the pressure. "He said this morning, in a half-joking way, that he would go out

Ex-convict Martin Delaney, alias Ed Morrell, wanted to be a desperado. *California State Archives.*

in a day or two and try his hand again on Evans. If he goes, and if he meets Evans, an interesting fight may be looked for, as Evans does not like him any better than he likes Evans."

Rapelje did take part in various Evans-chasing expeditions, but a confrontation between the two never occurred and both fugitives later surrendered peacefully, as previously related.

After Evans and Morrell escaped from the Fresno jail, a posse, including Will Henry, Lindsay Timmins, and several others stumbled onto their hideout in a large manzanita thicket in the mountains. It was a small shack built the previous year by Evans and John Sontag, of weathered boards up against a rock wall and blending into the rocky scenery. Snow was falling and the weather was bitterly cold. Evans and Morrell were huddled over a fire when one of the officers called for Evans to surrender. The two fugitives grabbed their weapons and quickly disappeared into the snow storm. The officers were too startled to do more than fire three shots after them.

Hi had been out with another posse and later talked to Timmins and the others about the incident. When Evans and John Sontag were at the shack the previous year, Evans had a big black cat as a house pet. Since then the feline had never left the area. When the deputies tried to catch him, he too disappeared into the heavy brush now being covered with snow. The lawmen did, however, manage to capture Chris Evans's wooden arm, before they burned the shack.

Back in Fresno, no one knew what to do with the arm, so Hi came up with an idea.

After Evans and Morrell's narrow escape, their crude shelter was destroyed, with only the fireplace and some utensils surviving. *Annie Mitchell Collection.*

Daily Evening Expositor, **February 12, 1894:**

> *Hi Rapelje intends to take Chris Evans' artificial arm to San Fran-cisco and exhibit it at the Midwinter Fair. But his cabinet will not be com-plete till he has secured the fine, slick, black cat which has made its home at the camp of Evans and Sontag since last winter....The officers were unable to catch the cat or they would have carried it away....Hi Rapelje intends employing someone to set a trap for the cat, and when he is secured he will be sent to the Midwinter Fair to keep company with Chris' artificial arm.*

It cost Hi nearly $25 to have the cat trapped and shipped to town and he was delighted when it finally arrived. His new pet warmed up to him immediately, and the lawman soon realized he would not be able to send it to San Francisco as had been planned. After only a brief period, Hi began to notice the cat had some curious traits. It would react to any unusual noise in the neighborhood and its hackles would rise until either Hi or his wife, Zella, went to the window and looked out. Then it would settle down again. A few such instances convinced Hi that the cat had been trained by Evans to warn him of danger.

Rapelje, his wife, and young son were living at 623 S Street at this time. At night, Hi would take off his belt and holstered pistol and put them on a bedroom nightstand where they would be easy to grab in an emer-gency. He was sleeping soundly late one night when the nearby house of John de la Fontaine caught fire. It was the custom in those days for some-one to fire a pistol several times to warn of a fire and when the alarm was sounded the Evans cat bristled, "its eyes like two balls of fire."

Daily Evening Expositor, **March 1, 1894.**

The cat jumped on the bed, but when Rapelje didn't respond it jumped down and rushed to the stand where Hi's pistol lay. Springing upon the stand, the cat seized the belt and pistol in its teeth and jumped to the floor, pull-ing the load toward his mas-ter as he peacefully slept. By the time the animal had made several unsuccessful attempts to jump on the bed

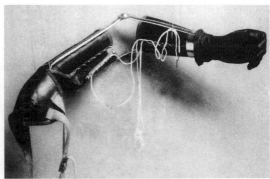

Evans' false arm, manufactured by the George Tieman Company of New York.
Fresno County Historical Society.

with its heavy load, Hi was aroused by the commotion. He was, of course, further amazed at the actions of his new pet.

Mrs. Chris Evans arrived in town on March 7 to see her lawyers about an appeal for her husband and she had her own comments about Rapelje's cat. Chris was sharing a Folsom cell with Dick Fellows, probably the most noted stage robber in California next to Black Bart. Dick had a good education and was the prison librarian. This pleased Mrs. Evans since her husband was an avid reader and would be able to get any book he wanted. In a long article in the *Expositor*, dated March 8, 1894, Mrs. Evans discoursed on a variety of subjects, including Hi Rapelje's new pet:

> "I know all about that cat," she laughed. "You tell Hi Rapelje that the cat he has, never saw Chris' cabin. The Philbert boys are full of fun and they let Rapelje pay the expressage on the cat and for her keep just for a joke. I know where the real cat is. In fact, she is in my possession now."

In Fresno, there was grumbling from the county supervisors indicating that august body had a vivid memory of the recent escape of Evans, while their recollections of the good work at Stone Corral were rapidly fading.

There were eight deputies, or sheriff's assistants, under Scott and it was suggested that other county offices were equally overstaffed. Despite his hard-won laurels at Stone Corral, Hi was low man on the totem pole and knew he would be first to go if the stories were true. He liked Fresno. He had many friends and did not want to move again. It seemed prudent to begin looking around for another job.

Fresno's Chinatown was situated west of the railroad tracks. It was also the town's red light district, and there were many white prostitutes and women of other races quartered there, as well as Chinese. The few Anglo-owned businesses were saloons: the Club, Brown's, Fagan's Golden West, and others.

There had been a segregated Chinese community at nearby Millerton, on the San Joaquin River, but when the railroad officials selected the Fresno locale for its depot in 1872, the Asians were among the earliest arrivals at the new town site. When Fresno became the county seat in 1874, Millerton became an overnight ghost town. Of the 600 residents of the new town, 200 were Chinese. Chinatown steadily grew as local farm and rail-road workers moved in and supported the Chinese shops and mercantile establishments.

As early as 1873, the Chinese had been rebuffed when they tried to purchase property east of the railroad tracks, however. This had assured their segregation from the rest of the community. The Anglo population needed the Chinese—for cooks, as farm and dairy laborers, for laundry work, and other menial tasks. The whites did not, however, want the Asians living in their midst.

Like much bigotry, this segregation stemmed largely from misun-derstanding. The whites could not comprehend their strange-speaking neighbors who dressed in unusual clothes, ate with sticks, and wore their hair in long braids. Not surprisingly, the Asians wanted little to do with the whites, either. Most Chinese were in this country for only long enough to make money to send home to their families, or to return in style to China themselves. Even when they died, their bodies or bones were often shipped back to China to be buried in their home provinces.

The question was compounded by the nation's labor problems, re-cessions, and other social troubles. The Chinese became the convenient scapegoat for these difficulties and were blamed for taking jobs from white men. As a result Chinese had little chance in a court of law or in business. In their own enclave, in Chinatown, they could rule themselves in their own world and survive.

Fresno's Chinatown supported many respectable Chinese merchants and families who also profited from the hordes of Oriental laborers patronizing the saloons, bordellos, and gambling dens. *Author's Collection.*

Fagan's, or China Alley, runs just behind the tall smokestack in foreground. The railroad tracks are barely visible in upper left corner. At upper right, G Street intersects with Tulare Street. China Alley, with all the awnings, was the heart of Chinatown and was a teaming tenement jammed with Chinese boarding houses, gambling dens, saloons, laundries, shops of all kinds, and the cribs of prostitutes. *Author's Collection.*

Most of the Chinese who settled in Fresno were peasants from Kwangtung Province. The majority were bachelors who had left their families behind in the old country. As a result, Chinatowns were largely male sanctuaries, made even more so by exclusionary federal laws and miscegenation policies. Given these circumstances, it was almost a foregone conclusion that American Chinatowns would also evolve into tenderloin districts—centers of illegal gambling, opium dens, and prostitution.

As in other towns, this exclusion of Fresno's Chinese quarter assured its status as a tourist attraction. The Tong Duck and Tong Sing general store was the first brick building and did a thriving business among Fresno's Chinese. There were restaurants, saloons, markets, and herb shops of all kinds. Strolling down China, or Fagan's, Alley was indeed like being in another world. Along with various specialty shops, there was a theater where traveling troupes from China entertained. Strange, melodious oriental music played, while brightly colored lanterns and signs added to the mysterious ambiance of the area. The aromas of burning incense and opium mingled with that of steaming rice cakes and other delicacies.

The Chinese New Year was a particularly colorful time, when fireworks were exhibited and pungent lilies in porcelain bowls lined every street.

But there was another side to Chinatown. When Sheriff Scott was apprised of the kidnapping of a young girl by highbinders, he put together a team of deputies and constables and conducted a massive search of the tunnels and rooms known to undermine Chinatown. A reporter went along on the search and was appalled at the sights and smells of this underground world.

Daily Evening Expositor, **March 21, 1894:**

> *...The smell first strikes the white man as something unendurable. It is a combination of smoke, dust, opium, rotten fish and meat, decaying vegetables, old clothes, leaking gas...and the only water ever present is the seepage from the earth beneath...After a few doors are passed all becomes dark. The officers lit matches to help them on their way...in one of the caverns they ran into a dead man lying on a pile of stuff....In another vault, which was a cave hollowed out under Tulare Street, a sick man was found lying on a miserable bed....The Chinese no doubt laugh among themselves at the white men who try to make thorough examination of these gloomy labyrinths.*

Despite the large group of officers engaged in the search, both above ground and below, the girl was not found.

Rapelje knew that Fresno's Chinatown was ruled by a merchant class representing various districts in the homeland. These "companies" were principally benevolent societies that helped new emigrants and travelers, collected dues for various charities, and otherwise protected members' interests.

Chinese lottery ticket, as printed in a San Francisco newspaper. *Author's Collection.*

The Tongs were quite different. These were secret societies that often preyed upon the companies, fought in feuds, and controlled vice in Chinatown. Their fighters were called highbinders, or hatchet men. Hi Rapelje quickly learned that whenever serious trouble was eminent, San Francisco highbinders would suddenly appear in town.

Although illegal, lottery and fan tan games flourished west of the railroad tracks. The lottery was simple to play; you could bet from ten cents up; it paid off the same day, and tickets were sold all over town. Chinese laundrymen, houseboys, and cooks sold lottery tickets to housewives while others covered the saloons and hotels. "Tan" games took place in hidden rooms in Chinatown, protected by heavy iron doors and watchmen. It seemed impossible for police to curtail the games. Still, when an opportunity presented itself, a posse of deputy sheriffs, policemen, and constables would pounce on an identified gambling den. The gamblers then paid a small fine and the system would begin again, the legal penalties being considered merely a "tax" to operate.

In the 1890s, the various Tongs in Fresno's Chinatown were each taking in at least $50 a day, amounting altogether to about $12,000 a month. Much of this money found its way back to China. There were ample assets for local payoff, but an even better system had evolved over the years. A Caucasian watchman, usually a spe-

A Chinese gambling game. *Author's Collection.*

cial policeman paid by the Chinese merchants, was employed. This watchman kept order in the Chinese Quarter, collected mail, represented Chinese merchants and gamblers in court to pay fines, and generally looked out for Chinese interests in a white man's world. Needless to say, the opportunities for fees and graft made it a lucrative position.

The Chinese tan games were raided whenever a gambling den could be located, but for a long time lotteries were given a pass since Anglo lotteries were also allowed. But the Caucasian lottery profits stayed in town, while much of the Chinese lottery money found its way to San Francisco or China. When the authorities finally realized that they could recoup much of this money in fines, raids commenced. An early foray was headlined: "Raiding the Lotteries, Four Wicked Mongolians Nabbed by Officials."

Daily Evening Expositor, **March 28, 1894:**

> *A raid was made on the Chinese lotteries last night, and four Celestials, Ah Fong, Ah Quin, Ah Fong and Ah Gin were put under arrest. The officers who came down to disturb the peace and quiet that have for so long settled over the heads of the Chinese gamblers were Constable Matheson and Deputy Constable Angel and Deputy Sheriffs Timmins and Rapelje...*

The article went on to expound on how much money was involved in these Chinese gambling operations. This raid might very well have stirred the interest of Hi Rapelje in the bustling entity that was Fresno's Chinatown.

It was probably after a county board of supervisors' meeting on April 17, 1894, that Rapelje decided he must make a move. Supervisor Letcher had suggested that Sheriff Scott could get along with "a deputy or two less," and although no formal suggestions or demands had been made, the handwriting on the wall seemed clear to Hi. He knew two of the largest Chinese companies were at odds with each other and each wanted its own watchman. If he could get the appointment as special policeman, he would be paid by the Sam Yep Company that employed him. Then, he could keep his deputy commission, but be off the county payroll, except for special sheriff's duty.

The See Yup Company watchman now on duty was a man named Joshua E. Ragsdale. A native of Tennessee, Ragsdale had lived in Fresno since 1887 and had been a watchman for most of that time. He was forty-two years old, spoke fluent Chinese and was generally respected by his employers. Needless to say, he was not happy about the situation, and when Rapelje received the appointment as a "Special" for the Sam Yep Company, Ragsdale blamed Hi for his salary cut.

There was trouble almost immediately. When Hi was called to Sacramento on business, he appointed a friend named Pat Reardon to take his place. Reardon had lost out to Rapelje for the watchman position, and Ragsdale had no love for either man.

A street scene in Fresno's old Chinatown a few years after Rapelje's time there.
Fresno County Public Library, California History and Genealogy Room.

A panorama of Fresno in 1901 showing a portion of the city east of the railroad tracks (upper left), and Chinatown on the western side of the tracks. A double row of trees lines Mariposa Street, with Tulare Street just beyond. G Street is the first street west of the tracks. *Fresno County Public Library, California History and Genealogy Room.*

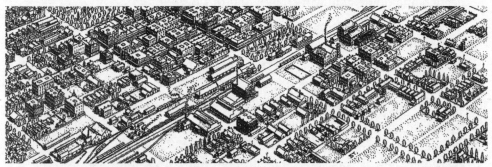

On the evening of April 24, 1894, Reardon was sitting on a bench near the entrance to China Alley when Ragsdale walked up to him while making his rounds. He roughly asked, "What are you doing here?" According to Ragsdale, Reardon growled "It's none of your business!" Then, calling Ragsdale a vile name, Reardon reached behind him as if for a pistol. Ragsdale immediately hit Reardon in the face, arrested him, and hauled him off to jail.

In mid-May, Reardon was tried in justice court on Ragsdale's charge of disturbing the peace. He was easily acquitted when he convinced the court that Ragsdale was the aggressor in the incident. A week later, a smiling Reardon charged a glowering Ragsdale with battery. When the watchman was convicted and fined, he was noticeably unhappy.

Instead of dropping the matter, Ragsdale now began telling anyone who would listen that there was a plot to get rid of him in Chinatown. He claimed that high public officials (presumably Sheriff Scott) were involved in conspiring to make Hi Rapelje the only watchman across the tracks. Ragsdale retained an attorney who finally wrangled a hearing before the board of supervisors. The hearing turned into a farce, as did a second one. Hi testified, as did Ragsdale, his attorney, and several others, but no one seemed to take the hearing seriously, and to Ragsdale's dismay it was ruled that no Chinatown special officer was to be appointed. Ragsdale had to scramble to obtain a deputy constable's commission to retain his job. The situation simmered in that summer of 1894, but it would not go away.

Ragsdale's primary jurisdiction was Chinatown and there is scant record of his venturing far from his domain even though he was a deputy constable under John Albin. Hi, on the other hand, was often called to other cities for help on criminal cases, while aiding the local police when needed and doing field work for the sheriff's office.

At the Fresno Republican convention in February, Hi was nominated to run for city marshal in the city's general election. Four others were nominated also, but in the balloting Rapelje made a poor showing and stable owner Martin Woy won with just over 32 votes.

In late February 1895, John Ashurst dropped into the sheriff's office to see Jay Scott. Ashurst ran a large cattle spread in eastern San Benito County and was being harrassed by rustlers. This was unusual since everyone knew it was not safe to steal anything from John Ashurst. The west side of the valley was a vast and sparsely occupied area that had not changed much since the early Gold Rush days. Where Fresno County bordered with San Benito County, in the foothills of the Coast Range, the law was a scarce commodity, and Ashurst made his own law when necessary.

Fresno Morning Republican, **September 21, 1897:**

> *It is said that on one occasion when he located a band of Mexican thieves whom he knew to have stolen many head of cattle from him, he went alone to their camp and without any ceremony entered it and began clubbing the thieves. He was armed and ready for deadly work had there been any need, but the Mexicans were so afraid of him that not one raised a hand against him.*

The newspapers often featured articles about vigilante and other types of "justice" in the area, much of it centering around Cantua Creek, Joaquin Murrieta's old hideout. John Ashurst knew the area well. Hi commented on him in the *Fresno Morning Republican*, March 5, 1895: "Rapelje says that he is surprised that the Mexicans would steal from John Ashurst. Ashurst is held in mortal dread by them on account of his reputation as a fighter. A brother of Ashurst, however, has had charge of the cattle and they were not afraid of him."

Ashurst strongly suspected that some of his current stolen stock had been disposed of in Fresno. Sheriff Scott assigned Deputy Rapelje to check local corrals and slaughter houses for any evidence of the rustled animals, then report his findings to Ashurst. It was several days before eight of the missing steers were found at Rogers & Pond's slaughter house. Four of the animals had already been killed and their hides were drying.

The other four were in the corral. The owners promptly offered Rapelje all the information they had. The Mexican who had sold them the steers proved to be one of the suspects Ashurst had mentioned.

After contacting Ashurst with his findings, Hi secured warrants and then took the train to Mendota. Obtaining a horse and buggy there, the officer headed for Cantua Creek, where he met up with Ashurst, a constable, and his deputy. It was night as the four officers proceeded up Cantua Creek. They stopped at the Mexican jacales (huts) inhabited by the rustlers and arrested twelve suspects, some objecting strenuously to the proceedings. By one o'clock in the morning they had finished the roundup. Ashurst and the constable herded their captives over to Hollister, while Hi and the deputy constable stayed to pursue two suspects, including the leader, who had managed to make their escape. During the night the two lawmen became lost in the mountains and did not find their way out until morning. Their quarry had escaped.

"Rapelje had a hard trip of it," commented the *Republican*, "and it probably brought up many memories of the Sontag and Evans chase. He returned to Fresno yesterday all the way from Cantua on horseback, except that his horse gave out and for the last 20 miles he had to foot most of it."

It was thought all of the gang had been captured, with the exception of Luis Pares, the leader, and one other. Deputy constable John Ashurst was back in Fresno a few days later. He wanted to make sure the four cattle being held by Rogers, the butcher, were his, and the two men proceeded to the San Joaquin River, where the cattle were pastured. The rancher was able to identify his stock and they began the ride back to Fresno.

On the way, they saw a young Mexican rider who was behaving suspiciously and stopped him. They asked him several questions, but his evasive answers and actions indicated he was hiding something. The three returned to Fresno and under hard questioning, the young man confessed that he was the son of Castro, at whose house Luis Pares was now hiding. Only about nineteen years old, the boy soon broke down under Ashurst's rigorous questioning and admitted he had been sent to Fresno to keep an eye on the rancher's movements. He also told them exactly where the Castro house was located, and Ashurst promptly looked up Rapelje and the two officers made their plans.

On the night of March 7, Ashurst, Rapelje, and Deputy Sheriff Ben Merritt, along with young Castro as guide, rode quietly out of town. They headed their wagon northeast toward Willow Creek, in eastern Madera County, where the Castro ranch was located. Stopping at a saloon along the way, the party was surprised to find the elder Castro well along on his way to a glorious binge. It was thought he was there as a lookout, but his nervousness led from one drink to another until he could scarcely stand. Afraid he still might be able to somehow warn their quarry, the officers loaded him in their wagon, where he promptly fell fast asleep.

Continuing on their way, the lawmen stopped some two miles short of the ranch house, then walked the remaining distance. Heavily shielded by thick brush and trees, the house would have been difficult to find without young Castro's aid.

Fresno Morning Republican, **March 9, 1895:**

> *It was now about 3 o'clock in the morning. Young Castro was compelled to lead the way into the house, strike a light and guide the officers to his bedroom, in which Pares was sleeping. When the latter was awakened two officers were standing over him and he was looking down the barrels of two six-shooters, and he wisely submitted to arrest without a murmur. He seemed to be considerably surprised, however, and had slept well with the belief that capture was almost impossible.*

It was thought by the officers that this particular rustling operation was now effectively broken up. At least, rustlers would probably avoid Ashurst's ranch for some time to come. "The prompt manner in which the gang was rounded up," commented the *Republican*, "is due to the efficient work of Hi Rapelje and John Ashurst."

Back on his beat in the Chinese quarter, Hi was reminded again why Chinatown was…well, Chinatown. In late May 1895, Ragsdale, the other watchman, was made aware of a man named Gutte who was living with two prostitutes. One of the women was said to be a sixteen-year-old French girl who was claiming to be nineteen. Although Ragsdale was a deputized constable, such matters were not in his domain, but he arrested the trio on a vagrancy charge, his real objective being an attempt to rescue the girl from the life she was leading. They were taken before a justice court, then released on bail.

Talking to the young girl and others, Ragsdale learned that she had only been in the country for six months. Gutte and the woman kept most of the money she made, and although she desired to quit her life, she never had enough money to do so. Although Ragsdale appeared "very much moved" over the matter, a few days later he appeared before Justice St. John and asked that the charges be dismissed. Saying there was not enough evidence for a conviction, the watchman offered to pay the court costs involved. When questioned by a *Republican* reporter about his contradictory actions, Ragsdale gave a surprising response.

He had desired to prosecute the case, explained Ragsdale, but the district attorney's office, Justice St. John, Constable Albin, and Policeman Russell had all advised that the case be dropped, that to prosecute these three and allow so many others of the same class to go unpunished was not right. He had yielded to the advice of his superiors. When the reporter questioned the named authorities, however, all denied telling Ragsdale to drop the case.

The implications of all this seem clear, then and now. It was Chinatown. While Ragsdale's concern was laudable, the fact is that tenderloins and Chinatowns were needed. In that Victorian time, they were tolerated, if not condoned, because if the Chinese quarter was not on the west side of the tracks, it might just turn up on the east side. The young French girl was a victim of the system and the time.

The Ragsdale–Rapelje feud was still smoldering. The difference in the two men's personalities was emphasized by Hi's acquisition of the sobriquet, "The Mayor of West Fresno," despite Ragsdale's longer service in the area. Neither was willing to give an inch or even discuss the situation. Both men had been discharged by their employers and both were now working without pay. When the two Chinese companies smoothed over their differences, they agreed to employ just one watchman in the future. For now, each officer was putting his best foot forward, hoping he would be selected at the next company election. Apparently the election finally took place that summer and both watchmen kept their jobs. Nothing had changed and the Asians hoped the two watchmen could work together for the benefit of their gambling revenues. They could not decide just what else to do.

In September 1895, Hi was hired as marshal at the race track during the county fair. He had no sooner finished this duty than he was called to Los Angeles as a witness in the Witty lawsuit pertaining to the rewards in the Evans and Sontag case. During this period, Fresno City Marshal Martin L. Woy had deputized one Stephen Watson to take Hi's place in Chinatown. Ragsdale objected before the city board of trustees, but the complaint was ignored.

In a letter to the local Democratic organ from watchman Ragsdale, a concern was voiced that a wager he had been appraised of might turn into a self-fullfilling prophecy. Hi was glad to respond.

Fresno Morning Republican, June 5, 1895,

> *Editor Republican—In the Expositor of June 1st appears a personal card signed by J. E. Ragsdale, in which he makes mention of some bet being offered that "he and I would have a shooting affray before the year ended," etc.*
>
> *I cannot imagine why the gentleman has thus rushed into print, except it be that he fears the long-suffering public of Fresno will forget that he is in town, and still occupying the highly moral position of "Exposer of Public Scandals," in addition to being a watchman for Chinese stores and other businesses in the Chinese quarter. However, I have no interest in the gentleman, and take this method of informing him that he need not be alarmed at the betting propensities of his friends. I have no intention of engaging in a personal difficulty with him or anyone else, and only ask that he leave me out of his personal cards in the future, for the reason that I do not care for the general public to know that we are acquainted....*

Chinatown could wear you down with the rules and routine that made you little more than a servant to your Chinese employers, and Hi must have enjoyed getting out of town when he could. And, there were too many saloons. Sometimes he would step into Brown's, or the Club and have a few drinks before going home. In 1892, there had been over sixty saloons in Fresno. There were even more now in 1895.

Early that month, word was received that two escaped inmates from the Madera jail had been spotted camping on Pine Ridge with some Indians. Hi remembered one of the fellows, a young mountain boy named William Laverone. He was only about seventeen in the spring of 1893, when he killed Elijah Ehart in a shootout. The incident changed his life. After stealing a horse in 1894, he was sent to Whittier, where what passed as the state reform school was located. A stretch in Folsom Prison was next, then a holdup put young Laverone and pal Jack Roberts in the Madera County jail on May 1, 1896.

William Laverone, the Madera jailbreaker. *Author's Collection.*

Madera was a new county whose residents did not see the need for an updated jail. Of course, they had to learn they were wrong the hard way. On the night of May 6, Laverone and Roberts managed to escape after a desperate struggle with a guard. The prisoners had dug out a brick from the wall and badly beaten the guard before escaping with his weapons into the night. The fugitives made for the mountains, with a posse of a dozen men hot on their trail. By the end of the month, the two outlaws had still not been located. Two Madera lawmen searched the area north of Madera around North Fork and O'Neals, Laverone's former home, but no clues could be found. The lawmen's opinion was that the fugitives "had gone further north, as it is impossible for them to subsist in the mountains without showing themselves in order to acquire food. There have been no robberies committed in the foothill districts for some weeks, and if the outlaws are there they must have laid up stores for such an occasion at sometime in the past."

The officers were right. Laverone and Roberts were at that time already 250 miles north, in Tehama County. The hills above Fresno and Madera, however, were still alive with rumors and false sightings. When a Yosemite stage was held up on June 18, there was no doubt about the robbers according to the *Fresno Republican*: "The robbery is laid at the door of Laverone and Roberts, who recently escaped from the Madera jail, but it is only suspicion....Sheriff Westfall arrived from Madera a few hours after the robbery and took up the trail." But there was still no sign of the fugitives.

When Sanger constable J. S. Irvine and his deputy John Perry received word that Laverone and Roberts had been seen in an Indian camp on Pine Ridge, they prepared for a trip to the mountains. Asked if he would go along on the expedition, Hi Rapelje jumped at the chance.

The three officers made their way to Toll House, at the foot of the road leading up to Pine Ridge. They acquired an interpreter, and every

Indian camp was searched and the residents questioned, but it quickly became obvious the mission was futile. There was a backup plan, however.

Jim Haslip, a fugitive Indian accused of a vicious murder and robbery, had also escaped from the flimsy Madera jail in April 1895. Jim Lawson, another accused murderer, escaped with him, as well as three vagrants. The authorities were so furious that Judge William Conley signed an order sending future prisoners to Fresno's jail until a proper jail could be built in Madera County.

Sheriff Westfall went to Fresno to ask Rapelje to join his search for the fugitives, to which Hi readily agreed. "When the conqueror of Evans and Sontag gets on their trail," trumpeted the *Republican*, "they will either have to get out of the country, fight or be captured." Despite frantic efforts by officers of both counties to recapture the fugitives, Haslip and the others remained at large.

Learning that Haslip had been seen at the Big Sandy Indian Rancheria, Hi and the other lawmen announced they were returning to town, then took a circuitous route toward the Indian village at Big Sandy. They stopped five miles short of the village, then crawling through thick patches of brush and manzanita, they approached the rancheria from the least-likely direction.

Jim Haslip, the Indian outlaw.
Author's Collection.

Fresno Morning Republican, **June 23, 1896:**

> *Just before reaching the Rancheria the officers had to cross a deep gulch. As they picked their way down the bank they were briefly exposed to view and a squaw standing by a hut outside the Rancheria spotted the officers. She quickly turned and ran into the dwelling. Haslip came out on the run and mounting a horse which stood near, dashed off into the brush.*

The officers were furious. Storming down to the hut, they told the Indian woman she was going to be arrested and go to jail. They managed to scare her enough so that she agreed to help them catch the outlaw. She told them where she left food when Haslip was in hiding and the lawmen set up an ambush for the following night. The food was set out and Constable Irvine and the interpreter hid for two nights, but the Haslip never showed up. Rapelje and Perry searched all the surrounding area for three days, but the Indian had vanished again. The disappointed officers had to return empty-handed.

In late August, Irvine went after Haslip again. This time he chased Haslip out of the mountains and into the foothills above old Millerton. Irvine was still on his trail when Tom Beasore, a half-blood deputy, recognized the outlaw and quickly had him in irons. Laverone was captured in Tehama County in late June 1896, and both he and Haslip were tried and received life sentences.

Meanwhile, the feuding between Rapelje and Ragsdale raged on in Chinatown. The matter had long since become hopelessly politicized, the *Expositor* editorially opposing any Chinatown comments made by the *Republican*—and vice versa. Ragsdale was nearly always the aggressor, while Rapelje, when necessary, attempted to minimalize the charges and accusations with which he was assaulted. Ragsdale would seem to have been the more legitimate of the two men since he would not likely have been constantly accusing others of actions of which he was guilty. Rapelje, on the other hand, never said anything more than he had to in print, and at this distance in time he seems to have been so deeply involved in Chinatown affairs that he no longer knew (or cared) where payoffs and salaries overlapped.

Typical of the squabbles taking place was an incident in late February 1897, when Ragsdale sent another accusatory letter to the *Expositor*. The missive was addressed to City Marshal Woy and complained that a Chinese merchant named Quong Chong was paying off city officials for the privilege of running a lottery that had, for the past few years, been ignored by Woy and other city authorities. Ragsdale's superior, Constable John Albin, was surprised at the charge. When he tried to raid the game, he was thwarted by a Chinese lookout posted outside the door. Albin warned the lookout that he would be arrested for vagrancy if he did not obtain legitimate employment, but the man stayed at his post and was arrested by the constable.

"He was defended in City Recorder Clark's court by Deputy Sheriff Rapelje," wrote Ragsdale. "He was convicted on November 27th, and sentenced to imprisonment in the county jail for ninety days.

The case was appealed on December 2, 1896, and has not yet been retried. This convicted Chinaman was on duty on the same day of his sentence..." Ragsdale concluded his letter, stating that through the window of his office he could still see this lookout on duty.

Quong Chong promptly presented a rebuttal in the next issue of the *Republican*:

> Ragsdale claims I told him that I paid the City Marshal and others for the privilege of conducting lottery and other games. This is not true. I never told him anything of the kind, and what is more I never paid the marshal nor anyone else a cent for that or any other purpose. It is also untrue that I offered Ragsdale any money for the privilege mentioned.
>
> The motive that prompted Ragsdale to make the charge against me was jealousy. I used to pay him money as Chinatown watchman, but when Rapelje circulated a petition among the Chinese to be employed as watchman, I signed it and have been with him ever since. Ragsdale wanted me to go back to him, but I refused...

Rapelje visited the *Republican* office and of course verified Chong's story. In the midst of all this, there were other Chinese skirmishes that reinforced the *Expositor*'s campaign against the lotteries. Taking the bull by the horns, an *Expositor* reporter bought a lottery ticket, then preferred charges against the sales agent. Constable Crutcher made the arrest and on the afternoon of February 16, 1897, Him Kee appeared before Justice St. John for his hearing. To the great expressed shock of the *Expositor*, the defendant's representative was Hi Rapelje, who had a long talk with the justice, pleading Him Kee's poverty and minor role in the lottery operation.

The reporter was startled! "Surely Hi Rapelje's reputation as a brave and efficient officer must suffer by such work as this. Not only is he darkening a creditable record made in past years that entitled him to the place he now holds under Sheriff Scott, but he is going farther and jeopardizing that position by such work in behalf of a Chinese lottery gambler." The newspaper continually ignored the fact that Hi was only doing what his employers paid him to do—right or wrong—represent the company. This was lawyers' work, and of course, Hi should have quit.

The newspaper's criticism begs the question: Why did not the *Expositor* criticize the prominent local lawyers who defended the Chinese in court?

There are indications that the steady complaints of Ragsdale and criticisms of the *Expositor* were affecting Hi more than was readily apparent. On a Tuesday night in mid-February 1897, a sullen and well-oiled Rapelje stepped into Tom Maloney's Laurel-Palace saloon. Maloney and the watchman had been at odds for some time, and now Hi suddenly accused the saloon man of furnishing information to the *Expositor* about Chinese lottery games. When Maloney denied it, Rapelje cursed at him and drew his pistol. Maloney was as willing as Hi to fight, but before anything could happen, a bystander stepped between them and prevented further hostilities.

Daily Evening Expositor, February 18, 1897:

> *Rapelje was taken outside, but returned to the saloon a few minutes later.*
>
> *"Have you got it?" he called out to Mahoney?*
>
> *"Yes," was the answer.*
>
> *And in a second two guns were flashed and Pat Conway rushed between the men, and again there was no fight.*
>
> *Then it was proposed that Maloney go out the side door of the saloon and Rapelje out of the front door, and that they walk to the corner and when they met again begin shooting. This was agreed to and the men started out. Constable "Coon" Crutcher had arrived in the meantime, however, and he proceeded to take Mr. Rapelje over to a room where he stowed him away and kept him safe until morning.*

It was a stupid move on Hi's part and liquor and his hot temper had done the talking. The *Expositor*, however, found the incident a wonderful opportunity to "pile on," and they took full advantage of it.

In May 1897, Zella was diagnosed with a serious health problem. Hi escorted her by train to San

A quiet moment in Fresno's old Chinatown, about 1910. *Fresno County Library, California History and Genealogy Room.*

257

Francisco, where a specialist placed her in a local hospital and scheduled an operation. Hi saw her situated, then had to return to Fresno for business. "Hi Rapelje left for San Francisco last night," reported the *Republican* on June 20. "Mrs. Rapelje is lying in a hospital, where she had an operation performed recently. The case was serious, but she is now improving." The nature of Zella's ailment is not known, but she made a complete recovery and Hi soon had her back at home again.

In early October, Hi learned of a sixteen-year-old Chinese girl named Fong Sim had been kidnapped. She was an inmate of one of the China Alley brothels and while on an errand was captured by four highbinders who threw her into a buggy, then disappeared. When Hi heard of it, he rushed to the depot to make sure they did not get on the night train. As usual, various stories circulated as to the girl's origins, one tale suggesting she was a previous kidnap victim sold into prostitution and her recent abductors were merely trying to rescue her. Attractive Chinese prostitutes were worth their weight in gold. In any case, rewards were offered and several other constables and sheriff's deputies were on the trail, also.

Hi and Constable Will Henry heard that three Chinese men and a woman had been seen on the West Side plains. By traveling all night, they were able to track and rescue Fong Sim and arrest three of her abductors some thirty-five miles southwest of Fresno. It was bitter cold, and the captives were all glad to return to the warmth of the city jail.

The new story was that Fong Sim had been rescued by a Stockton merchant named Wong Gong Chew who wanted to rescue and marry her. He had offered a $200 reward and Hi thought it best to keep her at his home, but she was soon back in China Alley, according to the report. What Zella thought about having a member of the local demimonde in her house was not recorded. Fong Sim said she was an actress who had come to this country several years earlier. "She is a rather prepossessing woman," commented the *Republican*.

By early 1899, Hi had lost his special deputy sheriff's commission, but he managed to obtain a deputy position under Constable Puleston to maintain his watchman job. Chinatown was changing. There were frequent raids on gambling games, although it was difficult to catch a game in session. Hi had to go along on the raids to make sure his clients were treated fairly, and he was constantly caught in the middle. And it was more dangerous. There were more strange faces along China Alley—highbinders from San Francisco trying to get a slice of the vice money derived from the hordes of teamsters and farmworkers looking for entertainment.

An idea of the money being generated west of the tracks was indicated by a gambling raid in September 1898. Dozens of games were shut down, at least momentarily, with one lottery operation having some "200 white men—mostly grape pickers—packed into a narrow hallway awaiting a chance to part with the money earned during the week."

The size of the Fresno police force had been reduced and other cuts were coming. It seemed like a good time for Hi to look around for a fallback position again. Although still a deputy constable in Chinatown, Hi invested in a rubber-tired hack, a buggy used around town, and set up a stand at a local hotel. He ran a small ad in the *Republican*, pronouncing that his innovative vehicle "rides like a Pullman coach. Just the thing for invalids and those desiring a comfortable ride. No jolting or jarring..."

Even a series of shootings in Chinatown had not slowed down the activity in the "quarter." The *Republican* reported on April 16, 1899, that when Dan Maloney was called to testify in a hearing relating to the recent shooting death of Chuck Hock, there were several surprises in store for the court. Maloney and his brother Tom were prominent white Chinatown saloon owners. Another brother, Jack, had been shot and killed in his Club saloon in 1893 during a dispute with M. C. Boyd over unpaid wages. Jack's enamorata , one "Edna," had tried to shoot Boyd in the jail but was disarmed. Boyd was glad to be sent out of town while on bail, along with Deputy Sheriff Timmins, to hunt for the escaped Evans and Morrell.

Dan and Tom Maloney's saloon operations enjoyed various vice-related perks while doing business in the Chinese community. Prostitutes, whose quarters lined up along F Street, next to Tom Maloney's place, included women of various races and served a clientele from both sides of the tracks. Saloons also were involved in gambling. The Maloney brothers, for a time, operated a dance hall as well.

When called to testify in the Chuck Hock murder case, Dan Maloney at first refused. Later he agreed to take the stand and was asked by one of the attorneys why he was afraid to testify?

"If you knew the habits of the Chinese you would not ask that question," replied Maloney. "When two companies are at war it is as much as a man's life is worth to testify against either of them. Within the last few days between 35 and 40 highbinders have come to town and before another week has passed there will be trouble in Chinatown."

When asked if threats had been made against him if he testified, Maloney replied: "Yes, by white men and by Chinamen, too."

The police, also, had seen indications of Tong activity and they had heard rumors of new faces among the Chinatown highbinders. Constables Dumas and Puleston, after discussing the matter with District Attorney Everts, planned a raid to arrest as many of the newly arrived hatchetmen as possible.

About seven o'clock on the evening of April 19, 1899, police officer James D. Morss went on night duty in Chinatown. Two Tongs, the Bing Kung and the Suey On, had been feuding for some time over the killing of Chuck Hock, and the resulting trials and hearings. The time for talk had now passed. As Officer Morss walked up Tulare Street, two smiling Chinese grabbed his arms and invited him to Fagan's Golden West saloon for a cigar. The cheerful trio was enjoying their cigars in Fagan's when the shooting began.

Hi was enjoying his evening eye-opener in Brown's saloon when he heard the first volley. Rushing out of the saloon and across Tulare Street, he sprinted down China Alley, where he could see two Chinese shooting their revolvers at a yelling man writhing on the ground. Farther up the alley, a dozen hatchet men were shooting and running around in an excited manner.

Fresno Morning Republican, **April 20, 1899:**

> *As Rapelje ran up to arrest the Chinamen who were shooting at the man lying on the sidewalk, a prominent member of the Bing Kung Company rushed by him, pursued by a highbinder. The fugitive took shelter in a hallway leading to a tan den. No sooner had he reached the door than the man who had followed him fired. The bullet struck Leong Tung in the forehead and he dropped dead. Rapelje caught the murderer by the queue and held him until other officers arrived. At the jail he gave the name of Wong Duck.*

The arrow on this 1893 Sanborn fire insurance map shows where Hi entered China Alley. Brown's Saloon is one-half block away, across the street. *Fresno County Public Library, California History and Genealogy Room.*

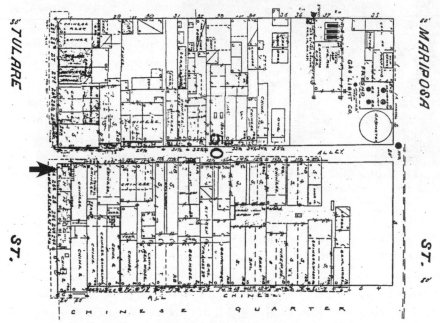

Meanwhile, the decoyed officer Morss rushed out of the saloon in the direction of the shots. As he reached the alley, he saw a Chinese man running diagonally across Tulare Street toward him. The man rushed up to Chin Chi, who was standing in a doorway and shot him dead. The gunman continued running toward Morss, who yelled at him to halt. Pointing his pistol at the officer, the man rushed on despite another shout to stop. Morss then fired and the man dropped to the pavement, shot in the liver and kidneys. As he was rushed to a hospital, an informer was secured and a general sweep through the area for highbinders was made by constables and police officers.

In the alley, another mortally wounded Chinese man was found. He died shortly after being admitted to the hospital. He was identified as one of the highbinders. The man shot by Morss was identified as a "bad man" nicknamed "Shorty." He had served as interpreter at several of the recent trials. Law Tang, a "ferocious-looking" Chinese was found in one of the G Street dens asleep in a bed. When his blanket was thrown off, he was wearing shoes and was fully-clothed. He was identified as a highbinder,

Inside China Alley, two Chinese men carry a roasted pig to a local feast. *CSUF Special Collections.*

also, and was taken to jail and charged with murder. The locked doors to other dens were broken down and found to be filled with excited Chinese men. Bulletproof vests, daggers, pistols and a great many cartridges were discovered, also. Soon the jail was full of suspects, but it was going to be a mess to sort out.

Chinatown was very quiet as the inquest began the following day. Wong Duck, the man Hi had caught by his queue, was arraigned and put in jail. He had blood on his hands when arrested and was thought to be the man holding down the shooting victim in the alley. Rapelje's testimony was extensive, but surprisingly he did not accuse Wong Duck of the Leong Tung killing as other witnesses had done. Instead, Hi's testimony was vague and evasive and District Attorney O. L. Everts was visibly upset. Later he would learn that Hi had told several friends that he (Rapelje) had shot Leong Tung that bloody night. Concerned about Tong retaliation, Hi had not admitted the killing, but his friends prevailed on him to tell the truth.

The next day D. A. Everts told Hi he knew the truth about the Leong Tung killing and reminded him he was still under oath. This time Hi related how he had run into the alley and broke up the men shooting at the man on the ground. He had "slapped" one man on the head with his pistol and when the others saw it was "Mr. Hi" they had fled. He had struck another in the head and when the fellow ran to an alley doorway, Hi yelled for him to stop, then fired. Shot in the head, Leong Tung was dead when he hit the floor. Hi then grabbed Wong Duck by the queue as he ran past.

INQUEST ENDED.

The Chinese Puzzle Solved.

Hi Rapelji Admits Killing Leong Tung.

The Night Watchman Gives a Revised Version of the Shooting in the Alley.

As predicted in yesterday morning's Republican evidence was yesterday introduced at the inquest over the remains of the Chinese killed in Wednesday night's battle which served to clear up much of the mystery surrounding the case. The triple killing is no longer a Chinese puzzle, for the Coroner's Jury yesterday returned verdicts fixing the responsibility for the death of each of the victims at the morgue.

The jury found that Hi Rapelje killed Leong Tung, otherwise known as Leong Chung; that Ah Yung killed Ah Tai and that Wong Duck killed Wong Gee. Promptly at 9 o'clock yesterday morning the inquest was resumed on the body of Leong Tung (Chung). District Attorney Everts was on hand to conduct the examination of the witnesses and was assisted by Attorney W. D. Crichton. Attorneys Dante K. Prince and E. A. Williams looked after the interests of Wong Duck.

RAPELJE'S REVISED VERSION.
Hi Rapelji, the watchman, was recalled. District Attorney Everts explained to him that he was expected to clear up some of his testimony of the day before and he proceeded to do so. Of course, it was understood that he should confess to having killed Leong...

262

"Rapelje's confession," reported the *Republican* of April 22, "was corroborated by a Chinese witness, and the jury accepted it and found that he killed Leong Tung, but failed to add the customary 'While in the performance of his duty' to the verdict."

It was an uncomfortable verdict for Hi, but it was the best the jury could do. In a gunsmoke-filled alley, at night, and peopled with yelling, shooting Chinese, he was in a dangerous situation. Tung was identified as a highbinder. No white jury was going to get very upset over the killing of one of the instigators of the trouble. The *Republican* seemed satisfied with the verdict:

"The jury found that Hi Rapelje killed Leong Tung, otherwise known as Leong Chung; that Ah Yung killed Ah Tai and that Wong Duck killed Wong Gee."

But the inquest and testimony made no difference. The Chinese defendants had the best lawyers in town and all the lottery money needed for their defense. Wong Duck alone had four attorneys. But the best part (for them) was that none of the Chinese witnesses against them could be found. "The acquittal of Wong Duck," wailed the *Republican* on June 22, "disposes of the last of the cases growing out of the 'late unpleasantness' in Chinatown. Over a dozen Mongolians were arrested at the time, but not a single conviction was secured."

Fresno's Tong troubles made headlines all over the country, with the *Omaha World-Herald* devoting ten inches of column space to the events.

Despite continued raids by the authorities, the Chinese Quarter still simmered and no one could be sure another Tong war could not erupt. Despite his killing of Leong Tung, Hi still felt safe in Chinatown, depending on his friends to warn him if there were any threat on his life. Actually, he was closer than ever with Charley Quong and other Chinese men and was no longer advised when a police raid was going to take place. He was paid by the Chinese and obligated to look out for their interests. He was walking a fine line

Two San Francisco boo how doy hatchetmen. They could show up in any California town on a murderous mission. *Sutro Library.*

and he knew it. Soon he would be forced to decide which side of the tracks he wanted to be on.

In January of 1901, Miss Donaldina Cameron, of San Francisco's Presbyterian Mission, made a late night stop in Fresno. Her Bay City mission was a prominent haven for Chinese slave girls trying to escape their grim life of prostitution and forced marriages. Cameron traveled throughout the state in her attempts to rescue these unfortunate young women. At this time she had picked up a girl in Bakersfield and was returning with her to San Francisco.

Cameron was sleeping in a lower berth when her train pulled into Fresno's Southern Pacific depot. It was close to midnight. A man entered the car with the conductor and she heard someone ask where the Chinese girl was. In a moment a heavyset man had pulled aside the curtains on Cameron's berth and again demanded the whereabouts of the girl. It was Hi Rapelje. Cameron barely had time to compose herself before Rapelje reached up into the upper berth and dragged young Gook Fong into the aisle. Cameron protested, but was shown a deputy constable's star and a warrant. In her nightclothes, Cameron begged the watchman to wait until she could get dressed, but Rapelje took his quarry off the train to his hack and several waiting Chinese.

Dressing as fast as she could, Cameron rushed from the train, but the hack had disappeared. A bystander told her that a Chinatown watchman and hack driver had taken the woman, and Cameron immediately went to police headquarters to report what had taken place. Phone calls to the two local justice court judges were unsuccessful, but policeman Henry Russell took her to Rapelje's hack stand where the watchman was questioned. He denied having the Chinese girl, but was identified by Cameron as the kidnapper. Hi said he was not the guilty party, but offered to try to locate whoever was involved. Disgusted, Cameron stayed in town to try to find her charge.

Much of the town was outraged on the morning of January 6 when news of the incident was published. Rapelje must have suddenly realized he had made a disastrous mistake. He was no longer an admired peace officer, but a pawn of his Chinese employers.

Hi Rapelje was clearly overmatched when he went up against Donaldina Cameron. *California State Library.*

Fresno Morning Republican, **January 6, 1901:**

INFAMY COMMITTED IN THE NAME OF JUSTICE

> *Hi Rapelje, Chinatown Watchman, Thwarts Efforts of a Presbyterian Missionary Woman to Rescue a Chinese Girl from Her Owners.*

> *The process of the law polluted to accomplish the outrage on public decency by recourse to the old subterfuge of getting out a warrant for the apprehension of the woman on a trumped-up charge of grand larceny. Rapelje denied his connection with the abduction plot – woman released on heavy bail furnished by Chinese.*

It was indeed the old brothel owner's dodge of charging an escaped Chinese prostitute with theft to obtain the return of his property. Recorder Cosgrave had issued a warrant for the girl's arrest upon the complaint of her alleged husband, one Charley Quong. Rapelje knew the scheme well, of course, but so long as he held his watchman job he had little recourse but to do the bidding of his Chinese employers. He should have refused to become involved in the dirty business and he found that this time he had painted himself into a nasty corner.

Fresno citizens were up in arms about the incident. Donaldina Cameron, however, was used to playing hardball and she would not go away. She solicited the aid of local ministers and public officials and swore out conspiracy complaints against both Rapelje and Charley Quong. A furious Quong was forced to bring the girl, Gook Fong, to court, where she was removed for her own safety to the city jail. She was quickly released on her own recognizance. That night Cameron and her charge outwitted several officers who still sought to seize her on new warrants before she left town.

Hi had been sucked into the Chinatown vortex and his "Mayor of West Fresno" days were far behind him. *Author's Collecton.*

Far from seeing the brutal heartlessness of all this, Rapelje tried to enforce several more warrants on Gook Fong, brought to town by Bakersfield's city marshal, but none of the local justices would sign them. Determined to make Hi feel the public's wrath over the incident, the Fresno city trustees met and dismissed all special policemen such as Rapelje. They made it clear that all could re-apply for their old jobs on an individual basis, but Rapelje would not be re-appointed. Donaldina Cameron, however, was not yet finished with the callous and mercenary watchman.

Returning to Fresno on January 10, 1901, Cameron was determined to prosecute Rapelje and Quong for their actions. She was met at the station by several deputy sheriffs, including Hi's longtime friend Johnny White. To press the conspiracy charges, Cameron appeared in Justice St. John's courtroom on January 25 for the preliminary hearing. Hi's attorneys, Walter D. Tupper, Dante Prince, and W. P. Thompson tried to justify Rapelje's lying to Policeman Russell and Miss Cameron that night by insisting they had asked if he had "kidnapped" a Chinese girl, rather than if he had "taken" her. It was a lame defense. Also, it was shown Hi had delivered the girl to Justice Cosgrave's house for safekeeping, but that he was told to look after her himself and bring her back at ten the next morning.

"Talk about your missionaries and good people," railed attorney Tupper, "Why you couldn't get the woman to heaven anyway according to the Westminster infant damnation creed believed in by the Presbyterians. If this 'crime' of abducting a Chinese girl from her Bakersfield home by a missionary had instead been perpetrated upon a white woman, the public would be indignant." Tupper's cynical attempt to tarnish Cameron as a kidnapper had few sympathizers.

Walter D. Tupper, Hi's attorney. *Author's Collection.*

The trial was scheduled for February 27, 1901. It lasted several days and was bitterly contested by both sides. Hi's counsel tried to put the best face possible on a bad situation.

Fresno Morning Republican, **March 2, 1901**

> ... *It was strange though that in a town like Fresno where murderers go unpunished that old time citizens like Rapelje, pursuing the occupation of hack driver and watchman, should be dragged before a court on a flimsy charge like this.*

In the end, the jury could not agree and the charges were dismissed. Hi, however, was out of a job. It was Ragsdale's domain now. Hi's Chinese employers would have fired him if he had refused to do their bidding and that is the way it should have ended. The only good to come out of the mess was the Chinese paying his legal bills. Times were changing and he must have been relieved that he was no longer a Chinatown errand boy... or worse!

In the summer of 1903, Hi and several other Fresnans invested in a Calaveras County mine. Although located close to the fabulously rich Utica mine, the great expectations did not pay off. In July, after staying a little too long in the White Fawn saloon, Hi was arrested for racing his hack up and down Fresno's main street.

The disgraced former lawman now put all his energies into his cab service, enlarging his Fresno Hack & Coupe Company with the addition of a livery stable. The 1904 city directory lists son Harry as one of his drivers.

In May 1910, Hi was called over to the oil boom town of Coalinga to fill in for a deputy marshal who was ill. There was a dispute between Rapelje and another officer named Keller that continued for several days. One day the two officers met on a street corner and again began arguing. When Keller called Hi a "liar," Rapelje smacked him in the face and a heated exchange of fists took place. By the time a crowd had gathered, the two had drawn their blackjacks and the blood was flowing freely. When several spectators stepped in and grabbed the officers' blackjacks, Hi and Keller went for their guns, but these, too, were seized. The two combatants

Coalinga was the heart of a booming oil field, filled with whiskey shops on every street corner. *Fresno County Library, California History and Genealogy Room.*

267

were then sent off in opposite directions, both still yelling threats at the other. The town marshal later fired both hot-headed officers.

When Chris Evans finally inveigled a parole in 1911, Rapelje was asked by a reporter if he was concerned that the old bandit would come hunting him. Evans had made threats against Rapelje, whom he considered a "blood money" hunter who had badly wounded him at Stone Corral in 1893.

"Chris is old, " responded Hi, "and has lost the sight of one eye and the use of one arm, and if his people will care for him, I see no reason why he should be forced to remain in prison any longer. It is true he has made threats that he would get revenge if he ever got out, but he is so old and feeble now that I don't believe he would attempt it..."

In December of 1914, Hi renewed an old disagreement with Phil Alveso in the White Fawn saloon. The two had stepped outside, but when Hi discovered his opponent was unarmed, the men went at each other with their fists until stopped by an officer. Later Hi was acquitted of an assault charge when Alveso admitted Rapelje had drawn his pistol only because he thought his opponent was going for his.

Hi watched for an opportunity and did watchman work on occasion and for a time was head deputy for the Huntington Lake Power Company. During the war he was again commissioned as a deputy constable and deputy sheriff while also acting as a railroad guard.

Chris Evans was a crippled old man living on charity in Oregon and was no longer a threat to anyone.
Tulare County Historical Society.

The old lawman was at his home at 730 L Street when he died of prostate cancer on July 4, 1919. He was sixty-eight years old. Besides his wife, Zella, and their son, Harry, he was survived by a sister and two brothers in Michigan. Although there was no will, probate records indicated his estate consisted of several pieces of property worth some $4,000, which was awarded to Zella.

Today, only a few of the original brick buildings of Fresno's old Chinatown remain scattered throughout a redeveloping area west of the

Southern Pacific tracks. The colorful days of visiting theatrical troupes, of Tong wars, fan tan games, and Chinese cultural celebrations are only a dimming memory of a time that has passed forever.

Also lost in the vagaries of history is the memory of a happy-go-lucky, pioneer Yosemite stage driver, trusted by his employers and lionized by his passengers. As a lawman he was tireless and conscientious, but his temper frequently got him into trouble. Although he participated in one of the more noted gun battles of California's frontier days, his recognition and respect as a peace officer had been tarnished irreparably in Chinatown. Hi Rapelje shamed the star he wore and he had to live with that, but it all occurred in a changing West that he had helped to tame.

The End

Chapter Six

David F. Douglass

"...One of the bravest men I ever met."

They came from all over. Delegations from the Knights of Pythias and Native Sons of the Golden West arrived on the train from Grass Valley and other areas and were met by local representatives. Lawmen and officials from around the state were also arriving. John Thacker, the Wells Fargo detective, made his appearance the night before the funeral. It was not often that Nevada County, California, had hosted such crowds. All business houses in town were closed and flags flew at half-mast. When all the lodge members had gathered at their respective halls, they assembled in the street and marched to the Water Street home of the dead sheriff.

The remains were then escorted to Armory Hall for an emotional funeral. Large baskets of flowers and displays were everywhere. Sacramento Wells Fargo employees sent a handsome piece reading, "Our old Friend Dave." Despite the large dimensions of the hall, the crowd had spilled outside and now strained to hear the eulogy and singing of the choir. Soon it was over and the crowd be-

Sheriff Douglass died under strange circumstances that were only resolved over 100 years later. *Author's Collection.*

gan assembling in the street. More than three hundred men now marched toward Pine Grove cemetery at the edge of Nevada City. Seventy buggies followed, as bells tolled through the streets. Another ceremony was held at the gravesite and David Douglass was then lowered into his grave. Soon, the crowds began breaking up and returning to town. "The funeral," commented the *Grass Valley Union*, "was the largest seen here in many years."

David F. Douglass was born on his father's farm near Stockton in 1858. Norval Douglass was from Tennessee and he married Joanna Dillon about 1855. They had come west with other family members during the early days of the Gold Rush. Perhaps he was just restless, but Norval Douglass moved his family to Merced County in 1868, where he continued to farm. The 1870 census shows nine children—six boys and three girls. David was twelve years old at this time and was in school, but he helped out on the farm as did the other older children. The family moved several more times before young David came of age and eagerly struck out on his own.

Like most young men starting out in life, Dave Douglass held a variety of jobs in those early years. In 1880, he was living at home while employed as a railroad laborer. Later, he worked cattle on a ranch in Nevada, then returned to California where he raised grapes in Solano County. In 1883, he obtained a position as stagecoach shotgun guard and messenger for Wells Fargo, his routes being in Sierra, Plumas, and Nevada counties. He learned his business well and in time was guarding bullion shipments on the Southern Pacific Railroad and a narrow gauge road between Nevada City and Sacramento.

Douglass liked Nevada City. Nestled in the pine and brush-clad hills, the town was the county seat and had a colorful history dating back to Gold Rush days. Mining was still a principal industry, but agriculture had be-

Nevada City as it appeared in the Gold Rush days of 1856. *California State Library.*

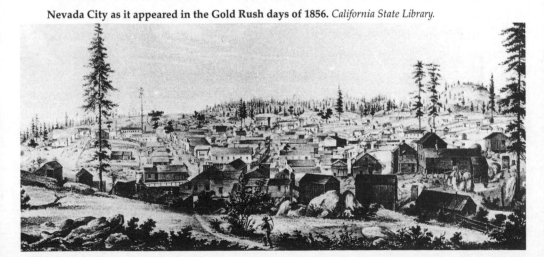

come very important since the Nevada Narrow-gauge railway had been completed in 1876. A group of Bartlett pear orchardists had recently established a colony in the county, naming their area "Chicago Park" after their hometown.

The Champion Mine, one of the many large operations in the county. Some $400,000 in gold was taken out in a three-year period. *Author's Collection.*

Douglass liked the people, also, and he made many friends in the area. His job as a Wells Fargo messenger put him in frequent contact with the Nevada County sheriff's office and he was soon spending off-hours visiting with local officers. Perhaps it was during a visit to the Wells Fargo headquarters in San Francisco that he met John A. Read, secretary to the Pacific Mail Steamship Company. One way or another, young David Douglass met Read's twenty-year-old daughter, Emily, and a courtship was initiated. On October 3, 1884, the young couple were married in San Francisco and soon after took up residence in Nevada City. Their son Aloyisius was born the following year.

The director of Nevada City's Union Hill School was William H. Pascoe, an immigrant from Cornwall, England. In 1888, Pascoe was elected city marshal and soon was considering higher office. When he ran for sheriff in the fall of 1892, his friend David Douglass campaigned for him and was elated when his fifty-year-old friend was elected. David also gratefully accepted the undersheriff's badge on the new sheriff's staff. It was better money than his Wells Fargo job, and probably no more dangerous, much of the work being court duty, rounding up jurors, and serving papers.

Nevada City was a typical wild Gold Rush town that evolved into an agricultural and cattle-ranching economy. *Searls Historical Library.*

An early sheriff had been killed, however. There were always risks in being an officer, but the new undersheriff looked forward to his occupation of protecting the residents of the county.

Nevada County was relatively peaceful during the first months of the new sheriff's term. Other sections of California, however, had been plagued with train robberies by murderous bandits who did not hesitate to shoot anyone interrupting their work. These train robberies, although not concerned with Nevada County, would still affect it in a disastrous way.

Near Seymour, Indiana, in early 1866, the Reno brothers committed what was probably the first peacetime train robbery in the United States. Following up on this coup, Jesse James and his gang wrecked a train at Adair, Iowa, in July 1873. The derailed express car was robbed first, then the passengers. Train robbery in America had blossomed and quickly caught on.

In 1870, the first train robbery in the far West took place near the California border at a spot called Verdi, Nevada. The robbers got away with $37,000, but they were quickly tracked down and captured.

It was more than ten years later that California got into the act. In Placer County, on August 30, 1881, just before midnight, five local desperadoes dislodged a track and derailed a Central Pacific engine and cars. It was at a location called Cape Horn, just above Colfax, in the high Sierra. The robbers were amateurs and panicked at the last minute, fleeing the scene in the darkness. They were promptly captured and the two ringleaders were convicted and sent to San Quentin, but they had set the stage for train robbery in the Golden State.

The scene of the attempted train robbery at Cape Horn in 1881. *California State Library.*

The story of train robbers Chris Evans and John Sontag has been told in Hi Rapelje's chapter. They had terrorized the San Joaquin Valley during the early 1890s, killing three lawmen and several others. When George Sontag joined his brother and Chris Evans for the Collis robbery on the night of August 3, 1892, he was quickly picked up as a suspect while his two partners escaped to the mountains.

George was convicted of the Collis robbery and was sentenced to life in Folsom State Prison. He was admitted to Folsom on November 3, 1892, and he was not happy. He had a wife and child and, although guilty, he probably felt he was taking the rap for his brother and Evans, who were still free in the mountains east of Visalia. Soon, all he could think about was escape.

In 1890, William Fredericks had been admitted to Folsom to begin a four-year term for a Mariposa County stage robbery. A German immigrant who spoke broken English and whose real name was never known, Fredericks's time was growing short when he met George Sontag shortly after the train robber's arrival. When not working, convicts have little else to do but plot escapes and talk about life on the outside. George and a group of pals were indeed planning an escape and they let Fredericks in on the scheme. With good behavior credits, Fredericks was due to be released soon and he had no interest in escape, but he did agree to help by stashing weapons in the prison quarry after his release.

Released on May 26, 1893, Fredericks had instructions from George Sontag to visit Chris Evans's family in Visalia and obtain guns for the planned break. Fredericks was to store the weapons at a secret spot in the prison quarry, then wait for the fugitives at a rendezvous above Col-

fax with clothes and food. The men did not have much of a plan; the five convicts involved were to seize a guard, then flee with him as a hostage. There were no walls surrounding Folsom, but the American River was on one side with Gatling gun-manned guard towers on the other three sides. Very few had ever escaped from the dreaded prison.

Fredericks fulfilled his end of the plan, then waited at Bear Valley, east of the railroad town of Colfax. On the afternoon of June 28, 1893, Sontag was chaining down some boulders on a rail car in the quarry. His four convict accomplices had already obtained the hidden guns and now waited for Sontag to distract the guard, Lieutenant Frank Briare.

William Fredericks's mug shot as it appeared in the *San Francisco Morning Call,* **July 27, 1895**

Stepping away from the railroad car, Sontag walked slowly toward the guard, who was watching him carefully. Suddenly, as Briare was seized from behind by convict Anthony Dalton, Frank Williams rushed up with two rifles and several pistols. The convicts now shoved Briare ahead of them, toward one of the guard towers. When he saw an opportunity, Briare, jumped over a precipice and the escaping prisoners were suddenly exposed.

Although they dived for cover in the gravel and boulders, the convicts were quickly shot to pieces, three being killed and others badly wounded. Sontag had numerous bullet wounds, but lived to testify against his brother and Chris Evans.

Fredericks was waiting for his convict pals when he heard news of the disastrous escape attempt. Keeping under cover, he promptly headed towards Dutch Flat where he could jump a train. He was heading west on top of a railroad car when the conductor spotted him. A brakeman named Bruce climbed up to the roof of the car and ordered the supposed "tramp" to get

The granite quarry at Folsom prison where the escape attempt was made. With all the open ground, they never had a chance. *California State Library.*

off. As Bruce closed in on him, Fredericks pulled a pistol and fired, hitting the brakeman in the chest. "Run, damn you," exclaimed the gunman, "or I'll give you another!"

As Bruce painfully scrambled down the ladder, Fredericks jumped to the ground on the other side of the car and disappeared into the countryside.

Grass Valley Union, June 29, 1893:

...Bruce was shot in the breast, the bullet entering the right lung. It is feared that he cannot possibly survive the wound....Shortly after the shooting the wounded brakeman was taken to the Railroad Hospital at Sacramento. ...

This incident took place about twelve miles from Grass Valley, and immediately a large manhunt was underway for the gunman who was assumed to be a tramp. For some years, tramps had been a problem in California due to the economic hard times in the country. They were walking on the roads and crawling into, or on top of, freight cars on the railroads. They stole or begged food at ranch houses or on the outskirts of towns. Most were looking for work, but when discouraged, many took to theft.

Officials were quickly getting a handle on the Bruce shooting, however. Folsom's warden, Charles Aull, was a former peace officer and Wells Fargo detective. He had also served as turnkey at San Quentin in the 1870s.

The warden had been alerted by guards that George Sontag was constantly in the company of a small group of tough convicts. Aull had suspected a break even before it had taken place. On the day of William Fredericks's release, the warden had called him into his office and cautioned him about getting mixed up in any escape attempts fostered by the older convicts. When the bloody escape attempt occurred, Aull was certain that Fredericks was involved in some way. He was also convinced that Fredericks was probably responsible for the shooting of brakeman Bruce at Gold Run.

On the evening of June 30, Sheriff Pascoe was helping to coordinate the search for the brakeman's assailant in Grass Valley. Officers were stationed at train depots throughout the area, while others were posted at bridges and road crossings. Warden Aull had promptly circulated a wanted poster for William Fredericks.

Shortly before ten o'clock, Sheriff Pascoe noticed a suspicious character emerge from the Pacific Saloon and begin walking down the street. His features matched a photograph of Fredericks in the sheriff's possession. Staying on the opposite side of the street, Pascoe followed the man. The two turned up a street leading to an old foundry, with the sheriff about twenty feet behind his quarry. At the sheriff's suggestion, Constable William Richards followed fifty feet behind the two men. Later, Richards recalled what happened.

Grass Valley Union, July 1, 1893:

> *...As the stranger came to the road leading to Lakeman's foundry he turned and seemed to increase his gait. Pascoe increased his gait, also. Tramp went around foundry, still followed by Pascoe and I remained at entrance near foundry to head off the tramp.*
>
> *Suddenly I heard a pistol report, followed by three others.*

Looking in direction of shots I saw a man approaching me at a rapid gait and after he passed me I commanded him to halt. He increased his speed and I aimed and fired one shot. I retraced my steps and came up street after assistance. Met officer Dennen and together returned to scene of shooting. I thought tramp was secreted among old iron about the foundry and made a thorough search for him. Could find no trace of him and we proceeded around foundry by the path taken by Pascoe when we came across his dead body.

During entire affair I did not hear a word uttered by Pascoe or tramp and did not have the least idea that he had been shot...

Richards was severely criticized for his actions, since about an hour had been lost in searching around the foundry and contacting the coroner and a physician. It did not make sense that Richards heard the shot that killed Pascoe. Also, since he thought the man he shot at was the fugitive, he certainly should have pursued him. It was a time for prompt decisions, and Richards made the wrong one!

Immediately, officers began arriving in town and posses were formed. As soon as he received the news, Undersheriff Dave Douglass left for Grass Valley, where he checked into the Holbrooke Hotel. A $1,200 reward was quickly offered with more in the offing. "Deputy District Attorney Riley and Deputy Sheriffs Douglass and Neagle," noted the *Union*, "started posses out in every direction about one o'clock this morning."

Most authorities were now convinced that Fredericks was indeed the man who had shot Bruce and who had now killed Sheriff Pascoe. Bruce had identified Fredericks from his photograph and others who had now seen the ex-convict, identified him also.

On July fourth, the fugitive was reportedly seen at Jones' Bar, on the Yuba River. There he broke into a house and, speaking in broken English to the family, denied shooting sheriff Pascoe. He also said he would never be taken alive. Posses sent to the area verified the sighting, but a thorough search of the brushy forest was fruitless.

Grass Valley Union, July 8, 1893:

Deputy Douglass Returns. Belief that Fredericks Crossed the Feather River.

Deputy Sheriff Douglass, who has been most vigilant in trailing the murderer of Sheriff Pascoe returned to Nevada City yesterday morning. He guarded the Yuba River bridge near Marysville Wednesday night and

Main Street in Grass Valley, shown here in the 1890s. On a street intersecting Main, Sheriff Pascoe was killed, probably by the desperate William Fredericks. *Nevada County Mining Review, 1895.*

had rather a rough experience. Nearly one hundred tramps crossed the bridge, all of whom he closely inspected, but three of them were obdurate and would not submit until compelled to do so at the point of a pistol....

There were continued reports of Fredericks moving north, and he finally managed to leave the state and vanish. Traveling about the West, he committed numerous crimes, but then foolishly returned to California in March 1894. While attempting to rob a San Francisco bank, he killed one of the tellers who had shot at him. Captured nearby after fleeing the scene, he was convicted and sentenced to hang after his trial.

Dave Douglass had done a good job as undersheriff in the pursuit of Fredericks. He was appointed by the county board of supervisors to succeed Sheriff Pascoe. It was a sad, but gratifying promotion. The new sheriff had been a good friend to the Pascoe family. The dead sheriff had left two girls and four boys in the family, ranging in age from fourteen-year-old Ruth to twenty-one-year old John. Sheriff Douglass knew the older children would look after their younger siblings and their mother.

When one of the Pascoe boys asked to be appointed a deputy, Dave did some hard thinking. "I made an oath over my father's body," remarked young John Pascoe, "that I would either see his murderer hanged or I would kill him." Dave Douglass knew

Headline in *Grass Valley Union,*
July 1, 1893

278

TERRIBLE
—
Sheriff Pascoe Murdered!
—
ASSASSIN UNKNOWN,
—
But Supposed to Be the Tramp
—
Who Shot Brakeman Bruce.
—
SEVERAL POSSES IN PURSUIT.
—
Testimony Given By Constable Richards.
—
The most atrocious murder ever committed in this city occurred last night about 10 o'clock. Wm. H. Pascoe, Sheriff of Nevada county, was killed. The shooting took place in the

this and was certain John would make a good officer. Perhaps to keep him from any rash act, he made the young man his new undersheriff.

When a date had been set for Fredericks to hang, Warden Hale, of San Quentin, sent an invitation for the three Pascoe boys to attend. They did, but the event had to be discomforting, to say the least. Brute that he was, Fredericks knew how to die. The headline in the *San Francisco Chronicle* on July 27, 1895, read; "He Died Like A Brave Man." The Pascoe brothers had to be content with a piece of the rope that hanged him.

No man likes to acquire higher office at someone else's expense, but David Douglass knew that he was best suited, by training, for the job. He now set out to prove it. When he ran for re-election that fall, Sheriff Douglass was retained in office by a healthy plurality of the voters.

The following summer there was a series of robberies near Nevada City. Houses were burglarized and pedestrians and buggies were stopped and robbed. Although tramps were again suspected, when a San Francisco police detective was stopped and held up on the road, he had other ideas.

Grass Valley Union, July 30, 1896:

> *He performed his work so coolly that the Detective was convinced he was an old hand at the business.*

Sheriff Douglass headed several posses that investigated the reported robberies, but with little result. On Saturday afternoon, July 25, Sheriff Douglass and Deputy Pascoe were on foot scouting in the vicinity of the Wells ranch following a recent robbery. Suddenly, Douglass saw a man who fit the description of the lone bandit. The man saw the sheriff at the same time and broke into a run.

Grass Valley Union, July 29, 1896:

> *...His horse [sheriff's] was tied up at Wilson's as on Sunday, so when he saw Myers running across a clearing up toward the top of the hill he ran toward the road and met a horseman whom he asked to dismount. Taking the horse Douglass chased Myers up over the top of the hill and fired two shots at him without hitting him. Myers did not return the fire...*

Myers, or Meyers, was later established as the robber's name. It was also learned that he had

Another Hold Up.

The expression of "hold up" is getting to be a common one and is generally now, is this county, applied to some point on the Ridge. Within less than a week there were two such incidents and they were all accomplished by "a lone highwayman." We learn from Mr. Thos. Howard that this morning a Chinaman was stopped at a point near Lake City and robbed of $50 in coin. The party who did the operating is supposed to be the same one who has been plying his vacation for the past several days. The officers are on his track. The expression is not a new one.

The Grass Valley Weekly Telegraph, July 25, 1896.

previously worked at a local sawmill. In the brushy, forested terrain, the fugitive quickly disappeared in the gathering twilight. The disappointed lawman again returned to town empty-handed.

As a Democrat, the sheriff was under fire from certain quarters for his lack of results in bringing in the fugitive bandit. Frustrated, Douglass had been "goaded on by adverse criticism of a local newspaper," complained the *Union*, "and certain individuals, [and] he was determined to spare no effort to capture the highwayman."

Late the following Sunday morning, the sheriff received a tip that the fugitive was hiding in the area of Sugar Loaf Hill, near the forks of the San Juan and Blue Tent roads. Mrs. Douglass was visiting her parents in San Francisco with their son. Douglass elected not to bother his deputies this time as it might be another false lead. Besides, one man in a light buggy was not likely to be as noticeable as several armed men on horseback. As Sheriff Douglass was leaving, neighbor Ed Schmidt's little dog, "Jack," was wagging his tail and looking up at him hopefully. Smiling, the lawman scooped him up and set him on the seat next to him. It was about eleven o'clock when he headed up East Broad Street.

Several miles from town, Sheriff Douglass tied his horse to a tree near the forks of the road and began cautiously scouting the area, working his way toward Wet Hill. A man named Towle lived nearby and happened to notice the horse and buggy standing off the road later that afternoon. He had heard some shots, but assumed hunters were in the area. When he saw the rig was still there the following morning, he went to town and informed the sheriff's office.

Nevada City Transcript, **July 27, 1896:**

> *Deputy Sheriff James G. Neagle and Martin McGrath at once procured saddle horses and started out to look for the Sheriff. The fact that the dog returned about 4 o'clock Sunday afternoon gave rise to further suspicions that something unusual had happened. Neagle had heard Douglass say that he thought the robber was camped near what is known as the cold spring, on the other side of the hill from L. H. Wells's milk ranch, and suggested to McGrath that they ride to the spot.*
>
> *McGrath was riding ahead and as they approached the place designated saw a man lying on the ground about 200 feet beyond the spring. He motioned to Neagle to keep still. As both men then stole cautiously and quietly up to where the man was, they were horrified to see two dead men lying upon the ground. Sheriff Douglass was one of them, and the other*

was a stranger. The men were within a few feet of each other. Douglass was lying on his face. His pistol had fallen from his hand and was lying near the robber's hand. He [the sheriff] had been shot twice, and from behind. One bullet passed through his back, between the fourth and fifth rib and ranged upward penetrating the left lung, passing through the vertebrae and coming out on the right side. Another bullet passed through his back at the right hand, severing the cords and lacerating the flesh in a frightful manner. There was a bad wound in the right eye, but this was probably caused by his falling upon a stump or stub....

The other corpse was assumed to be the much-sought highwayman. There was a black, cloth mask lying near the body. He had been shot twice, once in the heart and again in the stomach. His hands were on his .44 caliber Winchester and it seemed obvious the man was lying down when he was discovered and made a grab for his rifle, but the sheriff was too fast for him. Both bodies had been stripped of any money or valuables.

The dead robber was lying on his back with his coat folded under his head like a pillow, a further indication he had been shot while lying down. McGrath was sent to town with the news. He returned with separate wagons for the two corpses. Deputy Neagle had stayed behind to guard the bodies. Soon, there was a growing crowd of spectators arriving—on horseback and in buggies, with pedestrians bringing up the rear. It had been deduced that immediately after Douglass had shot the bandit, the robber's partner heard the shots and rushed to the scene. Coming up behind Sheriff Douglass, the second robber now shot the lawman in the back and after robbing the bodies, fled into the brush and disappeared. Liveryman Robert Salta, who had been held up two weeks previously, promptly recognized the dead man as the robber.

When the two wagons arrived for the bodies, the crowd began breaking up and trickling back to Nevada City. Coroner John Hocking had been telephoned at Grass Valley and met other officials at the funeral parlor on Broad Street to prepare for the inquests. A crowd was now gathering at the undertaking rooms, as groups in saloons

Sheriff David F. Douglass played a lone hand and lost. *Searls Historical Library.*

and on street corners discussed the shocking events. The inquest found that the sheriff had been shot in the back and killed by a second bandit. Posses had already been organized by deputies Neagle and Pascoe. They were now fanning out, looking for signs of the fugitive killer.

Meanwhile, many witnesses came forward to identify the dead robber as a character who had been around town for some time, begging meals from outlying houses. He had also worked at a local sawmill, and he had given his name as Meyers. Enough robbery victims identified the man so there was no doubt the sheriff had shot the sought-after highwayman.

Sketch of the dead bandit as published in the *San Francisco Call,* July 30, 1896.

Telephone and telegraph quickly carried the tragic news throughout the state. "He died a hero," shouted the front page of the *Oakland Tribune.* "Brave Sheriff Douglass Dead," cried the *San Francisco Examiner.* "Death Strikes from Ambush," chorused the *San Francisco Call.* It was the same up and down the great San Joaquin Valley, as the valiant sheriff was eulogized for his bravery.

The Sacramento Bee, July 27, 1896:

> "I knew him well," [Ex-Sacramento Sheriff Tom] O'Neill said, "and I consider him one of the bravest men I ever met. He did not know

Nevada City street scene in the 1890s. The sombre scene shown here certainly characterized the mood of the city in the days following the death of Sheriff Douglass. *Searls Historical Library, Nevada City, California.*

what fear was and his one idea while in performance of his duty was to get his man.

When Sheriff Pascoe was killed by Fredericks, Douglass and I spent several days together in the brush in Yuba County where the murderer was supposed to be hiding. We traveled over a good many miles and I found him to be a good fellow all around.

When Douglass met that Nevada County highwayman he gave the fellow a chance to surrender, I would bet on that, and when the man showed fight he barked up the wrong tree, because Douglass would die in his tracks before he would let his man get away.

"Very much grieved this afternoon to hear of the death of Douglass," said Wells Fargo detective James B. Hume.

San Francisco *Daily Report*, July 27, 1896:

I knew him very well and always found him to be a brave and intrepid man. If he believed he was doing his duty nothing on earth could stop him. He worked for Wells Fargo some years ago....I regarded Douglass as one of the most industrious, zealous and successful officers we have had in California for some years....

Strangely enough, there was little, if any, immediate talk of a reward for the sheriff's killer. The *Grass Valley Union* mentioned the reward offered for Sheriff Pascoe's killer, but noted that nothing was ever collected since Fredericks was not captured at the time. "Monuments to the bravery of such worthy officials," reported the *Union*, "should be erected, and to start a fund for this purpose the *Union* heads the list with a contribution of $10. That it will swell to many hundreds we little doubt."

Just how swollen the fund became is not recorded, but as the fruitless hunt for the murderer progressed, monuments were quickly forgotten and Undersheriff John Pascoe found himself in the same position that Dave Douglass was in when his predecessor was killed. Deputy Pascoe was constantly in the saddle searching for the killer, but without success. As undersheriff, he must have harbored some kind of hope that he would be selected as the new sheriff, but his youth and inexperience were against him.

Actually, Coroner Hocking was now the defacto sheriff, awaiting a permanent appointment by the county supervisors. "It is rumored here today," noted the Grass Valley *Weekly Telegraph*, "that possibly Dana Getchell will be the choice of the Board....Dana Getchell would make a good officer and would meet the approval of the citizens of the county."

Getchell, the Nevada City city marshal, was very active in the hunt for Sheriff Douglass' killer and was indeed appointed to the sheriff's post. A popular businessman of the city, Getchell was a good marshal and highly respected.

The newly widowed Emily Douglass settled her affairs in Nevada City and moved to San Francisco to be near her parents. The Douglasses owned various parcels of property in Nevada County. Besides several mining claims, there was a lot in Stockton, also, as well as a partnership in a local ranch. The sheriff had also presented his wife with a mining property as a gift in May 1894. Much of this was still being paid for on time, as was a houseful of new furniture. There was little left for the widow when her husband's estate was settled. So far as is known, Emily Douglass never re-married.

Dana Getchell, the new sheriff. *Nevada County Mining Review, 1895.*

Sheriff Pascoe's widow never recovered from her husband's death. When she became further depressed after Sheriff Douglass was killed, her family sent her to Oakland to visit a sister, where she committed suicide in October of 1896.

In time, the deaths in the line of duty of three Nevada County sheriffs faded into the haze of history. The proposed monuments to sheriffs Pascoe and Douglass faced a similar fate, but there were those who would not let the past die. One man, Dr. C. W. Chapman, was deeply concerned about the obligations of history. The stories of these martyred lawmen should be remembered and perpetuated for future generations and Dr. Chapman would see to it.

He took up his campaign in the early 1930s, and those who stood in his way only served to spur him on. After acquiring the support of the Native Sons of the Golden West, of which Sheriff Douglass had been a member, it was finally announced that a monument would be built and dedicated on October 18, 1936. Invitations were sent to officials and dignitaries around the state. Los Angeles Sheriff Biscailuz vowed to attend the event despite the short notice.

SHOT BY AN OUTLAW!

Sheriff Douglass Kills the Daring Lone Highwayman

AND FORFEITS HIS OWN LIFE.

Murdered by an Assassin Who Fired From the Rear.

POSSES IN EVERY DIRECTION.

The Tragedy Occurred Sunday Afternoon in the Vicinity of Wells' Ranch on the Purdon Road.

Grass Valley Union, July 28, 1896.

"…From Los Angeles," noted the *Grass Valley Union* in October 1936, "the irrepressible Eugene Biscailuz and Eldred L. Meyer, a high officer of the order [Native Sons of the Golden West], and party, will drive all night in order to reach Nevada City for the dedication."

A few days later, in another reminder of the forthcoming dedication, the *Union* prompted its readers that there was still an unresolved issue. "Did those two men," editorialized the *Union* on October 17, " shoot it out, face to face, or did a third man, a shadowy figure believed by many to have been an accomplice of Meyers, participate. The intervening forty years have not served to formulate a positive answer to that question."

The occasion was attended by a large crowd. The area had changed a good deal during the past forty years…in fact, the Nevada City airport now dominated the historic spot. Behind an old hangar, the monument stood stark and ominous on the northwest slope of Cement Hill. An approximation of the exact site was the best that could be made. The memorial, still standing, was a crude affair, a concrete base studded with stones and topped by a slab of granite on which was mounted a brass plaque. It is dedicated to "David Fulton Douglass" and makes no mention of the other two martyred sheriffs.

Repeating the conclusion of the coronor's inquest at the time, the plaque states that "It is believed that Douglass was pitted against two and that one escaped."

Just as Dr. Chapman refused to accept the reticence of the county and others to participate in the monument project, there were those who felt there was more to the story of Sheriff Douglass' death. Al Trivelpiece, a

The modest monument as it stands today in a wooded spot on the outskirts of Nevada City. A small plaque to the left of the monument marks where the dead bandit fell. *Searls Historical Library.*

Sacramento Bee newspaper reporter, in researching the story, received word that the long-dead sheriff had been killed by a twelve-year-old boy. In his article, Trivelpiece described how the boy had befriended Meyers and was a short distance away when he saw Douglass shoot his friend. Not knowing the sheriff or the circumstances, the boy had then shot the lawman in the back after seeing him shoot Meyers. Approaching his victim, the boy then robbed both dead men and hurried from the scene.

In 1961, Nevada County sheriff Wayne Brown received a letter from a Sacramento lawyer engaged in gathering evidence for a divorce action. During his investigation, the attorney had discovered that the father of one of the respondents in the case had admitted that he had killed a Nevada County sheriff when he was a young boy.

This was indeed startling news and indicates Sheriff Brown was the source of reporter Trivelpiece's story. Sometime later, Sheriff Brown received a late-night telephone call from an excited, younger man. The caller stated that his grandfather had confessed that when he was a boy he had shot and killed a Nevada County sheriff. After investigating the youth's story with the local district attorney, Harold Berliner, Sheriff Brown decided not to pursue the case. There was no witness and no real proof other than the old man's statements. He was in his seventies or eighties by this time, and his name was never revealed. "Even if the lad had been arrested at the time of the killing," stated the district attorney, "he would have been processed through juvenile channels and would probably have been sent to reform school."

SHERIFF DAVID FULTON DOUGLASS
ON THIS SPOT SHERIFF DOUGLASS, A NATIVE SON OF THE GOLDEN WEST, GAVE HIS LIFE JULY 26, 1896, BRAVELY PERFORMING HIS DUTY. ALONE HE TRACKED A HIGHWAYMAN TO THIS RETREAT AND BOTH FELL IN BATTLE. IT IS BELIEVED THAT DOUGLASS WAS PITTED AGAINST TWO AND THAT ONE ESCAPED. THE BODIES LAY PARALLEL.

DEDICATED OCT. 18, 1956, UNDER THE AUSPICES OF THE NATIVE SONS AND NATIVE DAUGHTERS OF THE GOLDEN WEST, THE COUNTY OF NEVADA AND THE CALIFORNIA PEACE OFFICERS' ASSOCIATION

Close-up view of the Douglass plaque.
Searls Historical Library.

Although few names are mentioned in this perhaps final chapter of a tragic story, does it really matter? Names would not change anything. Although as it stands, it is still circumstantial evidence, chances are we now know the final chapter of this tale of Sheriff Douglass's tragic showdown.

The End

Bibliography

Chapter One Sources

Articles

"He Helped Kill Murrieta," *San Francisco Examiner*, December 17,1893.

"Last of the California Rangers,"*San Francisco Chronicle*, April 21, 1907.

"Pioneer Days in the West with a Soldier of Fortune," *Duluth Sunday News Tribune*, January 29, 1922.

"Survivor of the Rangers who Killed Murrietta [sic]," *San Francisco Bulletin*, December 3, 1899.

Books

Boessenecker, John. *Gold Dust and Gunsmoke: Tales of Gold Rush Outlaws, Gunfighters, Lawmen, and Vigilantes*. New York, etc.: John Wiley & Sons, Inc., 1999.

Cossley-Batt, Jill L. *The Last of the California Rangers*. New York and London: Funk & Wagnalls Company, 1928.

Chamberlain, Newell D. *The Call of Gold*. Mariposa: Gazette Press, 1936.

Cunningham, J. C., *The Truth About Murietta* [sic]. Los Angeles: Wetzel Publishing Co. Inc., 1938.

Hilk, Thomas D. *Gleanings from the Mariposa County Newspapers: The Early Years (nine volumes) 1863–1935*. Merced, California: self published.

Latta Frank F. *Joaquin Murrieta and his Horse Gangs*. Santa Cruz: Bear State Books, 1980.

Outcalt, John. *History of Merced County*. Historic Record Company, 1925.

Pinkerton, Scott, and Leroy Radanovich. *Mariposa County Courthouse, "Shrine to Justice."* Mariposa: Mariposa Heritage Press, 1989.

Secrest, William B. *The Man from the Rio Grande, A Biography of Harry Love, Leader of the California Rangers Who Tracked down Joaquin Murrieta*. Spokane: The Arthur H. Clark Company, 2005.

Documents

California State Archives: Joaquin Murrieta Papers, criminal mug shots and prison records.

Mariposa County Archives.

U.S. Census Population Schedule: 1870, Buena Vista Township, Stanislaus County, California

Newspapers

Duluth Sunday News Tribune
Fresno Daily Morning Expositor
Fresno Morning Republican
Merced Express
Merced San Joaquin Valley Argus
Mariposa Chronicle
Mariposa Gazette
Fresno Expositor
Fresno Morning Republican
Merced San Joaquin Valley Argus
Merced County Sun
Portland Oregonian
Sacramento Daily Union
San Francisco Bulletin
San Francisco Chronicle
San Francisco Daily Alta California
San Francisco Examiner
San Francisco Daily Herald
Sonora Union Democrat
Stockton San Joaquin Republican

Chapter Two Sources

Articles
Corcoran, May S. "Lafayette Choisser's Ride," *Fresno Morning Republican*, September 30, 1917.

Dearinger, Lowell A. "An Illinois Family," *Outdoor Illinois*, November 1967.

Reynolds, R. S. "Punch Choisser's Ride," *Overland Monthly*, November 1897

Secrest, William B. "Punch Choisser's Wild Ride," *True West*, August 1965.

Books
Chamberlain, Newell D. *The Call of Gold*. Mariposa: Gazette Press, 1936.

Hilk, Thomas D. *Gleanings from the Mariposa County Newspapers: The Early Years (nine volumes) 1863-1935*. Self published, Merced, California.

Latta Frank F. *Black Gold in the Joaquin*. Caldwell, Idaho: The Caxton Printers, Ltd, 1949.

Pinkerton, Scott and Leroy Radanovich. *Mariposa County Courthouse, "Shrine to Justice."* Mariposa: *Mariposa Heritage Press, 1989.*

No author given. *Representative Citizens of Northern California.* Chicago, Illinois: Standard Genealogical Publishing Company, 1901.

Secrest, William B. *Lawmen and Desperadoes.* Spokane, Washington: The Arthur H. Clark Company, 1994.

Documents

California State Archives, prison records. Notice of Application for Pardon of Lafayette Choisser, June 30, 1859.

California Reports: The People vs. Choisser, October Term, 1858.

U.S. Census Population Schedules:

1840, Current Precincts, Saline County, Illinois.

1860, Corte Madera Township, Marin County, California.

1870, Township No. Two, Mariposa County, California.

Mariposa County Archives

Minutes of Mariposa County Court of Sessions, 1858: The People vs. Lafayette Choisser - Murder.

Various District Court papers: The People vs. E.G. Laird, et al., for the murder of Teacha, Charley, Amos and Sam, April Term, 1879.

Mariposa County Coroner's Inquest and Certificate of Death of Lafayette Choisser.

Newspapers

Merced Express

Mariposa Gazette

Fresno Morning Republican

Merced *San Joaquin Valley Argus*

San Francisco Chronicle

Chapter Three Sources

Articles

Burnham, Frederick R. "The Remarks of Major Frederick R. Burnham," *Annual Publications, Historical Society of Southern California,* 1927.

Gutierez-O'Neill, Ava. "Fighting the Tongs and Outlaws," *Los Angeles Herald-Examiner,* September 15, 1974.

Newmark, Marco R., "Calle de los Negros and the Chinese Massacre of 1871," *The Quarterly, Historical Society of Southern California,* June–September 1944.

Rasmussen, Cecilia. "A Forgotten Hero from a Night of Disgrace," *Los Angeles Times,* May 16, 1999.

Stern, Norton B., and William M. Kramer. "Emil Harris: Los Angeles Jewish Police Chief," *Southern California Quarterly,* Historical Society of Southern California, 1973.

Widney, Judge R. M. "Chinese Riot and Massacre in Los Angeles," *The Grizzly Bear,* January, 1921.

Books

Bell, Major Horace. *On the Old West Coast, Being further Reminiscences of a Ranger,* edited by Lanier Bartlett. New York: Grosset & Dunlap, 1930.

Crongeyer, Sven. *Six Gun Sound: The Early History of the Los Angeles County Sheriff's Department.* Fresno: Linden Publishing, Inc., 2006.

Ditzel, Paul. *A Century of Service/1886–1986, The Centennial History of the Los Angeles Fire Department.* Privately printed, 1986.

Edwards, Harold L. *Train Robbers & Tragedies: The Complete Story of Christopher Evans, California Outlaw.* Visalia, CA: Tulare County Historical Society, 2003.

Gidney, C. M., Benjamin Brooks, and Edwin Sheridan. *History of Santa Barbara, San Luis Obispo and Ventura Counties, California,* Volume II. Chicago: The Lewis Publishing Company, 1917.

Greenwood, Robert (compiler). *The California Outlaw TiburcioVasquez, Including the Rare Contemporary Account by George Beers.* Los Gatos, CA: The Talisman Press, 1960.

Guinn, J. M. *Historical and Biographical Record of Southern California.* Chicago: Chapman Pulishing Co., 1902.

Newmark, Harris. *Sixty Years in Southern California, 1853–1913, Containing the Reminiscences of Harris Newmark,* edited by Maurice H. and Marco R. Newmark. Boston and New York: Houghton Mifflin Company, 1930.

Secrest, William B. *Lawmen & Desperadoes: A Compendium of Noted, Early California Peace Officers, Badmen and Outlaws.* Spokane: The Arthur H. Clark Company, 1994.

Documents

California State Archives:
List of Convicts on Register of State Prison at San Quentin, State Printing Office, Sacramento, 1889; Reward documents pertaining to More murder.

U.S. Census Population Schedules: 1870, 1880, 1900, 1910, 1920. Los Angeles Township, Los Angeles, California.

Newspapers

Los Angeles Daily and Weekly Star

Los Angeles Daily News

Los Angeles Evening Express

Los Angeles Herald-Examiner

Los Angeles Herald

Los Angeles Republican

San Francisco Daily Alta California

San Francisco Daily Evening Bulletin

Ventura Signal

Visalia Weekly Delta

Chapter Four Sources

Articles

Boessenecker, John. "The Browning-Brady Gang," *Real West*. DATE??

Edwards, Harold L. "Bullets and Bicycles," *Real West*, March 1988.

Kildare, Maurice. "Hellish Years at Ashurst Run," *True West*, January, 1975.

Secrest, William B. "Bicycle Bandits at Reed's Crossing," *Wild West*, June 2000.

Sweeney, J. D. "Thrilling Crime Chapter in Early Tehama History..." Typescript in Tehama County Library.

Books

Duke, Thomas S. *Celebrated Criminal Cases of America*. San Francisco: The James H. Barry Company, 1910.

Grimes, Mary Lee. *The First Fifty Years: A Pictorial Essay of Tehama County*. Red Bluff: Tehama County Heritage, 1983.

Lewis, E. J. *Tehama County, California. Illustations Descriptive of its Scenery, etc*. San Francisco: Elliot & Moore, 1880.

Secrest, William B. *Lawmen and Desperadoes*. Spokane, Washington: The Arthur H. Clark Company, 1994.

Documents

Henry Family Collection; Jeanne Henry, and her son Richard, descendants of Sheriff Bogard, provided many clippings, official documents, photographs, letters, Bogard family reminiscences, and otherwise were most helpful.

California State Archives: criminal mug shots and prison records.

U.S. Census Population Schedules: 1870, Merrills Township, Tehama County, California; 1880, Tehama Township, Tehama County, California.

John Boessenecker Collection: Will Smith Scrapbook of newspaper clippings pertaining to Smith's activities.

Newspapers

Wells Fargo Bank Historical Services: large collection of newspaper clippings reporting on the train robbery and killing of Sheriff Bogard.

Corning Daily Observer

Fresno Morning Republican

Marysville Daily Appeal

Modesto Evening News

New York Times

Oakland Tribune

Sacramento Daily Bee

San Francisco Call

San Francisco Examiner
San Francisco Post
Redding Republican Free Press
Woodland Democrat
Yreka Journal

Chapter Five Sources

Articles

Chacon, Ramon D., "The Beginning of Racial Segregation: The Chinese in West Fresno and Chinatown's Role as Red Light District, 1870s–1920s." *Southern California Quarterly*, Winter 1988.

Secrest, William B., "A Gunfighter of the Old San Joaquin." *Fresno Past & Present, The Journal of the Fresno County and City Historical Society,* Summer 1999.

Books

Dillon, Richard. *The Hatchet Men.* New York: Coward-McCann, Inc., 1962.

Duke, Thomas S. *Celebrated Criminal Cases of America.* San Francisco: The James H. Barry Company, 1910.

Edwards, Harold L. *Train Robbers & Tragedies: The Complete Story of Christopher Evans, California Outlaw.* Visalia, CA: Tulare County Historical Society, 2003.

Hamm, Margherita Arlina. *Famous Families of New York, etc.* New York: Heraldic Publishing Co., Inc., 1970.

Outland, Charles F. *Stagecoaching on El Camino Real: Los Angeles to San Francisco, 1861–1901.* Glendale, 1973.

(No author given). *History of Merced County, etc.* San Francisco: Elliott & Moore, Publishers, 1881.

Reynolds, Annie and Albert Gordon. *Stage to Yosemite: Recollections of Wawona's Albert Gordon.* El Portal, CA: Big tree Books, 1994.

Robinson, W. W. *The Story of San Luis Obispo County.* Los Angeles: Title Insurance Company, 1957

Documents

California State Archives:
Criminal mug shots and prison records.

Minutes of Fresno County Board of Trustees., 1890–1900.

Records Management, Fresno County Clerk's Office: Constable and Deputy Sheriff appointments.

Superior Court Archives: Estate of H. L. Rapelje.

U.S. Census Population Schedules:

1900, Third Township, Fresno County, California.

Ontario, Canada Census: 1851, Middlesex / 1851, Elgin.

Correspondence with Elbert H. Ayres, Rapelje Family genealogist.

Newspapers

Fresno Daily Evening Expositor

Fresno Morning Republican

Mariposa Gazette

Merced Express

San Francisco Chronicle

San Francisco Examiner

San Francisco Evening Bulletin

San Francisco Call

Stockton San Joaquin Republican

Chapter Six Sources

Articles

Agar, Vin. "The Mystery of Sheriff Douglass." *Crime Prevention News*, San Bernardino Sheriff's Department (no date).

No author cited. "66 Year Old Murder Solved." *Nevada City Nugget*, October 17, 1962.

No author cited. "Act of Brave Sheriff to be Memorialized on Cement Hill." *Grass Valley Union*, October 17, 1936.

Books

Best, Gerald M. *Nevada County Narrow Gauge Railroad*. Howell-North Books, 1965.

Cloud, Janice G., editor. *The California 1890 Great Register of Voters Index*, Vol. 1. Heritage Quest, 2001.

Prisk, W. F. *Nevada County Mining Review*. Grass Valley: *Daily Morning Union* , 1895.

Documents

Searls Historical Library:

Location Notice for Douglass Ledge; Douglass purchase agreement for Belle Quartz Claim; Douglass purchase agreement for lot in Stockton; Douglas indenture agreement transferring title of mining claim to wife, Emily; Douglas indenture agreement for purchase of 41 acres by Douglass and Loughridge.

Four letters concerning settlement of Douglass estate; three letters by Emily Douglass concerning estate.

U.S. Census Population Schedules:

1860 O'Neal Township, San Joaquin County, California; 1870 Snelling Township, Merced County, California; 1880 Colfax Township, Placer County, California; 1900, 1910, 1920 San Francisco Township and County, California. 1880; Grass Valley Township, Nevada County, California.

Newspapers

Butte Weekly Miner

Fresno Weekly Republican

Grass Valley Daily Morning Union

Grass Valley Weekly Telegraph

Nevada City Transcript

Oakland Tribune

Mariposa Gazette

Los Angeles Daily and Weekly Star

Los Angeles Daily News

Los Angeles Evening Express

Los Angeles Herald-Examiner

Los Angeles Herald

Los Angeles Republican

San Francisco Call

San Francisco Daily Alta California

San Francisco Daily Evening Bulletin

San Francisco Examiner

Ventura Signal

Visalia Weekly Delta

Index

305

About the Author

Born in Fresno, California, in March of 1930, William B. Secrest grew up in the great San Joaquin Valley. After high school he joined the Marine Corps where he served in a guard detachment and in a rifle company in the early years of the Korean War. Returning to college, he obtained a B.A. in education, but for many years he served as an art director for a Fresno advertising firm.

Secrest has been interested in history since his youth and early began comparing Western films to what really happened in the West. A hobby at first, this avocation quickly developed into correspondence with noted writers and more serious research. Not satisfied in a collaboration with friend and Western writer Ray Thorp, Secrest began researching and writing his own articles in the early 1960s.

William Secrest with John J. Bogard's 44-40 Merwin & Huber April 12, 2007

The author holding Sheriff Gogard's Merwin & Hulbert revolver during a visit with Rick Henry and his family. *Kathy Henry.*

Although at first he wrote on many general Western subjects, some years ago Secrest realized how his home state has consistently been neglected in the Western genre and concentrated almost exclusively on early California subjects. He has produced hundreds of articles for such publications as *Westways*, *Montana*, *True West*, and *The American West*, while publishing seven monographs on early California themes. Secrest's many books on California history include *Day of the Grizzly*, *California Badmen*, *California Feuds*, *Dark and Tangled Threads of Crime*, *When the Great Spirit Died*, *California Desperadoes*, *California Disasters*, and *Perilous Trails, Dangerous Men*.